Secret Selves

how their changes changed me

a mother's story

JAMIE JOHNSON

T TRANSITIONS STUDIOS
238 Lynx Hollow Road
Pakenham, Ontario, Canada, K0A 2X0

Copyright © 2011 by Jamie Johnson
All rights reserved.

ISBN: 978-0-987-84500-9

Cover Design by Greg Banks

Note to the reader: In order to respect the privacy of individuals mentioned in this book, the author has changed their names.

Every effort has been made to ensure that the information contained in this book is accurate; however, neither the publisher nor the author is engaged in rendering professional advice or services to the individual reader. The ideas, procedures, and suggestions contained in this book are not intended as a substitute for consulting with your counselor or therapist.

Without limiting the rights under copyright reserved above, no part of this publication may be reproduced, stored or introduced into a retrieval system, or transmitted, in any form, or by any means, without the prior written permission of both the copyright owner and the above publisher of this book.

Publisher's Note: The scanning, uploading, and distribution of this book via the Internet or via any other means without the permission of the publisher is illegal. Please purchase only authorized electronic editions, and do not participate in or encourage electronic piracy of copyrighted materials.

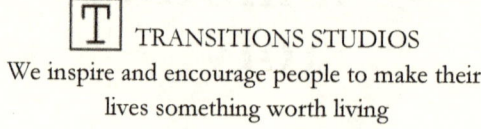

T TRANSITIONS STUDIOS
We inspire and encourage people to make their
lives something worth living

Praise for
Secret Selves

"*Secret Selves* is a compelling story that will change the way you look at life and parenting. As a mother, it's common to worry that your teenagers may experiment with drugs or become pregnant. It's not common to think that they will develop multiple personalities or be trapped in the wrong gender. This book is eye opening and riveting, and Jamie is a prime example of someone who is living her *Second Vision* and doing it well."

Kristin Macdonald
Author of *Second Vision: An Interactive Journal*,
radio show host & motivational speaker

"A brave tale about the hidden rewards of life with a challenging family."

Lenore Rowntree
Author and anthologizer of mental health issues

"*Secret Selves* is the remarkable story of a mother. In her journey to understand and support both [her children], Jamie has to let go of the image she had of what her family would be. Along the way, she learns the biggest lesson of parenthood: to love your children exactly as they are."

Joan Ryan
Author of *The Water Giver* & *Little Girls in Pretty Boxes*

"Candid and courageous, Jamie Johnson shares a deeply personal and inspiring account of raising her two [children]... Our children can help us find courage that we never knew we had. This is a story about love and acceptance, a true gift for anyone who is raising an exceptional child."

Cherie MacLeod
PFLAG Canada Executive Director

Jamie Johnson and her family share their struggles and triumphs with courage and honesty. A heartwarming story about what it means to love."

Janet Rowe
Homemakers magazine

"I loved this book! Jamie Johnson has a wonderful way of sharing how she felt while keeping her reader in suspense. The end of each chapter left me wondering what would happen next. But the greatest thing about this story is that it will help people."

Mike Jan
Group Facilitator, PTS Ottawa

Table of Contents

Prologue *11*

Chapter 1: Me *15*

Jul: Birth-2002: Chapter 2 .... *20*

Chapter 3 .... *28*

Chapter 4 .... *38*

Chapter 5 .... *47*

Joey: Birth-2002 .... *54*

Chapter 6 .... *54*

Chapter 7 .... *58*

Chapter 8 .... *63*

Chapter 9 .... *68*

Jul: 2003-2004: Chapter 10 .... *73*

Chapter 11 .... *80*

Chapter 12 .... *90*

Chapter 13 .... *97*

Joey: 2002-2005 .... *104*

Chapter 14 .... *104*

Chapter 15 .... *108*

Chapter 16 .... *115*

Jay: 2004-2005: Chapter 17 .... *123*

Chapter 18 .... *130*

Chapter 19	136
Chapter 20	143
Chapter 21	151
Chapter 22: Joey: Summer 2005	166
Chapter 23	166
Chapter 24: Kip: 2005-2006	185
Chapter 25	185
Chapter 26	195
Joey: Fall 2005 to Spring 2006: Chapter 27	203
Chapter 28	214
Chapter 29	225
Chapter 30	235
Chapter 31	243
Chapter 32	252
Chapter 33	263
Chapter 34	267
Chapter 35	274
Chapter 36	279
Chapter 37	285
Kip: Spring 2007: Chapter 38	292
Chapter 39	300
Me: 2007: Chapter 40	306
Epilogue	317
Acknowledgments	327

AUTHOR'S NOTE

My biggest fear, as a mother, is that in writing this book, I will somehow bring harm to my children. One cannot deny the fact that prejudice exists. And with prejudice, there is always the real danger of violence. To protect my children, I have changed names and places in this book. This too, is the reason I have published using a pseudonym. Other than the alterations of identifying information, the events are true to the past, written as I remember them. I have recreated all conversations and incidents to the best of my ability. Were it not for my children's strong belief that people would benefit from our story, I may not have had the courage to write it. This book is for them.

Secret Selves

Prologue

As Shakespeare so eloquently once asked, "What's in a name?"

Does your name make you who you are?

The little hospital bracelets my two children were given at birth should have contained some type of advice or alert... instead of a name. I saw a magazine advertisement once where a baby wore one that read, "Warning: Some rearrangement of priorities and beliefs may be required." That might have helped.

I think putting the name I gave them on their tiny arms was really a misrepresentation of what I was about to take home with me. Why? Well, by the time my oldest child was twenty-one, she had changed her given name, twice. By the time my youngest was eighteen, he had been called Joey, Troah, Jay, Inner Strength, The Darkness, Mr. Giggles, Tray and Leon. None of these were nicknames. *That* isn't something a mom sees coming. A word of caution might have saved at least some of the feelings of panic.

On second thought, it probably wouldn't have. It would have taken more than that to prepare me for what was to come.

So, should a mom feel differently about her kids because their names did not remain the names they were given at birth? Should I care?

I did care... at least in the beginning.

If you are a parent, you probably know what I was feeling. I'm sure you have, at one point or another, looked at your children and thought... *hmmm, this is not what I thought I was signing on for.* Hours of pacing with a baby who is screaming, for no obvious reason. Coming home from work to find out you're going to spend the next six hours working on a project that is due the next day and hasn't been started yet. Hearing your teenager use that tone on you: the one that says, "Mom, you're an idiot. You know nothing."

You can't help but feel that this parenting thing isn't exactly what you had planned. This can't be your kid! What follows is probably guilt. And that thought that crosses all our minds — *God, am I a bad parent?* But guilt was only one of the exhausting emotions I felt on the path to accepting my two young-adult children.

When I decided to have a family, I thought my children would grow up to be like me... you know, a bit quirky maybe, but, a regular Jane. Don't get me wrong. I'm not saying that that's a bad thing. I just didn't think a child of mine would grow up to be anything out-of-the-ordinary. Boy, was I wrong.

I had their lives all planned out for them: college, marriage, giving me grandchildren. And, until the teen years, our life was reasonably on track, pretty run-of-the-mill. So, I spent my days building this beautiful, typical, middle-class nest. Well, it was during those fragile teen years that fate decided to shake the hell out of me.

The day Jul told me that she wasn't like other girls took me down hard. I couldn't stand, or function; I could barely breathe. You would think that a day like that, a day that totally destroyed a parent's dream for her daughter's perfect life, would be the hardest day that a mom would ever have to go through. But it wasn't my toughest moment as a parent; unfortunately, I was just getting my feet wet. Thank God, I didn't know that at the time. I needed to ground myself and find my legs again before her brother, Joey, took his turn at knocking them out from under me. If I had had to deal with Joey taking little breaks from reality at the same time I tried to accept what Jul was, I probably would have felt like a victim — someone fate had decided to toy with, just to see how much one mom could take. I mean, the odds of having the two children I have must be inconceivable.

My nest didn't turn out at all like I had planned it. Inside, there should have been two fluffy, little robins that grew into beautiful, red-chested birds. I forgot that watching an eagle soar can stop the world for a moment. That the sound of a loon can calm me. That watching a chickadee flit, or a hummingbird float, can instantly put me in a better mood. They are all beautiful in their own right. The same sun shines on all of them. The same wind lifts all their wings. And children are the same. They are all different, and they are all special. It just took me a while to figure that out.

Chapter 1
Me

My childhood was filled with secrets.

My mom shook her head at me a lot. I was a handful at times. I did pray; it's just that I couldn't seem to set myself on the timer that my mom had managed to put my older brothers and my sister on. Why did I have to pray at ten o'clock on Sunday morning? I felt as though I was being pushed and pressed, and forced into a mold that just didn't fit. I hated the dusty smell of the church. I sat looking at the angels on the ceiling during Mass, wishing I were outside, feeling the sun heating my skin. If I squirmed too much, I would feel her heavy hand press firmly on my leg.

This is stupid. Why can't I just pray when I need to?

I wondered how these thoughts would make God feel about me. Why couldn't I just be a good girl?

I was definitely a willful child. But even so, I knew I could never tell my mom that I didn't want to go to church on Sunday. She would have reacted with shock and disgust, as if I had told her I wanted to grow up to be a serial killer. It was something I was forced to keep to myself. We weren't allowed to question our religion.

My siblings and I were raised to follow the Catholic religion to the letter. My mom would constantly teach one of life's strict guidelines: present yourself well, especially every Sunday in church. Perception was important. Obey all the rules of the church and follow the commandments verbatim. Don't let anyone see that you are anything less than what you were taught to be by these rules. There were no exceptions, even if it meant letting your youngest daughter marry at eighteen to a boy you were not at all sure about. What else could you do? Living together was just not tolerated.

If there were a scandal in the family, you did your very best to cover it up, or, at least, to keep it as quiet as possible. What the neighbors thought of you seemed as important as being a good person.

In a town of 7000, your "neighbors" were everywhere. I could easily walk from one end of my town to the other. People would recognize me and wave as I passed. Friendly eyes keeping a watchful guard.

Beginning with the smell of the river, I would follow a street filled with the sound of rustling leaves from 100-year-old trees until I hit the downtown core. The movie theatre was my favorite place. There was a bowling alley, and two hotels: one filled with the draining sounds of country music, the other vibrating from the thud of its rock beat. A smattering of various small shops fell in between. I would hear greetings: casual toot-toots from cars passing by.

Next, I would see the newer part of town, with its proper bungalows. I remember the smell of the grass, each lawn sporting a fresh new buzz cut. The street was wide and the traffic unhurried here. A car might pull up beside me, its familiar driver offering me a ride.

I would eventually hit the mall — there must have been a dozen stores!

Past the mall were merely fields, waiting for something exciting to come to town.

I could make this walk safely in a half hour at any time of the day. It seemed, however, that I could not do it without someone who knew my family seeing me and knowing exactly what I was up to. I didn't realize back then just how tiny our town was, and just how many eyes followed me around. If I hadn't been wrapped up in my adventures, I may have known that many of my secrets weren't secrets at all.

I remember one example of *that* vividly: before I really had the knack of hiding the truth, I "rescued" a kitten from a poor family who lived close by.

Their house was on my way to grade school. They lived up the street... quite a piece up. Our street was a real mishmash of homes. Mine was a bungalow built by my parents in the fifties. A few were A-frames that looked like they outdated the turn of the century and really hadn't held up so well. The family with the cats lived in one of those.

Their A-frame looked like it was ready to collapse. The yard had a few rusting vehicles with flat tires, a variety of furniture that looked ready for recycling and out of place in the outdoors, and an whole lot of other stuff you might see in a junk yard. It made me feel uncomfortable to walk by.

There was one up-side of having to pass it, however — I looked for their little balls of fur as I walked by each day. I had one of my own, but she was fat and lazy. Their cats were scruffy and skinny. And hungry looking. If the old man that sat out front smoking wasn't there, I'd try to pet one as I passed, but most of them would dart off if I even got close.

Then this family, which already had more cats than was fair for one home, hit the jackpot — kittens. I didn't like it... the ones they already had didn't look like they got fed very often. I had to do something.

There was a big pine tree in my back yard. On one side, at the bottom, was a hollowed out part. It was perfect for a little secret home. So, I padded it with a blanket, snuck over to the poor family's house and grabbed a kitten.

The little wriggling fur ball fit nicely under my sweater. The whole run home my heart pounded. My eyes darted from house

Secret Selves

to house looking for witnesses. When I hit the safety of home, I cooed to my new little pet and headed straight out to my backyard fort. I vowed to love it and care for it; sneaking bits of food outside for the little guy whenever the opportunity arose.

I thought I was so sly.

Until the family knocked on my front door and told my parents that I had stolen one of their pets.

Well, I might have slipped up once in a while in my early years, but I think I managed to keep a fierce guard on the important secrets. At least in my mind, I had parts of my life that were kept private and out of sight from the neighbors.

That was hard to do when everyone knew you. It was mostly due to the fact that everyone in town knew my father. I often drive by the volunteer firefighter's hall just to see his name posted on the dedication to the building. It makes me think of the nights my mom spent chipping him out of his frozen fire chief's suit in the middle of winter. I'd stumble out of my room, rubbing the sleep from my eyes, trying to see what the strange tap-tap coming from the kitchen was. I'd find my mom holding a hammer in one hand and a long pointy thing in the other. "Go back to bed, honey," she'd say. "Everything's fine."

Sometimes, my dad would take me on drives in the country to take photographs, so he could paint the bubbling water, quiet trees and fringe of mountains surrounding our hometown. As he raised the camera I'd get a whiff of the oil-based paint embedded deep under his finger nails. It was probably a safe estimate that at least a third of the homes where I lived had one of his paintings hanging on the wall. Because of a bad heart, he was forced to retire from his day job at 62, when I was barely a teenager. He filled his time with art. I spent the odd Saturday with him, tending his exhibits at local craft shows.

My mother spent her days clicking at the keys of her typewriter and scribbling shorthand at an insurance office. Her free time was spent volunteering. Most people knew who I was because they knew my parents.

I was fresh out of college when I moved back to that small town. It seemed even smaller by then, but somehow felt like a shelter from the cold, anonymous anger of the cities. It was a place to start a family. My kids would be safe here.

And my husband, Earl, just couldn't wait to get started. I became pregnant less than a year after we were married. Julia Marie was born healthy, only four days before Christmas, just six weeks before my twentieth birthday. A special Christmas gift to us!

Barely an adult myself, I had this fresh little human being who was totally dependent on me. A huge responsibility, but the love I felt was incredible. It was a feeling I would experience again, four and a half years later, when Jul's brother, Joey, was born.

There is no denying that instant, incredible love; every mother knows it. And you want to give your children everything you missed out on in life — whatever that happens to be... opportunity, understanding, love, material things. What I didn't think about at the time is that I'd already given them something. The thing we all give our children automatically — genetics. And oblivious to me, my children had inherited a trait I would not learn to overcome until much later in life. Just like their mom's, my children's young lives were filled with secrets. Big secrets.

Jul: Birth-2002
Chapter 2

Secrets. For years I thought secrets were a normal part of life. Everyone had them. No harm done. I didn't realize that what my children would one day conceal was in a completely different league from what I considered important to keep private. I'm not sure when, but somewhere along the way, I realized that hiding away those truths can have a damaging, life-changing effect.

Looking at my daughter when she was young though, you would have seen a happy, easy going child. She gave off a carefree, tomboy vibe. There was no evidence of the painful secrets.

From the moment Julia was born, there was a very natural closeness between us. She was an easy baby, but being a girl was never easy for Jul. She didn't play with dolls, or dress up in my jewelry and heels, or do anything any other little girl did. She played with cars, climbed trees and spent her time with boys. Having happily climbed my share of gnarly trees and constructed dozens of assorted forts, I didn't even bat an eye. Dolls were boring in my childhood mind. Catching a soft, wart-covered toad and finding a secret home to hide him in was much more interesting to me. Dressing like a cowboy or a gruesome, ugly troll was more appealing than wearing anything pretty. I thought it was wonderful. Jul was just like me! I saw no sign of the awful childhood pain she would share with me years later.

* * *

Maybe I should have been able to see hints of it early on. At five, she wanted desperately to play hockey.

"It's today, right, Mommy?" Excitement trickled through her voice.

"Yes, honey, it's today. We're going to the rink right now." I looked at her babysitter and rolled my eyes, smiling and shaking my head a little.

"Will I get to wear my skates *today*?" She hopped toward the car.

"Yep, that's what we're going there for."

"When, Mommy? When will I get to wear them?"

She was so eager. I looked at her and ran my hand through the silky feel of her shoulder-length, shiny brunette hair. "The first thing we're going to do is put your skates on."

"Will it be a *real* hockey game, Mommy?"

The ad said Power Skating would teach the kids the skills they needed for the local hockey league. "They're going to show you how to hold your stick and pass the puck, stuff like that. It'll make you a better hockey player."

That first night was one of my all-time, most embarrassed mom moments. We arrived at the rink (Jul in a matching sweater-and-mitten set my mom had knit her) to find a bunch of little boys in pretty much full hockey gear. It was a couple shades of pink, her sweater set. I remember it clearly. Probably because you could pick Jul out of the group in a second, no matter where she was on the ice.

I sat on the bleachers, shaking my head. *Good God, why hadn't they warned me when I'd signed her up?!* Maybe people would think the cold of the rink was causing my scarlet cheeks, not the fact that I felt like a total moron.

It didn't seem to discourage Jul, though. She got out on the ice with her hockey stick, teetering unsteadily, and gave it her all, solid determination showing in every shaky movement. At the end, she wobbled off the ice toward me.

I took her little chin in my hand. "I think we'll have to get you some hockey gear like the boys, won't we?"

Her eyes sparkled with excitement, and her face broke into a huge smile.

With a bit of detective work, I managed to find some second-hand equipment. On night number two, Jul was one of the boys. She looked absolutely adorable in her little helmet, shoulder pads and jersey. And that look of pride — priceless! I chuckled to myself as I watched her show the boys she was worthy of the uniform.

The course only lasted a few weeks. Toward the end, I thought maybe I should get some information on what the next step was. It was starting to look as though I would have to learn how to be a hockey mom. If Jul had wanted to play basketball, Earl, her dad, might have done his part, but hockey was not his thing, so I was completely on my own.

My inquiries led to crushing news that changed Jul overnight. Only boys were allowed in the hockey league. After learning that she had to play ringette, a girl's game where you chased a ring with a straight stick, her interest in skating vanished. Her tomboy attitude stuck around, though.

Viewing those years in hindsight, I had a naïve confidence — almost a cockiness about parenting. I was in control. I would eventually learn that things aren't always as they seem; that even the sunny disposition of my Jul could turn into a storm cloud, hovering. It could even suddenly drop a bolt of lightning, striking close enough to stop my heart for a second.

But when Jul was five, parenting seemed easy. All I had to do was redirect her energy. So she couldn't play hockey, so what? I introduced her to soccer. There was a co-ed league in town and she could run around with the boys and be as rough as the rules allowed. She loved it. Problem solved.

Back then, there was certainly no adventure to being Jul's mom. The biggest challenge she offered me was asking me to say goodbye to her long, brown hair. Her dad took her to our hairdresser, and she came home looking like a cute little boy. It startled me. The cut was shorter than I'd pictured when she left for the appointment, but it was what she wanted.

It would have to grow on me a bit. Her beautiful hair had been shiny and wonderful to touch. It had looked just like mine had when I was a tyke. I would miss it. Jul, on the other hand, beamed with her new look. She was starting to make decisions; I could see the first signs that she wasn't my baby anymore.

*   *   *

In some respects, as Jul was growing up, her dad and I were growing up with her. Having married so young, Earl and I had both gone through major changes since our vows. Our marriage, which had started out filled with love, now harbored resentment and anger.

I worried about the atmosphere my children were growing up in. I remember one day in particular. It was a summer day, the ninth summer we had spent as man and wife. Jul was 7; Joey, her brother, was 3. Earl arrived home from wherever he had spent his day; I never knew where that had been.

He was carrying a large bag of dog food, about the size of a full pillow case. He hadn't even set it down yet and I asked, "Did you get paid today? That hydro bill is due tomorrow." Money was a constant battle.

"Jesus, Jamie, would you get off my back for one fucking minute." He threw the bag of dog food down hard.

Secret Selves

The impact tore it open, sending kibble flying across the entire kitchen floor. They were big nuggets, the kind for full-size dogs. It sounded like a large truck had just dropped a load of gravel in my kitchen.

Jul was standing close to me, on the opposite side of the room from her dad. As the nuggets rolled across the cushion floor toward us, covering almost every inch of floor space, her little eyes seemed wide as dinner plates.

How did you become such a jerk? What happened to you?

He snarled out the next line. "It's *my* construction company. I'll use the money for whatever I feel like."

Sure, and I'll use every cent I can scratch up to pay the bills? That's fair.

I was tired of these fights. Taking in a deep breath first, I tried again. "Earl, the marriage counselor said that if we're going to stay together, we need to work together. You have to be honest with me. Did you get paid?"

He stood with his head to one side, looking annoyed. "Fine. Yes, I got paid."

"How much did he give you? All of it?"

He looked straight into my eyes. "I told you I got paid. And I'm going to be *honest* with you — that's all I'm going to tell you."

Jul and her toddler brother were seeing too many arguments, hearing too many harsh words. It was no environment to grow up in. It was no way for anyone to live.

Earl's life choices had squashed out any feelings of respect and trust I once had for him. I felt as if I was spending my life trying to convince him to change, while I covered up his habits. We gave counseling a miserable attempt. It didn't help. I guess he tried to save the marriage, but that would have involved a major transformation in his life. And that's a pretty difficult task — to change who you are.

Finally, having reached my limit, I found a nice house to rent, with a big yard bordering a field. I moved my two children into our new home, and started over. Everything in my 5 foot 2 inch frame told me I was doing the right thing.

I have to admit, I was a bit scared. Could I make a go of life on my own? Well, I was going to give it one hell of a try. I was surprised by my attitude, though. I had been raised to believe that when you marry, it's for life. I thought I *had* married for life, but *this* just felt right.

My little house was barely affordable without child support. I'd have to swing it, though. Earl was not about to help out. I mean, really, at the end of our marriage, he didn't seem to care if our bills were ever paid. Why would he care if I now missed a bill or two? I'd have to watch my pennies, but I'd be fine. I worked full-time for a manufacturing facility and I'd get a second job if I had to. I'd make it work.

That experience was a turning point in my life. I decided if I was going to start my life over, why not start off right, a real fresh start. I'd spent my life keeping the peace. I finally made the decision that if I was going to do this alone, it was time to be me, not the person everyone expected me to be. It looked as if it was up to me to be the role model for my kids, so I committed to being an honest one. No more hiding my husband's habits — it wasn't my job to protect his reputation anymore. I wouldn't go around bashing him (well... I would try not to, anyway), but I wouldn't protect him either. No more pretending to get something out of going to church — I am definitely a spiritual person, just not a religious one. That's all. No more worrying about people's whispers either. They were going to get the real me. If that made them gossip, so be it. I decided life was too short to live it only to please others. I had been suffocating. It was time to let myself breathe, experience life without binding.

Freedom didn't come without a price, however. Even though I felt I was doing the right thing, I worried about what our split was doing to the kids. The separation had to have had an effect on Jul. How could it not? They say the younger the children are, the more resilient they are. Joey had only just turned three. I'd keep my eye on him, but he seemed okay. He was a handful, that was for sure, but he had been since he was born. No changes there. I worried about Jul, though.

When I notified her school, they put her into a program designed to help kids deal with the challenges of life in an upset home. It was called Rainbows for All God's Children. She seemed fine, but I figured there must be things she was going through that I couldn't see, so I asked her what they talked about at Rainbows.

In her cheerful way, she casually replied, "They tell us our families might be different than other people's, but that's okay. And they give us ice cream! I *like* ice cream."

She was so cute. She was just that type of child: adaptable. We were moving from the country into town. Jul seemed to see it as an opportunity to make friends. She found a playground down the street with tall trees, high swings, a play structure to climb on, and some neighborhood boys to go to it with. She taught her little brother to climb the big tree in our yard. It was a massive Maple, with branches in all the right places. Joey thought his sister could do anything, so he eagerly watched. Sitting on the front porch, enjoying the sweetness of the fresh cut grass, I would watch my daughter demonstrate the art of climbing a tree. On Sundays, she would go to church with my mom, and, then afterwards, sit with my dad while he painted his landscapes. She loved being with him, surrounded by the smell of oil paint and turpentine. Once in a while, as she sat on his knee, he would put his long paintbrush in her hand. I will never forget how high she held her head the day she brought home her first Julia original.

Things seemed to be working out just fine. After about a year, I started dating a great guy who the kids were comfortable having around. Life was normal enough, I thought, except for one small, very important, hidden detail.

Chapter 3

I spent the next eight to ten years correcting people who thought Jul was my son.

We'd be at the mall. A colleague from work would stop pushing her cart down the aisle of the grocery store. "Hi, Jamie, how are you?" And then turning, "And you must be Joey?"

I tried my best not to look embarrassed. "No, actually this is Jul." She was twelve and it was *still* happening.

My friend looked at the floor, horrified, and then lifted her gaze back up to Jul. "Oh, of course, where *is* my head today?"

It wasn't her fault, really; Jul looked like a boy. It was an honest mistake.

Poor Jul. She must hate this? I looked at my daughter, but when I searched her face, she didn't look the least bit uncomfortable. Strangely enough, she looked, somehow, content.

Everyone thought she was a boy. You couldn't blame them — she wore a ball cap and jeans constantly. There was always something to do with sports on her un-tucked, oversized T-shirt. She wanted her hair cut if it reached anywhere close to two inches.

It was much more than a look, though. It was an attitude. She had the outgoing, aggressive nature of a boy. Throughout my children's early years, one of my everyday battles was to break up stubborn bickering, calm flared tempers, and tear my daughter and her brother away from each other. They were constantly at it. As Jul put it later in life, "Not even my dad could control us when we were on a roll!" Jul would assert herself as if she was Joey's big brother, tackling him and forcing him to do things her way. Her personality matched her boyish look.

When puberty kicked in, I became a little worried. Shouldn't she have some female friends who she could talk to? I knew her feelings and thoughts were about to get more complicated, and her body was changing. It didn't look as if she was going to have the overly curvy shape that I fought with every time I shopped for clothes, but she definitely had a figure. It was more athletic than mine, but it was obviously changing, and she certainly wouldn't be able to talk about *that* with the boys she spent all her time with. She'd spent a bit of time with a few of the girls in her grade, but it looked as though she felt uncomfortable with them.

She seemed tense. I wondered if it was the new surge of hormones, or the frustration of not fully fitting in with any of the little cliques at school. Whatever it was, it intensified the battle between my children. Dealing with Joey had always required a certain amount of patience. As my dad would have said, the boy was more of a whipper-snapper than I'd ever been, and he could wind Jul up without even trying. It seemed as if there was a whole year that I could count on her to meet me as I came home after work, every single day. I'd barely have one foot through the door before I heard, "Mom!"

"Joey erased the Nintendo game I was playing. I worked on it for hours and now it's completely gone!"

Or, "Joey keeps standing right in front of the TV. I'm watching it. He wants me to change the channel, and he won't shut up!"

Or, "Joey spilled a Coke in the living room and he won't clean it up. I told him he couldn't have one, but he did anyway!"

I'd take a long, frustrated breath as she spoke. "Jul, could you *please* just give me five minutes when I get home before I have to start refereeing... *please?*"

I had to find a way for her to be more relaxed, and find friends who she could talk to... either that or I might just choke the two of them.

I needed advice. How do you help a kid who has spent her whole life doing boys' stuff, suddenly fit in with girls? It had happened naturally with me. It did take me a while to find friends that I felt natural around, but I transitioned into "girly" stuff effortlessly. I liked jewelry. I wanted a purse. I couldn't wait to get my first kiss from a boy. But Jul seemed stuck.

I needed a second opinion from someone I respected and trusted.

I turned to a psychologist I'd seen when Joey was five. Joey had stopped sleeping in his bed because he was convinced there was a hand living in it, and this hand wasn't friendly. (Jul and Joey had watched The Addams Family together — I think Jul had something to do with that particular phobia.) I assumed that the fear of this imaginary hand was a temporary thing. Every once in a while I'd try to convince him there was nothing to be nervous about. I'd give it my best shot, but nothing worked. After six months of him curling up on the mat beside his bed and reaching up to pull his blanket down over him, I began to worry.

My counselor told me not to stress over it. "He won't sleep on the floor for the rest of his life, Jamie. It won't hurt him. He'll get back in when he's ready."

He'd been right. It took quite a while for Joey to brave the sheets again; it was probably another year, but he got back in. Sometimes, things just need time. Maybe Jul's difficulty fitting in was one of those things, but I had to find out.

My cool, calm therapist listened attentively while I explained my concerns.

"I hate this. It's giving me flashbacks. It took me forever to find close friends who I clicked with. I didn't fit in with the brainy group or the jocks. It seemed so hard to find friends I really connected with. I guess Jul's having the same problem. I wish she could find some girlfriends. Especially now. Don't you think that's important?"

I wanted her life to be perfect. Somehow, as parents, we seem to think that we have some level of control over that.

The doctor had an opinion right away. "I think you're right, Jamie."

My heart sank. I had secretly hoped it was just paranoia on my part.

"Don't worry about Jul having a lot of friends who are boys. That's just fine. But I think some closeness with girls is important right now."

I sat in thought for a moment. "Any idea how I would do that?"

"Well... how about something like a pizza and movie get-together after school some day... just girls, and maybe, if Jul is open to it, she could take off her ball cap while the girls are over." He knew she wore that damn thing every day. "They just need to see she isn't that different after all."

* * *

I sat in my rocking chair; swinging back and forth relaxed me. Jul sat on the couch. Her eyebrows were scrunched together. "I don't know, Mom."

"Dr. Bill says he thinks it'll help. It's worth a try. I'll get whatever kind of pizza you want... and snacks. You'll enjoy it."

"But why do I have to take off my cap?"

"It's only for one night, honey. Just to show them you're just like any other girl."

"But it's just a cap, Mom." She looked annoyed. Her cap was part of her identity.

"Dr. Bill thinks it's a good idea."

"Fine." It sounded like she knew I wasn't going to give up.

Taking off her ball cap for the party did not miraculously make Jul "like" the other girls. As I fluttered around the room, delivering drinks and filling chip bowls, I could see that it would take more than a pizza party to make her fit in with these girls. She looked as if she was trying to feel like a part of the group, awkwardly adding something to the conversation when she could (which wasn't often). She didn't share their interests; she had nothing in common with them. They were concerned with fashion. They were all starting to pay attention to boys; many had started to date. Jul couldn't hide the fact that she had no interest in either of those things. How could she just suddenly fit in? The girls were polite to her for the most part, but that was about as good as it got. And the ball cap, well, it was back on her head the minute those girls stepped out the door.

Things went back to normal. I wondered exactly why she didn't fit in with the girls. I didn't think it was her personality. She was easygoing and she had absolutely no trouble making new friends who were boys. She was dyslexic, a fact that everyone knew, but surely that had nothing to do with it… they wouldn't judge her for that, would they? Her grades were fine.

Then what was it?

I came up with an idea. Although filled mostly with boys, there were a few girls in her class. One seemed very sweet and I thought she may be able to offer some insight into the problem.

"Jul, why don't you call Margaret and ask her why you're not seen as 'one of the girls'?"

Maybe it is that damned cap.

Jul was horrified. "Mom, I can't call Margaret and say that. She'll think I'm a freak!"

I pressed. "Honey, it won't hurt to ask. If you find out what it is that makes you seem a little different to them, it might be something you can easily change."

"Mom…"

"Come on, honey. Give it a try. Please… for me."

Jul sighed. "It's not going to help."

"There is only one way to find out."

I stood a few feet away as she looked hesitantly at the phone. She just stood there for a few minutes, looking. She turned to me and wrinkled up her forehead. "I hate this, Mom."

I felt for the kid. "I know, honey. I hate this too, but it might give us some answers."

She looked at the phone again.

"Come on. Take a deep breath and do it. You'll feel better when it's over."

She slowly dialed the number. The poor thing looked terrified. "Hi…um…Margaret? It's Jul. I….I'm…okay. You? Yeah, I'm calling cause, well…um, I need to ask you something." Her eyes darted nervously to me and then flicked back to the floor. She took a deep breath. "I don't quite know how to put this. It's just that… well, uh… I feel like the girls think I'm weird or something. Do you know why?"

There was a short pause and then "Yeah, I know, it's stupid, never mind. I'll see you tomorrow." Jul hung up quickly and turned to me with an exasperated look. "She doesn't know, Mom, okay. Can we please just drop it now?!"

The only thing I accomplished by that phone call was to embarrass two girls in grade seven. This young girl *was* very sweet: too sweet to tell Jul anything. My obsession with making Jul belong had probably only made things worse.

* * *

Finally, in grade eight she seemed to find her way into one of the little cliques. Hallelujah! It was a co-ed clique; a group of boys and girls who would hang out together. Jul grew close to a girl in that group who was a "little person."

My kids had grown up seeing her regularly and thought of her as anyone else. But having lived her life in such a small town, this

Secret Selves

girl, who had a body so much smaller from everyone else's, had most likely experienced her share of sideways glances and cruel snickers, just as Jul had. Especially once they hit high school.

Diversity just didn't exist on our streets. Jul and her friend were part of a very small minority of people who were different, and some of the kids in high school fed on those differences.

"Nice hair, Jul. Did the clippers get out of control?"

"Where'd you get that shirt, Jul? What's wrong, did nothing in the *women's* section fit?"

"You coming to the prom, Jul? No, what was I thinking, that would involve having a *date*."

I think most people who knew my teenage daughter thought she would eventually share with the world the fact that she was a lesbian. I certainly did. She not only looked masculine, she gave off a strong male vibe.

In high school, she enthusiastically acted in three plays — always playing a male role. Her first part was the mayor in the short story, "The Lottery." I sat in the audience, musing about how the artsy side of my family was showing up on that stage. She had no acting experience, but she was pulling the role off beautifully. It just seemed to come easily to her.

During intermission, I overheard a conversation behind me. In an overly dramatic voice, a young girl said, "Interesting that Jul got a *male* role, isn't it?"

Luckily, the kids around her didn't bite at this conversation opener.

She tried again, snickering as she spoke. "Playing a *guy* really seems to work for her, doesn't it?"

Her friends didn't get caught up in her insinuation. It was a good thing, too. I held myself back, but if they'd jumped on board, I probably would have turned around and said, just as over-enthusiastically, "Hi there. I'm Jul's mom!"

I told myself to smarten up. I knew what was on this rude girl's mind. There are people everywhere who get a kick out of making fun of homosexuals and our high school was definitely not immune. Kids love to make fun of unique people. Being such a small town didn't help, either. There were probably fewer than ten kids in our schools who didn't have white skin. If you were the least bit different, you stood right out. It seemed as if many of the kids couldn't grasp the simple concept that being different shouldn't matter.

And in everything Jul had ever done, she was a little different from the norm. Sometimes it would be something subtle. When she was little and played Barbies with her cousin, Amber, she *had* to be Ken… always.

She would only play sports that were co-ed, challenging the boys every chance she got. She joined the school band with the hope that she would play the drums, something no girl had done in the history of the school. She auditioned and succeeded. She simply was not like every other girl.

I began to realize that it was probably time for Jul and me to have some type of talk about sexuality. Despite being raised to follow the strict rules of the Catholic church, I'm a pretty open-minded person, and I figured everyone who knew me would have to know this fact, including Jul.

I had remarried by then. Both her new stepdad, Will, and Joey were open-minded people. There was no reason for Jul to feel uncomfortable about telling us she was gay. But maybe still, in her teenage mind, there would be hesitation to talk about how she felt if her feelings were different from the norm. That's a pretty tough thing to bring up with your parents. It would be up to me.

I tried to let it happen as naturally as possible. We were very close, so we spent considerable time together. Finding time to talk usually wasn't difficult. One day we were watching a show about relationships on television. It seemed to create the perfect opportunity to open that door.

"Do you ever feel attracted to girls, honey?"

Her answer sounded slightly embarrassed. "Yes."

It came out so naturally that even though it was what I had been prepared for, it kind of surprised me. I guess it was just the newness of being open about it.

"Well... it doesn't matter who you're attracted to, honey. It won't change the way we love you. It's perfectly okay to feel like that and you don't have to feel uncomfortable talking about it."

The relieved look on her face assured me that I had done the right thing.

To hear the closest person in the world to you say that she didn't care if you were different, that it was perfectly fine, had to feel good.

And I felt great!

Open, comfortable, honest communication with my teenager — I must be doing something right.

So... if we were that close, if we were that honest with each other, how did I make such a mess of things? Why didn't I know that my child's youth was filled with pain? Why didn't I see the signs?

I had no idea that later in life, as an adult, my daughter would look back at her youth, and write about those early years with these words: *Life sucks. How can people tell me that life is filled with happiness, and all these great things are ahead, when all I feel is pain and hate toward the world? Why does it hurt so much all the time to be me? Is this normal?*

My mom always told me that for all the bad things in our life, something good is to come, but as far back as I can remember, I don't have good thoughts. Not that every day has been terrible, but then again, at the same time, it has. I hate me. I hate to look into the mirror. I hate the sight of myself. I go to bed every night crying, praying for God to take away the pain that I feel every day.

It's like I'm wearing this costume that doesn't have a zipper for me to take it off. My heart aches with the thought of waking up tomorrow, and having to live this life I hate again and again. Will I wake up someday from this nightmare to find out that it was all a bad dream? Wouldn't that be great? I pull the covers over my head and try to quiet my cries. How can I live like this every day? After all, I'm only ten years old....

Chapter 4

The phone was ringing *again*.

Shortly after *the talk*, the thing began to ring constantly. It was Jul's line. We had two — one for us, one for the kids. It's one of those things that seem necessary in a blended family. Since I'd taken Will's name, my last name was different from the kids'. I wanted my children's friends to be able to find them. It just seemed like the right thing to do — to have a line with a listing in the phone book using their last name.

Most of the time, we ignored the ring of their line, but lately it had been relentless. That line didn't have an answering machine, and the person on the other end seemed to believe in letting it go for twenty rings or so. They would wait ten minutes and try again — another twenty rings. *Jesus!*

Not being able to stand it any longer, I reached for Jul's phone. "Hello."

"Could I please speak to Mark?"

We didn't have a Mark in our home. "I'm sorry, you've got the wrong number."

The first half a dozen or so times I answered, I would politely give the young girl on the other end that same response. The calls didn't stop. It was the same girl *every time*. Why could this person not get it?

The sound of the phone started to burrow in and eat at my nerves. I would roll my eyes and drop my shoulders. *What is wrong with her?* "Hello."

"Uh… could I speak to Mark, please?"

Annoyance edged its way into my voice. "Look, what number are you trying to reach?"

It didn't add up. She was trying to reach us.

"I'm sorry, but, like I keep telling you, no Mark lives here. We have a Jamie, a Will, a Julia, and a Joey. That's it. No Mark. We've never had a Mark."

She sounded desperate. "But that doesn't make sense. I know it's the right number; half of the time Mark answers." She sounded as confused as we were as she described the long conversations they'd had together from this number. You could hear her frustration.

"Well... no Mark lives here. Sorry."

"Okay... whatever."

I certainly didn't blame her for sounding discouraged and a bit angry, especially since every time she reached us she was paying a long distance charge. She was calling from several hundred miles away.

Still she kept it up. It didn't take long before the constant telephone ring was not the only bell grating in my head. This Mark mystery was setting off loud alarms. Jul was on the phone a lot. She had a lot of Internet friends, spent countless hours sitting at the computer, and a few of the friendships had developed to the point that phone conversations began.

With two lines, we didn't have to keep track of who owed what on the phone bill. Joey wasn't old enough to be interested in the phone yet, so the total bill for their line was always one hundred percent Jul's.

Lately, it had been a bit of an issue. It was sometimes pretty outrageous. Jul had two part-time jobs, so she did have the money to pay the bill. It just seemed that several times, every cent of her pay was ending up in the pocket of the phone company.

I'd decided months back that Jul must need these phone and Internet friendships — friends who couldn't see her, couldn't judge her. As long as she kept the bill paid, what was the harm? I would turn a blind eye. But this Mark mystery was making me crazy. I was suspicious. Now that we knew where this long distance caller was from, it was time to take a closer look at that bill.

The alarm bells were ringing for a reason. Jul was making a lot of calls to the same place that Mark's girlfriend had called from.

What the hell was going on?

It triggered a memory of something that had happened when Jul was somewhere between ten and twelve. She had become Tom in a letter to a girl. The girl had been a friend of one of the guys Jul chummed around with, and the words Jul had written in that note were distinctively flirty. It was signed with her male alias, Tom. I had found that letter.

Why I didn't question why a young girl would do this is beyond me. It must have been denial. All I saw was total dishonesty. It was the only time I can remember being angry enough at Jul to let my temper get away from me.

She says the "F" word even made its way into the conversation that day… something that never happened. I swore the odd time, but not in front of my kids, and never at them.

I screamed at her as I tore up the note and threw it into the trash. I vividly remember the size of her eyes, so I must have really let her have it.

She wouldn't dare do something like that again, would she?

It was time Jul and I had a little talk.

She was in her room, playing a video game. I tried to control my tone, but it came out forcefully. "Jul, could you pause that, please?"

She looked up nervously.

I wasted no time. "Are you pretending to be a boy named Mark?"

Her eyebrows lifted. "No."

I looked at her hard and cocked my head. "Tell me the truth. I've talked to her. She calls a lot when you're not home."

Her eyes quickly moved to a spot on the floor. She lifted them for a second, but they were filled with big, sad tears and when she met my eyes, she quickly looked away again.

"I'm sorry, Mom."

Those words crushed my spirit temporarily. I felt like I had lost a long battle. "What's going on, Jul?"

She took a deep breath and closed her eyes. "She's a girl I met on the Internet. I couldn't help it, Mom; I have a crush on her."

I could feel the blood rush to my face, my whole body growing tense. "How long has this been going on?"

Jul opened her eyes, but continued to stare at the floor. She shrugged, "I don't know… a few months."

I saw red. I was angry with modern technology for providing the opportunity for this. I was angry with myself for somehow letting it happen. I was angry with this damn girl for being so naïve. But most of all, I was angry with Jul.

"Jesus, Jul."

My daughter wasn't a rebellious teen. When I was upset, she was upset. You could tell my anger, which didn't surface often, was causing her seams to let go. Big tears ran down her cheeks.

"Why did you do it?"

She could only sob out the words, "I don't know… I don't know." Each convulsive breath sounded like it tore off another piece of her heart. I could hear that she hated that it had to be like this. I could hear the pain.

I did feel for her; all she wanted was to enjoy the connection she had made with this girl. But I couldn't let her tears change my reaction. I had to teach her that her actions had consequences. I knew she was going through a difficult, internal identity struggle, adjusting to life as a lesbian, but she had to realize that everything we do has an effect on someone else.

"Honey, you can't keep doing this. You just can't. It isn't fair. You are lying to this poor girl. Keeping the truth from someone is exactly the same thing as lying. You have two choices — end the relationship or tell this girl the truth!"

Jul was an emotional mess. "I can't, Mom. I need some time. *Please!* I didn't mean to hurt anyone. I just… I really like this girl. Please, Mom. I need some time to think."

My old feelings of anger toward Jul's father resurfaced, worsening the rotten feeling developing in the pit of my stomach. At the end of the marriage, it seemed as if lies were a part of our daily life.

Those feelings that came from being lied to had stayed with me like a bag of old garbage I couldn't quite get to the curb. His stories had made me feel not only deceived, but also unloved and un-trusted. Respect for people and honesty were qualities that I'd tried hard to instill in my kids. How could Jul intentionally deceive this poor girl? I imagined how shredded her heart would be when she found out the truth.

Jul wasn't a mean person. She was usually caring and sensitive. She must not have been thinking clearly. I tried to reason some sense into the situation; I needed to slow the momentum of my anger.

I guessed that she must have figured it would be easier to get girls interested in her if they thought she was a boy. Maybe she just wasn't comfortable with the idea of being a lesbian yet. She probably didn't think there were too many teenage gay girls talking about it freely, either.

Obviously, her scheme had worked.

All I could think was, *Oh, that poor girl. She'll be crushed when she finds out.* I wondered what effect this experience would have on a fragile, lovesick, young teen. I slowly shook my head.

I thought I had taught Jul the value of honesty. I had to find a way to give her a shove into reality. She seemed to be wearing blinders.

Instinctively, I felt I had the answer.

Jul and I often watched movies together. Wednesday night was chick-flick night in our house. Jul and I would pick something out, watch it and talk about it. We shared a lot of things and one of them was the love of a good movie. As if being helped by fate, I remembered a story that to me personalized the impact of lying to people. It just so happened that the circumstances of the movie, although different, had similarities to Jul's situation.

It was called "Boys Don't Cry," a heart-wrenching, true story of a transgender girl living her life as a boy. When the main character had been born, the doctor had looked at her reproductive organs and said, "It's a girl." She, however, identified completely with the opposite gender. It made life horribly difficult.

The movie depicts a very disturbing re-enactment. It unfolds a true-life story with unflinching realism, no matter how tragic. It might just show Jul that this sort of thing could not be taken lightly.

The night we watched the movie brought mixed feelings for me. Although I wanted Jul to see the horror lying could bring, I hated exposing her to such tunnel-visioned hatred. It is everything I despise, but the movie is presented in a way that would, no doubt, leave a strong impact on her emotions and her intellect. She would understand the cruel realities of the story. The movie would drive home my point — in serious relationships, honesty is a necessity. If she were a lesbian, she needed to be upfront about it. She needed to understand that lying about being a boy could even be dangerous.

"Boys Don't Cry" begins with the main character, Brandon, meeting a girl named Alanna, and the two falling in love. Alanna believes Brandon is one hundred percent male. Brandon, who has lied about his identity before, has always paid a price for it. He decides to tell Alanna the truth, describing himself as having a sort of "weirdness — a birth defect." Alanna seems to accept the problem, and shows him love regardless of the difficult news. Unfortunately, it is too late to undo the lies.

Brandon's *friends* have found out. They have clearly decided that he is some sort of freak, and is no longer their friend. The two *friends* take turns savagely punching and shoving him while tearing at his clothes. They rip his pants down, Brandon screaming for them to stop the whole time. They yell back cruelly, "Well... what the fuck are you?"

I looked over at Jul. Her eyes were wide with fear.

When his friends see that Brandon does not have a penis, they grab Alanna and forcefully hold her face at his exposed crotch, yelling, "Look at your boyfriend."

I blinked repeatedly as I watched, trying to keep my eyes from filling with tears. My hands automatically came up to cover my face. I hated seeing such unnecessary suffering. It was horrible to watch. No one should have to be treated like those two young people were treated. It certainly did get my point across, though. Jul had to be re-thinking her Mark charade at this point.

When Brandon tries to escape, they throw him into their car. Fearing for his life, Brandon desperately tries to calm them by explaining that he is still the same Brandon that they were friends with. The car stops at a deserted parking lot.

The two *friends* take turns getting on top of him and raping him. They stop periodically to step back, and take a punch or two, the whole time laughing and hooting. You can hear Brandon continuously pleading for them to get off. The scene is one of the hardest I have ever watched.

Our living room was silent as the scene played out. I was more than a little uncomfortable. I had forgotten how incredibly painful and well done this story was. This time, even more than the first, the movie had me in quiet sobs. I wanted to look over at Jul but couldn't. The story had me too shaken. At his young age, the lead character Brandon endures more types of pain than I had experienced or would hopefully, ever have to. The images on the screen placed a heavy boulder solidly in the pit of my stomach. It felt like I had taken my teenage daughter to the site of a horrible, bloody automobile accident, in order to teach her to drive safely. *Had I done the right thing?*

After the rape, Brandon fights to hold himself together, denying (even to himself) that it had happened, but his bruised, torn and bleeding skin expose the truth.

When the legal official begins to take his statement, the cold questions come at him as if he is still being beaten. "Did they fondle you? Did he stick his hand or a finger in you? So, you are saying that you are a virgin and they didn't stick it in you — just pop you one?" As Brandon struggles to retain his composure, the man continues his attack of questions. "Why do you run around with guys if you are a girl yourself? Why do you go around kissing the girls?"

As I watched, I imagined how Brandon felt, desperately needing to be a boy but facing arrogant, uncaring questions about the parts of himself he had tried so hard to hide from the world: the parts of himself that he hated. I imagined how hard it would be if you had a boy's brain, and a cold-hearted cop kept asking you about being touched like a girl. Brandon looked crushed. His look of defeat made me feel just how much he hated being treated like a girl.

Instead of receiving the empathy and the help he deserves, Brandon is treated with a disgusted demeanor and apathy. The conclusion to the movie ends with this teen being brutally murdered by his two *friends*.

I had forgotten that horrible detail.

It was so hard to sit through. The story's depiction of humiliation, betrayal, merciless rape and finally, murder literally makes you look away at times, but its message is about looking at life with unprejudiced eyes. It is a story about having the strength to find the incredible courage to be yourself. Jul had to learn to be herself and honest about who she was. Lying to people wouldn't make the problem go away; it would only make it worse.

Jul didn't say much as she watched. I tried to steal looks to get a read from her face. Her brain appeared to be approaching overload. I could see the concentration in her face. A person couldn't help but be completely moved by this story.

I hoped the harsh realities of the story were teaching her that lying in such a passionate area of life could have devastating effects. I wondered what was going through her head.

It wasn't until years later that I learned what *was* going through her head. The whole time, Jul sat thinking, "Holy crap! So, *that's* what I am!"

Chapter 5

Eight years later, when Jul was 24, she told me that watching that painful movie at 16 was almost like a gift to her. She experienced gratitude for having seen it, and felt an amazing closeness to the lead actress. It helped Jul to find herself. At 24, she still had dreams about meeting that actress. I guess it was fate that made me choose it.

I, on the other hand, continued life in my little bubble. Jul didn't say anything to me about her new discovery, and somehow I couldn't figure it out for myself. Jul had always been a boy. I couldn't recognize that then, but I can see it clearly now. I am not sure if I blocked out the possibility that Jul was a transgender, or if I really didn't see it. When I think back, I remember times when I don't know how I could have missed it.

Jul was 12 when Will and I got married. For the ceremony, I wanted her to wear a beautiful, dark teal dress covered in the same color of lace. Jul begged to wear a suit. Her cousin Amber couldn't understand why she complained over and over about having to wear this dress. Amber would have gladly worn it. But Jul desperately wanted to wear a suit. How could I not see the significance of that?

Maybe I didn't want to.

I remained in my protective little bubble for some time. Every once in a while, I could see hints that Jul had something important that needed to be talked about, but I was left to wonder what it was.

She did give me clues every once in a while, though. At 18, Jul had been getting the same boyish haircut for years. She liked the way it gelled into short spikes — the shorter the cut, the better the spikes.

She was on her way out to get it trimmed one afternoon in October. "Honey, you've had your hair the exact same for so long. This time, why don't you try it cut short like that, but with more feminine lines, like the girl across the street? I think her name's Nikki. You know the girl I mean, right?"

Jul looked back at me, saying nothing, her face expressionless. It was obvious she wasn't convinced.

I didn't hate her hair; it's just that I was getting tired of having to explain that to people that she was a girl. "I think it'd be really sharp on you. It'd really show how pretty you are. It's almost the same cut, just styled a little differently. Rachel knows Nikki, tell her to cut it like that; she'll know what you mean."

"Yeah, maybe, Mom. I gotta go."

While she was gone, I popped a pan of lasagna in the oven; it was for Jul, Joey and Will. I was going out for dinner. The pharmaceutical company I worked for was throwing a service award party to honor long term employees. Having reached the 15-year mark, I was excited and ready to celebrate.

My first service award party (at five years) had been so much fun. They always threw a great party! Pulled out all the stops. Open bar. Elegant dinner. At my ten-year mark, I'd had the flu and had missed it. I felt overdue to enjoy an evening on their tab, and this year, my boss was even giving me a drive so I didn't have to worry about how much wine I drank.

I ironed my fancy navy blue suit while the lasagna was baking. The glittery jewelry I picked out added a little something to the outfit. I touched up my eye liner and added a bit of blush and a rose-toned lipstick, making me feel more dressed up than usual. I was happy with the end result.

When Jul arrived home from her haircut, I stood at the counter in our big country kitchen. Enjoying the aroma of lasagna, I sliced French bread, trying not to get crumbs on my suit. She was barely in the door when I blurted out, "I thought you were going to get it cut a little more feminine this time?"

It looked the same as always.

Jul looked at me with the strangest expression. She instantly burst into tears, and ran off, up the stairs.

My mouth dropped open. Shock wiped the frustration from my face. *What the hell was that?*

It was almost time for my boss to pick me up. I'd have to deal with *this* first, though.

The door to Jul's room was closed. I knocked. "Can I come in, honey?"

She was lying on her double bed, tears running down her face.

I sat down beside her. "What's wrong, honey? I don't understand. What did I say?"

She just shook her head. Her heartsick eyes conveyed shame, and the pain of rejection. *Why does she look ashamed? I don't get it.*

This was about more than a haircut; I knew that. I could tell there was something hidden there in that look, but what? I wanted to help, but her hazel eyes became dark with fear when I tried.

I gently put my hand on her leg. "Jul, no matter what's bothering you, you can tell me. You can trust me. No matter what it is, I'll understand. I love you so much; it's killing me to see you hurting like this."

She looked up at me with big tears spilling out of her eyes, and just shook her head back and forth, saying, "I can't. I can't"

My guilt, fear and curiosity blended into a sickening feeling, making me desperate to know this secret. I lowered the tone of my voice, trying to emphasize my sincerity. "Honey, you know what a good problem solver I am. Let it out. I can probably help."

She just repeated her painful phrase. "I can't."

I couldn't get her to budge.

I didn't make it to my 15-year service award party. I called my boss and cancelled at the last minute, saying I had a family problem that needed me. I knew that, if I went, the whole evening would be spent reliving Jul's hurt look as she ran up the stairs to her room.

Years later, she told me that fear had kept her from sharing the feelings that ran through her head over and over that night. Her hair was one of the only things she really liked about herself, and I wanted her to change it.

She figured if I couldn't even accept her haircut, there was no way I would ever accept her for who she really was.

* * *

About six months after that night, fate used a standard dental checkup to try to push the fog from my eyes, and quiet the distractions of life long enough for me to see and hear what was plainly in front of me. Jul was having her teeth cleaned. It was July. We were trying to get all the little things taken care of before September came and it was time to move Jul into her college dorm. As I waited in the chlorine smell of the sitting room, I was approached by Jul's dental hygienist.

"Jamie, could you come with me for a minute, please?"

"Okay." I knew this hygienist; she did my teeth too. But she sounded different than usual, more serious.

She led me into a private little meeting-room; one I'd never been in before.

"Have a seat there, Jamie." She pointed to one of the two chairs that were pretty much the only furniture in the tiny room. She looked at me intently, her face knotted in a frown.

I wondered what could be so serious that it required this privacy.

"I wanted to tell you that I've found some disturbing telltale signs in Jul's mouth."

Signs? Signs of what?

"Jul's tooth enamel is dissolving. Her front teeth are getting thin and they're shiny smooth on the inside. You can almost see through them at the biting edge. There's also some damage there. It's usually typical of someone who grinds or clenches. Some people do that in their sleep. It's often a coping mechanism."

Coping mechanism? I couldn't think of anything that she'd need to "cope" with.

She hesitated before her next sentence.

I looked at her face to try to understand this conversation. I was distracted by the way the strain in her eyebrows made it look like the trunk of a little tree was growing right there in her worried forehead between her eyes.

Finally, she asked, "Do you think Jul could be vomiting intentionally?"

That startled me back to the conversation. I hadn't been prepared for that.

"Bulimia?" I answered in shock. "No." It came out like she had just told me my daughter had secretly been married and I didn't know about it. "I don't think she'd do anything like that."

Jul had never complained about her weight; there was no reason to. The maturity level in the senior grades seemed to help many students accept her differences, and she had made a few good, close female friends, but I'd never heard any of them talking about their weight.

The hygienist was obviously not convinced. "I usually see this sort of thing when a patient is dealing with significant family problems, or personal issues. Are there family problems right now?" She looked directly at me and waited.

Damn, it's stuffy in here.

"No, nothing out of the ordinary. Things are normal."

"Is she under a lot of stress?"

"No. She's heading to college this year, but she got into the program she wanted, she's got the finances all organized, and she seems really excited about it."

The hygienist's face still hadn't relaxed. "I'm sorry, Jamie, it's just that I've noticed some body language that suggests Jul isn't comfortable with herself. Most often these telltale signs indicate bulimia," and she looked at me again.

I could see she was studying me, trying to tell if I was giving her the truth or not.

I really was telling the truth. I searched my memory for something that should have tipped me off.

Nothing.

"I'm *sure* Jul wouldn't deal with stress like that."

I suspected, from the concern the hygienist was showing, that she thought her gut feeling was a more reliable source than I was.

"Well… I have experience in this. You should pay attention to Jul for a while — her habits, any weight change, if she's absent after eating. And I really think you should visit your family doctor. The only other explanation for what I've seen in her mouth is a condition called acid reflux. The acid eats away the tooth enamel. It isn't common in young people, though… unless they're under terrible stress."

Great, this just gets better.

"I don't know what to tell you. The school she's chosen is a few hours away. She could have picked one that's closer, but the one she's going to has the better program. It was her choice. We're close, so it'll be hard on her to be away from home at first maybe, but she seems ready. I can't think of anything else."

"Well, if it *is* acid reflux, it requires treatment. You better get her checked."

I booked an appointment to see our family doctor. He was a very reserved man: the type of person who usually seems to be able to separate all emotion from his daily dealings with people. I thought it odd that his face seemed to mimic that of Jul's dental hygienist. The same knotted frown, the same look of concern.

He had a strange, puzzled look as he confirmed that Jul was suffering from acid reflux. The damage in her mouth was being caused when her stomach acid didn't stay in her stomach. It had been eating away at her teeth.

What would cause her to be under enough stress to develop an illness that resembled an ulcer? It seemed worse than an ulcer, really. I wondered why this would happen. I was at a total loss. I am not usually totally blind to things around me. Now, though, when I look back, I can see how all the clues were there.

It makes me think of when the kids were little. One Christmas, I bought a video gaming system for them to share. I wrapped up a note, dressed it up like a special gift, and placed it under our Christmas tree. That note sent them to another note. Each time Jul would read another note to her little brother, they would giggle and smile, knowing that they were getting closer to something big.

My clues had been laid out for me like a well-thought-out treasure hunt. Why could I not understand them?

Maybe I wanted to leave my big surprise well hidden in the closet, covered with its pretty protective wrapping. Maybe I was running away from what I didn't want to know, or could I simply not find a way to discover the truth? Maybe it was simply a mother's denial. Denial can certainly be a very tricky little devil.

Joey: Birth-2002
Chapter 6

By the time Jul was four, I had grown accustomed to thinking that when it came to raising children, it was all about a parent's reaction to things. If you react to a child's behavior appropriately, the outcome is pretty much within your control. I was only 24, mind you, so I knew I would hit some speed bumps along the way, but besides those little learning experiences, parenting seemed like a skill you could learn and hone, in order to mold your kids into great human beings.

Then came Joey. My two children could not have been more different. They both had a dry wit and a quirky, sometimes sarcastic, sense of humor: something passed down to all three of us from my dad. Other than that, though, they were total opposites.

This was apparent from the moment Joey was born. I had tried to breast-feed both of them. With Jul, I had lasted six weeks; with Joey less than six days. The very first time I tried, Jul had latched on to me like she had been doing it for years. Joey, on the other hand, had fussed and struggled. He would eventually settle in, nurse for a while, and then fall back to sleep. He would awaken an hour later, and be hungry again. Assuming it was because my milk wasn't quite right yet, I persevered for a few days. Every time I tried, I hoped that it would be the time he finally became satisfied, and would sleep for more than a short period of time. That never happened. I lasted less than a week, and in an exhausted state, switched him to formula.

If I had been paying attention, I would have learned something from those early days with Joey. Jul had been a relatively easy child to raise. No overwhelmingly enlightening moments there. Until Joey arrived, I saw parenting as a learning experience. One that was sometimes challenging maybe, but not much of an adventure.

When Joey hit 18 months, I was given my first serious dose of reality. He developed this strange little habit. He would be tottering along, and suddenly drop to all fours, rub his face into the carpet, and make a grunting sound. The first time I saw it, I stood there kind of dumbstruck, thinking *What the heck? What's he doing?* It didn't last long enough for my brain to process much past that point. He got up, and began playing as if nothing had happened.

The second time I witnessed this drop, rub and grunt routine, I wanted a reason to attach to such a weird behavior. I thought he must be getting teeth, and this thing he did was probably giving him some type of relief. It lasted a little longer than the first time, but still seemed like nothing to get worked up about.

After a couple of days, not only was this strange little activity not going away, it was becoming more frequent. Then, while walking past his room one night after putting him down to sleep, I heard something coming from inside. Concerned, I put my ear to the door. It sounded like the same grunt. I opened the door, and looked at my little baby doing the same unusual thing — but in his sleep this time. That didn't seem right at all.

I had wanted to believe it was nothing, but this was a little too unusual to ignore. It was enough to warrant a call to our family doctor.

After hearing my description of the episodes, our doctor decided that Joey should be checked out. He headed us in the direction of the children's hospital an hour away. The head of neurology was waiting for us.

To my amazement, Joey was admitted. I spent the next five nights sleeping beside his hospital crib in a large, wooden chair covered with cold, vinyl padding, and the days accompanying him to tests and meetings with doctors. On the second to last day, I called my parents to fill them in. My mom asked me if anyone had brought up epilepsy.

"Epilepsy?" I questioned. And then, in a slightly indignant tone, "No, there hasn't been any mention of that." I hadn't meant for it to come out like that. It was just a gut reaction. I mean really, one of my kids couldn't have epilepsy! How would that have happened? It was crazy. Besides, what happened to Joey didn't resemble an epileptic seizure at all.

Joey was diagnosed with petit mal epileptic seizures the next day. I had firmly believed that no child of mine could be epileptic. My children were in perfect health. But experience is stronger than beliefs. It was fate's first hint to me that I wasn't in control here. Would I learn from this experience? Well, it might take another little nudge or two from fate to reinforce this new concept.

Joey was put on medication that controlled the seizures. After six months of being seizure-free, we were told to wean him off his meds. I learned that a lucky thirty percent of infant epilepsy cases outgrow the condition. Joey was one of the fortunate ones. I was so relieved. Epilepsy seemed like such a terrible thing when I was 25. It's amazing how I now see everything so differently. Compared to what we went through in the end, petit mal seizures don't seem that bad at all.

Being a parent that year had taken a dramatic twist that I hadn't seen coming. What I didn't know was that it was only the first little turn my roller-coaster car would take. We were barely out of the gates. But that might not be the best way to describe life with Joey. A roller-coaster ride was the right way to portray a few of my future years with Jul. Life as the mother of Joey, however, would eventually become more like riding a bull. Short bursts of fear and adrenaline that would end in me being thrown down hard. More dangerous than a roller coaster. More complicated.

Sometimes, it is a very good thing that we don't know what's ahead of us in life.

Chapter 7

Joey challenged my authority right from the age of four, and always in a way that seemed beyond his years. I remember one morning, as we got ready for our day, I waited for him as he brushed his teeth, trying my best to be patient. When I asked him to hurry, he looked up at me and scowling, he said, "What are you looking at?" He used a rebellious tone that could have come from a teenager. Jul had never done anything like that.

Joey, on the other hand, often seemed to think he was in charge. I knew I had to show him who was boss. It was the "how" that I was struggling with. Making him go to his room did no good. He would simply wander out as if he had a right to. Spanking was fruitless. He was a strong little bugger. After fighting to hold him down just long enough to get a smack or two to his bottom, a feat that usually took at least a full five minutes or so, I realized he was winning most of the battles. I was a single mom then, and I needed help. I decided to consult a psychologist.

After meeting Joey, my counselor (a parent of four), explained that he had one just like my little four-year-old fireball. He said that a strong-willed child will instinctively fight for control. If he gets it, he is miserable because he doesn't know what to do with it.

The doctor then proceeded to give me what I thought to be unorthodox parenting advice. He instructed me to install a lock on the outside of Joey's bedroom door! I sat stunned. *Did he just say what I think he just said?* I'd never heard of *that* before.

When Joey misbehaved, I was to put him inside, lock the door and leave him for twenty minutes. It had to be long enough for him to know I meant business. If Joey threw his toys around in a temper tantrum because of it, I was to remove everything he was strong enough to lift, and close the door again. I had to win — whatever it took, I had to win. It seemed extreme, but I had to do something. I was reluctant, but I was desperate.

After listening to Joey cry, and pound on the door for the first full twenty minute time-out, and crying along with him from the next room, I opened his bedroom door. His little, tear-streaked face looked up at me, and said nothing. I knelt down beside him, and stroked his silky, sandy-brown hair. "Mommy's sorry to have to do this, honey, but if you're a bad boy, you're going to get a time-out like this for your punishment. You can come out now. I'm going to go downstairs, and make us some dinner."

He looked back at me with complete understanding, and said, "Can I help you, Mommy?"

I was amazed. It had worked! He would challenge me every once in a while to see if I was really serious about this time-out thing, but I got the control back (most of the time, anyway).

I wondered how two children with the same parents could be so different. With Jul, all I had to do was show her I was disappointed in her, and she would change her behavior. I was starting to think that, where Joey was concerned, there might be surprises around every corner. And they wouldn't be quiet, little learning experiences. Whereas Jul had a quiet disposition that drama seemed to be drawn to, Joey had a boisterous way of creating it. I suspected that if I learned something from Joey, it would land like a bombshell. In everything he did, he was loud, busy and overly energetic.

When I remarried, my husband, Will, learned quite quickly not to get him started. All it would take for Joey to wind up to an unstoppable level was a little poke or squeeze. Will's way of showing affection usually involved body contact. He would give Joey a little tickle, or tousle his hair in a playful way, and Joey would be all over him. That brings a pleasant mental image, doesn't it? Stepdad and stepson playfully rough-housing together.

Well, it was pleasant — at least for the first five to ten minutes. The following hour, a totally draining hour, would be spent trying to turn Joey off.

The length of this scene varied a bit, depending on if the boy consumed sugar or red food coloring, something that I put considerable effort into avoiding. Think of a small boy after he has eaten a bag of chocolate-covered espresso beans — that pretty much describes it. Even with only the healthiest consumption of food, though, once you flicked that switch, you had to let him run his course. By the time he had tired himself out, all parties involved would be exhausted. Telling him to settle down did no good whatsoever.

Actually, no amount of telling Joey anything seemed to do much good. He was a determined child, with very firm beliefs and opinions about everything. Once he made up his mind about something, there was no changing it. There had been countless times he was punished at school for standing up for the rights of others.

You see, if Joey decided some kids were being treated unjustly, their battle became his battle. The fact that these fights were often between a student and a teacher was irrelevant to Joey. He would stand up confidently, and tell the teacher exactly how he or she was being unfair, and he would not try to sugarcoat it. He definitely hadn't inherited my diplomatic way of doing things.

He would help out the "innocent" parties right through to the end, if he felt they were being wronged. Can you guess who the loser usually was in these battles? Joey would give it his all, though. Nothing would slow him down: not even being suspended for getting in the middle of something that had absolutely nothing to do with him. During those early years, it didn't ever cross my mind that Joey may have picked up this obsession because of something that had happened to him.

Maybe he had a very personal reason to protect the world from bullies.

The first time we saw Joey's fearless passion to right the wrongs of the world was in grade one. He was bound and determined he would convince his teacher that his class was getting too much homework. He was very serious about his opinion, and intended to make his teacher see he was right. Have you ever tried to explain appropriate and inappropriate to a six-year-old? It was no use; there was no stopping him.

Joey must have made a compelling argument, though, because he somehow convinced his cousin Eddie that the workload was far too much. Joey had been sitting in the living room, working at an assignment one evening when Eddie was babysitting. Eddie had asked him what it was. Joey hadn't ranted or complained. He had simply told Eddie that it was homework, and then convincingly shared his feelings on how homework in grade one wasn't fair.

Joey's cousin was roughly thirteen at the time. Quite swayed by Joey's arguments, Eddie wrote a serious letter to the teacher. It explained how six-year-olds were too young for this amount of evening work. That children needed time to enjoy family activities, and outside play. More than a few minutes of homework should be saved for higher grades. Eddie finished his sober advice with, "Thank you, and may the force be with you."

Even Eddie was a bit shocked when he found out that Joey had actually delivered the letter. Unfortunately, the cute Star Wars reference at the end of his note had not helped the situation. I received a very stern call from that teacher. This strict, seasoned teacher did not appreciate a six-year-old's criticism of her teaching methods one bit.

I could just picture it, too. He would be standing tall with his tensed-up, little face as he said something like, "We are too little for homework, Mrs. Smith. It's just mean. It's just really mean!"

I hoped he hadn't gone as far as to tell her *she* was mean. From the anger I heard in her voice, I figured he probably had. That call was the first of many during Joey's elementary school days.

As a divorced parent, I did what all of us do: I wondered if it was the divorce that might be causing this rebellious behavior from Joey. He'd been three when I had moved the kids out. They say children that age are resilient. They bounce back better than older kids. We tried to make it easier for Joey and Jul by making sure they saw both parents often. Joey seemed to take the move like it was just part of life. I hadn't noticed any immediate changes in his behavior. It was more like a steady, growing frustration with authority. He certainly tested me with more attitude than my nerves could handle at times.

I began to look into the effects of separation on young children. It had been proven that divorce could cause fear of loss, or fear of conflict and betrayal. He seemed to be anything but afraid of conflict, though; that was for sure. When confronting an authority figure, he had a confidence that was scary. He didn't appear the least bit intimidated.

Maybe it was a "parent-hate" transference thing? If kids are angry with their parents, sometimes they will transfer that rage onto any unsuspecting authority figure. Maybe that was what this was. What did I know? I just wanted him to stay out of trouble.

It didn't occur to me that there might be something I didn't know about. I was only trying to analyze what I knew. It didn't ever cross my mind that there might be a reason for Joey to want to protect others when he thought they were being bullied. Maybe someone hadn't protected him when he had needed it. Maybe Joey fit right in with Jul and me, and like us, had his own share of secrets.

Chapter 8

Almost as strong as Joey's passion for justice was his love for animals; he was drawn to all living things, except for worms and spiders. Those were the creatures from his nightmares. Because of this fear, he would not go into our basement at all. Being a century home, the basement was unfinished and very rough. Numerous spiders lived down there, many of them daddy-long-legs — a very large, therefore, very terrifying variety. I tried to tell him that they were harmless. Actually, I told him that over and over, but I've already mentioned how easy it was to convince him of something when he had his mind made up. You might as well forget it. Spiders and worms were horrifying, and that was that.

Joey wasn't the least bit intimidated by any other living thing, however. He was a natural with animals.

That year, as Jul waited on her acceptance into college, Joey made an announcement. "Mom... I *really* want a rat. Billy has one and it's so cute. He licks me, and he jumps up on the wires of the cage when we go by. I can take him out and he'll go under my shirt and sleep while we play video games. He's so cute."

I didn't want another expense. "Animals cost money to keep, Joey. We have Wiggles, Kissy and Sandy... that's enough."

His description of these misunderstood little guys had me kind of curious, though. I'd never met a pet rat before; Joey gets his love of animals honestly.

And the kid loved animals. He'd won best dog costume at the community fair one year when our dog, Sandy, let him parade her around in a curly, pink wig and clown costume. Joey loved that dog.

His fondness for the animal world went far beyond our walls, however. When he was ten or so, I walked through the living room one day as he watched television. Tears streaked his serious face. On the screen a woman held a skinny, feeble looking dog. She pleaded for donations to help the suffering animals she was trying to save. Joey looked up at me, and asked, "Can we send some money?"

The boy was almost too much of an animal lover, for Will's liking, anyway. We had two cats and a dog, but Joey wanted more. He wanted a lizard. He wanted a snake. The year he was 13, he really, *really* wanted a rat.

And if Joey was passionate about something, he could take annoying to an amazing level. Easter rolled around and Joey announced, with obsession pounding in his words, "I want a rat for Easter, Mom, and that's *all* I want.

I'd been listening to his pleas for months and I couldn't help thinking about the idea. The kid was wearing me down. It sounded kind of cool.

I waited for my opportunity to make the pitch to Will. One morning, as I dished omelets onto our plates for breakfast, I gave it a shot. "Hon, do you think it would be okay if we got a rat?"

The look on Will's face said, *Here we go. They have a new crazy idea.*

I could tell he thought we were both nuts. I was a grown woman, and Joey, well, he should have outgrown this desire for furry little friends by thirteen.

Guess again.

Joey was insistent. I really didn't see the problem, but Will didn't want a rat living with us. He should have known to say that, in those words. But he was so easy going, he wouldn't say no. What did he say? "A rat? We can't have a rat; we have cats."

Well... maybe we could.

I remembered Jul telling me that she had a close friend who was moving away from home, and couldn't take her pair of rats with her. She was looking for a good home for them. Jul said they were fun little guys. Maybe we could rent them for a week or two — see how it went. Rent-a-rat. It sounded like something I'd do.

I knew Jul would be game to help out. Along with having my dad's dry wit and quirky sense of humor, there was one other personality trait my children shared: they both had my love for animals.

Jul had taught Sandy to roll over. She'd even managed to get her to play dead when she made a gun shape with her thumb and forefinger, and said, "Bang." It was so cute.

Jul asked her friend right away, and it was confirmed – we were having two female rats in for a sleep over. Jul and I went to pick up Slinky and Jupiter for a weekend visit.

I had to admit, I was a little worried about the cats. When we'd lived in the country, Wiggles and Kissy had both been real mousers. How would these two hunters react to rodents sharing Joey's bedroom?

The weekend went off without a hitch. The cats were fine. Although a little curious, they seemed to recognize that these new things were pets. They would sit at the cage for a few minutes, and then wander off, having lost interest.

Actually, Will seemed more curious than the cats did. I remember walking by Joey's room the second day, and hearing something unfamiliar. It was baby talk — that soft, high-pitched voice that just often seems to come out of nowhere when you talk to an infant.

I laughed as I entered to find Will squatting at the side of the bed, smiling innocently, and talking softly to the rats as they ran around investigating the corners of the bed, coming back to lick his fingers every once in a while. I think he was realizing that the rats were quite personable, quite charming and very entertaining.

Joey sat beside him, looking rather pleased with himself. I think he knew that those rats were not going anywhere.

As the summer wore on, we got ready for Jul to go off to college, Will and I preparing ourselves for that partially-empty-nest feeling. But we had two new family members ready to at least fill a portion of that hole, even if it was a tiny, rat-sized portion.

* * *

When Jul left for college, I looked for something new to do as a family outing. It seemed even more important to do special things with Joey than it had been with Jul when she was younger. When Jul was eight and Joey was three, I had taken a second job. I spent the odd Saturday working as cashier for a local auctioneer.

Jul, who was always easy to have around, started to come with me. She won over the auctioneer right away, carrying boxes of junk people had bought to their cars. She even started bidding for me once I was bitten by the antique bug. Jul loved coming to the sales with me.

Joey, on the other hand, I'd never even considered bringing. I knew he would be bored stiff, and driving me crazy before we had the very first hour in. But, at the same time, I didn't want Joey to be jealous of the time I spent with Jul. I wanted Joey to get his share of one-on-one time. It made discovering fun things that Joey and I could enjoy together something of a priority.

By the time he was in his early teens that had become a bit of a challenge. We went to movies together, but really weren't drawn to the same ones. That summer, I found an article on a reptile zoo with a hands-on area that was only a forty-five minute drive away. It sounded like something that would be right up Joey's alley. It sounded fun to me, too, so the two of us headed there one Sunday afternoon… neither of us having any idea that it would be a life-altering experience.

Chapter 9

We landed at the reptile zoo without preconceived expectations. It didn't occur to either of us from the look of the place that anything special could happen here. It was boxy and boring, and ours was the only car in the lot. It was late afternoon, however, so I thought maybe the crowd had already gone. We paid our admission, hoping we wouldn't be disappointed, and headed in to see what types of strange and unusual creatures we could find.

The humidity hit you the minute you walked through the door. The place smelled of earth, water and unfortunately, jungle pee. The glassed-in displays we found were small enough that the inhabitants couldn't get too far away, offering us a pretty good close-up view. There was quite a variety of lizards, large snakes, a tank of piranha, and a reasonable selection of tortoises, toads and frogs. It was all very well and good, but we wanted the barrier-free experience. Then we found it — the "hands-on" room.

A young man entered behind us, wearing an African safari-type getup. He carried a small alligator, and asked if we wanted to see what it felt like. Its mouth was bound, so it didn't really get my adrenaline going, but it was pretty cool to touch, just the same.

Joey loved it. Whether it was holding a lizard or a frog or touching whatever was offered, he was all over it.

I got a couple of good pictures of him holding snakes about two or three inches in diameter, and long enough to be a challenge to hold on to when they started winding themselves around him. He held a chameleon for I don't know how long, letting it crawl up his shirt onto his shoulder. In the photo of that experience, he is face to face with the bulgy-eyed, little beast.

The next offer from safari guy changed Joey's facial expression in a split-second. His eyes widened as our zookeeper friend asked if either of us was arachnophobic.

I motioned toward my son, and then heard Joey quickly say, "Oh no... no way!"

Zoo guy laughed. "Oh come on, tarantulas are really not dangerous. You'll like it."

Joey looked him right in the eye, and said with dead seriousness, "If you bring a spider out here... I. Am. Gone!"

Our zoo guy began his pitch. He explained that some spiders are dangerous, but tarantulas only look deadly. They still have their venom, but it isn't strong enough to hurt a person; it isn't even enough to harm a dog. Besides, if frightened, the first thing they would do would be to use their legs to flick their coarse hair at you, hoping to get their little, irritating curls in your eyes, so you stop what you are doing and rub. If that happens, they run. They are as afraid of you as you are of them.

Joey was still shaking his head and saying, "No way, man!"

Zoo guy was not even close to giving up. "Come on, Dude. If you let me, I'll get the most docile, easy-going species on the planet. I'll stand on one side of the room, and you can come to me. No pressure."

I could tell Joey was considering this idea. He seemed curious, but he wasn't by any means convinced. He just stood there with his head cocked, looking serious.

Zoo guy gave it another shot. "You know, we use these things to entertain at kid's birthday parties, and I've literally helped dozens of people overcome their arachnophobia. And believe me, I know how you feel. I was arachnophobic when I started working here. We're talking really, *really* scared, of *every* type of spider. Now, I can hold them without even batting an eye."

He made getting past that fear sound pretty amazing.

Secret Selves

Joey looked at him suspiciously. "Well... okay... you can bring it in... but you'd better not come near me with it! I'm telling you, I'll be gone!"

Joey hid behind me when our safari friend came back. "This is Rosie. She's a Rose Haired Tarantula."

She was about three inches across and very hairy. I stood there motionless, and waited for Joey's rapid breathing to return to something that resembled normal. I wanted to get closer, but I knew I would have to do it very slowly.

I eventually said, "Okay, you ready?"

I took one step, with Joey still clinging to me from behind, and heard him quickly say, "Okay — stop, stop, stop!" He didn't say it too loud, though. I guess he didn't want to alarm that beastly tarantula.

As zoo guy told us about Rosie, I gradually made my way right over to the thing, taking one step at a time, and waiting in between until Joey's grip on me loosened.

I have to give it to the young lad, he was good with kids. "Listen Dude, I'll give you a quarter to hold her?"

Joey rolled his eyes and laughed. "Are you crazy? I'm not doing *that* for a quarter!"

Our new friend was a born salesman. "It's pretty hot out there, and it's almost closing time. How about doing it for a slushy?"

Joey's mouth and eyebrows made the expression he makes when he's considering something.

I think this guy knew he almost had him. He delivered his final catch line. "Tell you what: Mom will go first, so that you can see it will be okay."

The inside of my head burst into activity, but I tried not to show anything. I didn't want to ruin it, at this point. But inside I was thinking, WHAT? *Wait a minute! How did I become part of this deal? You want me to hold that tarantula? Shit... I don't really have a choice here, now do I?*

Outside I kept on my best, no-fear poker face. I think I might have actually pulled it off, too, because Joey came out with, "All right, if Mom holds it, I'll start with just touching it, and then we'll see."

Okay, that got my adrenaline pumping!

I like animals a lot, but I really had no desire to hold a tarantula. I'm really not the thrill seeker-type. But, I was screwed. If I said no, I was sure Joey wouldn't get anywhere with this fear. And I wanted to help. So I said, in my best attempt at enthusiasm, "Sure, I'll do it."

As zoo guy put the big bug in my hand, I thought he could probably see my heart pounding. I worked on keeping my facial expression in check — just like it was nothing. Like it was fun. Actually, it kind of was, really.

The intimidating little beast didn't sit still. As its long legs extended out across my hand, I could feel its tiny claws cling to me with each step it took. It didn't feel like a pin prick: more like it was holding on for fear of falling. Behind it was a silky-looking strand of web.

I guess I was concentrating more on not dropping this big, hairy bug as it crawled over my hand than how zoo guy's finish to his sales pitch went. How I can't say, but somehow before long, he had managed to get that tarantula from my hand into Joey's. Joey held his breath the whole time.

After that, once the giant spider was safely back in her box, it was closing time.

The drive back home was wonderful. Joey was oozing with self-satisfaction. Not only had he had a great time, but he had faced his biggest known fear and won. He was glowing. His smile was so big, it would have been contagious to even the nastiest bystander. That cherry slushy was probably the sweetest drink he had ever tasted.

I felt like a pretty cool mom, too. How many moms have held a Rose Haired tarantula? That day was definitely one for the books. I certainly had a story to tell Jul the next time I called her.

I actually felt a little envy inside for that young man in the safari costume. Man, what a wonderful job — helping people past their fears like that. I wondered if that kid knew how lucky he was. There wasn't a much better way for a young animal lover to earn some cash. I thought I would have enjoyed that as a teen. Heck, I'd enjoy it now.

My mind seemed to take off with that thought. Entertaining children at birthday parties would be a wonderful way for Joey and me to spend amazing, one-on-one time together. Unfortunately, if I ran the idea past Will, he would probably think that I had finally totally lost it. We would have a house completely filled with cages if we did it. Maybe I should think about it for a while. Maybe it *was* crazy.

But I couldn't make the damn idea go away. The thought of helping people with their fears — I loved it. I'd always wanted to help people in some way. Maybe this was it?

Or maybe this desire in me, this want to help others past their deep-rooted phobias… was a mother's intuition of what was to come.

Jul: 2003-2004
Chapter 10

I'm still not sure if I was in denial of, oblivious to, or afraid of what Jul was. But it wasn't completely my fault. Without even realizing it, Jul contributed to my blindness.

The next summer, during the months she was home between the two years of her radio broadcasting program, just before she turned twenty, my poor daughter attempted to be a lesbian.

I thought she was finally beginning to feel comfortable with who she was. I prided myself on the fact that I was being open and compassionate to this new concept. There was one little detail that I was missing, however. I was totally unaware that Jul had to make quite an effort to try to fit into this role. But she thought maybe she could make it work.

She had a close childhood friend who was gay, so she began spending her weekends in the city where he lived. She felt comfortable in the city. There was so much diversity; being different didn't matter to anyone.

At night, they would go to the gay clubs. Jul looked like a cute, baby-faced, butch lesbian; the girls loved her look, and her witty charm. She was an instant hit. She told me about the experimental relationships that she'd attempted over the summer — carefully leaving out the details that a mom wouldn't want to know about. I was glad to see her finding her fit in the world — at least, that's how it appeared to me.

Jul was making new friends. She'd been able to get a job where I worked, in the summer student program. It paid well and her savings for her second year of college were growing beautifully. Life was good.

We'd drive to work together. One day, on our way home, I had a few errands to do so I dropped her at our driveway and headed out to shop. When I landed back with my groceries Jul was watching The Oprah Winfrey Show.

Jul *never* watched Oprah.

She found most talk shows boring. In fact, she didn't watch much TV at all; a little sports and, of course, movies, but that was it. Actually, once my two kids were both in their teens, I knew exactly where to find them at the end of each day. It was almost as reliable as the sun setting. Joey would be playing a video game in his room; Jul would be on the computer.

Seeing her in front of the TV like that made me instantly curious.

I came into the living room and stood beside the couch where she was sitting. "Watcha watchin'?"

"Oprah. It's about transsexual people."

"It must be pretty interesting if *you're* watching it." I sat down in the chair next to her. I had no idea how difficult this show would be to sit through. But the emotional content pulled me in and held me there.

All of Oprah's guests were male-to-female transgenders, meaning that they were born with a male body, complete with penis and testicles, but felt, with all their heart and soul, that they were women inside.

The television screen was filled with Oprah's guests, each at a different stage in their transformations. They had all started hormone therapy to make their faces more feminine, reduce body hair, soften their skin, and begin the growth of breasts. I knew cosmetic surgery was common to improve facial features or increase breast size, but I began to squirm in my chair as they described the other surgical ordeals these guests had tackled.

I'd never really thought about the Adam's apple before: about the fact that it's a dead give-away that someone is male. I learned that day that some male-to-females have the cartilage in that area carved away until it is flat enough to resemble the more feminine neck of a woman: a very painful and very risky surgical procedure. Even though I don't have an Adam's apple, the thought of having it, or anything else for that matter, being scraped away gave me goose bumps.

This was nothing compared to the almost unthinkable, irrevocable, final step, though — sexual reassignment surgery. Even a woman cannot help but cross her legs when she hears the description of how the penis and testicles are first removed, and then reconstructed into female genitalia. It was fascinating, but completely terrifying. And the possible complications were horrible.

The guests of the show had all suffered through so much, but it was not just physical pain. It was the pain inflicted by people who couldn't see past their outer appearances.

Each of their lives had been bruised by the effects of being judged, of being ridiculed, of being labeled. Some of them had been disowned by their families — people who were supposed to love them unconditionally. Some of them had bounced from job to job because relationships with co-workers were so hurtful. Others lost lifelong friendships, or had trouble finding love because their looks hadn't turned out quite like they had hoped. Being brutally beaten was not uncommon in their stories. It reminded me of the horrible scenes in "Boys Don't Cry."

I didn't hear much during the last bit of the show. I couldn't help but put myself in the place of these poor people. I tried to imagine how I would feel if I woke up the next morning with a penis, no breasts and a body covered with hair. If society saw the new me as a man, I'd be expected to be tough and hardened, not soft and caring. I would need to hide my emotional side, or I'd be seen as weak. I would be viewed as someone's son, not their daughter, and if I continued to be attracted to men, people would consider me gay, even though I'm not. I would still be me on the inside. It would only be my packaging that had changed.

What would I do if society expected me to fit into the role of this foreign body even though I still felt like a woman inside? Could I possibly make that work?

Of course not. How could anyone expect anyone to make that work?

I would do whatever I could to make my body right. I'm the type of person who will do whatever I can to fix something that makes me feel uncomfortable about myself. If I had a terrible rash and I could get it cleared up, why would I just live with it? That is obviously simplifying the situation of a transgender, but, really, it's the same thing. If only the people who had hurt Oprah's guests could try to put themselves in their shoes, and see things from the eyes and heart of a transgender.

That was *not* what had taken place for these people. The theme of the show was clear. Life had started out for Oprah's guests as though they were stranded on the sidelines, watching life as spectators. Their change was supposed to have given them inner peace and self-acceptance. It should have allowed them to join in, to finally, really experience life. It looked to me that in the end, it had only brought more pain.

They all felt that people had turned their backs on them because they had chosen to become their true selves. Oprah was trying to help people glimpse into the unnecessary pain these people had suffered. I sat gulping back tears as the stories wrenched at my heart.

Jul decided this was the time. She looked at me apprehensively and quietly said, "Mom, I think *that* is what I am."

It came like a blow that knocked the wind out of me. All the air seemed to leave the room. I could no longer hear the TV.

The pounding of my heart filled the horrible silence as Jul waited for me to reply.

I felt like I was going crazy. All I could think was, *Oh, my God, how could you want a life like that, honey? A life filled with prejudice, betrayal, anger and pain. The surgical procedures will be different, but they'll be just as frightening. And people's reactions; they'll be exactly the same.*

Stories about the only female-to-male transgender in our hometown popped into my head. The range in comments about him had been everything from, "She must be somehow mentally disturbed" to "Something had obviously gone wrong in her upbringing." Some people even connected it to perversion. People just didn't understand. Why would Jul choose a life with so much pain?

The answer was simple... she didn't "want" this life. It *wasn't* a choice. But I couldn't see that.

My mind was spinning like a whirlwind fireworks display: illogical little thought fragments flicking off in every direction like sparks. The theories were gone before they could get too far, though. My mind didn't give me time to process each idea before going into protection mode and putting them out. We didn't want any fires starting.

But the sparks kept coming. What would people say? What if something went wrong? What if she did change her sex to male and afterwards realized that she had been wrong, and was still unhappy? These steps were permanent. Once a person makes this type of change, there's no way to go back.

I tried to figure out how to save her from every possible painful scenario that ran through my head. I *had* to save her.

Realizing Jul was watching me, waiting, I began my persuasion. "No, honey... you're not like that." I pleaded with my eyes. "You're just young. You're just... uncomfortable about being a lesbian because it's so new to you. You'll get used to being open about it; it'll just take a little time." I tried desperately to find a compelling argument as to why she just had to be wrong.

Jul's reaction was much more mature than mine. With hurt in her eyes, she said, "Mom, I know I'm not a lesbian; the dates I had this summer were enough to prove that. I experimented with touching, you know, and... it was awful." She looked down at the floor for a minute and then lifted her head sheepishly. "I hate my body, Mom. It's the wrong body. The girls I dated liked, well... you know... touching. It was horrible. It made me feel sick."

"Honey, that doesn't mean you're a transgender."

Her voice got firmer. Her chin quivered as she spoke. "I can't stand the thought of a girl, or anyone for that matter, touching *this* body; it's humiliating. It's not a choice, Mom. I have the wrong body."

To Jul, her breasts felt like two hideous growths. She couldn't relax while someone touched the parts of her body that repulsed her. It was then that she knew she had to somehow tell me she was a transgender.

I sat listening, trying not to hear.

I didn't want it to be true. I wanted her life to be perfect, and easy; well, as easy as it could be.

But her words had brought up things I hadn't thought of and didn't want to think about. I felt like I was living a nightmare.

The show ended, and to my horror, Oprah explained that it was a two part show. It was to be continued the next day and Jul was planning to watch the second half.

Oh, God, I don't know if I can do it.

I didn't want to think about it anymore; it was too frightening. And I *really* didn't want Jul thinking about it anymore.

The next day Jul didn't watch Oprah. A cool wave of relief washed over me. The panic was swept away in the undertow. I didn't ask any questions; I wanted to enjoy the water.

Even if I *had* wanted to, I couldn't ask why she hadn't watched it; fear had a good solid hold on my tongue.

When I think back to those days, I feel such shame. I didn't want to listen; I just wanted the whole thing to go away. I'm sure most parents of teens have felt that at some point. If your teenager wants to quit high school, you don't want to hear the reasons; you just want to convince your child that it would be a mistake. Panic takes over, and panic had definitely found its way to me.

I was so glad she didn't watch the second show.

She must have thought about it overnight. She must have come to the realization that she was wrong: that changing into a man was not the route to her happiness. It'd be too difficult a road to take.

I was on cloud nine. Back to my little bubble of denial. The walls of my comfortable bubble were, however, growing thin, and it didn't seem quite as cozy as it had been before.

But denial, my new best friend, was right there for me every time I needed her.

Chapter 11

Later that summer, Jul headed to the city for a first date with a girl she'd met on the Internet. She looked so cute — filled with excitement and nerves. I'd never seen her so jumpy. It should have struck me strange that she was suddenly comfortable being a lesbian, but I was just glad to breathe easy again.

As I enjoyed watching her fuss while she got ready to go, it occurred to me that the situation was a little strange. How many parents would feel relieved that their child was becoming comfortable with being gay? But I was. I was filled with that wonderful release you feel when your child makes a good decision. I didn't let myself think about the panic I had felt during the transgender episode of Oprah. It didn't seem necessary. The topic hadn't been brought up again.

Now Jul had a date, and with a girl who made her feel jittery! I so hoped it was a memory maker — the good kind, of course. I wanted my daughter to find love. I silently said a prayer that this date would go well.

That first date led to a second, a third, and well, you get the idea. Jul had a girlfriend. Her name was Cally.

Thank you, God.

* * *

During Jul's second year in radio broadcasting she would come home on the weekends whenever she could. We didn't see her much, however. She spent most of the weekend in the nearby city where Cally went to school. She'd stop in for dinner on Sunday nights before heading back to school. She still hadn't ever brought up the "T" word again.

Then, early one Monday morning, as I sat at my desk in my cubicle with a cup of coffee, the phone rang. "Hello, Jamie speaking."

It was Jul. I recognized her voice, but I could barely make out what she was trying to tell me. Her sobs were so intense that her voice was barely audible. "Mom... I can't live... like this."

"What? What do you mean, honey?"

"Just listen... okay, Mom? I want to be a boy. I *am* a boy. I need the body that I should have been born with. There's no room for discussion here. I'm sure. I just can't live this lie any more. I want to tell you everything. I need to."

I'd like to tell you what I said to my daughter. I'd like to share what thoughts went through my head. But the memories won't come.

I was numb.

As I held the receiver in my hand, I realized it was time for me to face the truth. The pain in her voice forced me to finally burst my safe bubble of denial. I later realized that that phone conversation somehow taught me that Jul was a true blessing in my life. She taught me what strength and real honesty actually are.

I needed to put my arms around her, squeeze her, and tell her I loved her, no matter what. I knew the five-hour bus ride from college would probably seem like an eternity, but I needed to see her. "Come home, honey. We'll talk. I love you."

The day Jul told me her news is still a mystery to me. I'm really not sure how I made it through my work day. Somehow I managed to stay at work, albeit in a somewhat altered state of quiet shock. I would no longer be able to pretend that life was normal. Having a lesbian daughter was within the limits of my brain's pre-programmed standard as far as normal was concerned.

But she was a transgender. It seemed a step beyond even conceivable.

But it was really happening.

I spent the day trying to prepare myself for the details I would face later that evening. How would I deal with this news? Fear of the future plagued my mind all that day. The memory of that Oprah show was like a hungry mosquito. It followed me everywhere: sucking my blood, leaving me drained, nervous and annoyed. I couldn't shake it.

Normally, when faced with a problem, I instinctively get to work trying to find the best solution. I never cower from a challenge, but this was like no other I had faced before. I had no idea where to begin.

When I got home from work, my first priority was a big hug. I needed some grounding. My husband, Will, always seems to have the ability to do that.

I'd wondered all day what the expression on his face would look like when I told him the news. I was pretty sure how Joey would react — total acceptance. It was how he always treated people whom others judged. I was not completely sure about Will. He reacted to almost everything in an easy-going manner, but was, at the same time, no-nonsense when the need arose. He didn't get upset often, but when he did, you could see and feel the intensity instantly. This news might be a real test of his good nature.

Will did not disappoint me. In his calm way, he said, "Well, I can't say that it's a big surprise to me, Sweetie. She's had the nature and characteristics of a boy her whole life. The calls for 'Mark' made me wonder if she was experimenting with living a different life." He'd never mentioned anything to me about his suspicions, but that's just his way. He quietly processes information, and shares it only when asked to, or when it becomes necessary.

I dug my head into his shoulder. "All day the same thing has run through my mind over and over. What the *hell* do we do now?"

I still felt as if I was in "protect" mode. Will jokingly refers to me, at times, as The Fixer. I think as moms, we tend to believe that it's our job to make things right when our kids have a problem.

"I really have no clue how to fix this, hon. I'm not even sure what needs fixing." If I could figure out some path to take, some part of the problem to work on, maybe I wouldn't feel so panicky about the whole thing.

Will's answer was difficult to hear. With calm confidence, he said, "Jamie, this isn't up to you. This is something Jul has to do. If you let *her* do it, when she is a man, she'll feel good about having done it for herself."

But… I was always the lead. Giving it to Jul would be a serious adjustment for me. My shoulders rose and fell with the deep sigh that accompanied the hateful realization that he was right.

A short while later, I got into my car and headed to the bus stop to pick Jul up. It wasn't a long drive; straight down the street, only a dozen blocks away. Any longer would have required Will behind the wheel. I wasn't feeling very focused. But I forced myself. I wanted to be alone with my daughter.

It was a snowy, early-winter evening. In a numbed state, I noticed how the moon made the snow sparkle in the darkness. It seemed surreal, as if I were in a dream.

When I saw her, the damp coldness somehow seemed to disappear. I watched her get into the car. From the bus stop to our home was a quiet, five-minute drive; neither one of us could figure out quite what to say.

Secret Selves

The minute we stepped through the door into our kitchen, I put my arms around her and held tight. We stood there, tears running down our faces, for what seemed like forever. I could feel the tension melting out of Jul's body as she softened in my arms. I couldn't bring myself to let go. I wanted her to feel how much I loved her; saying it didn't seem like enough. The pain in her voice earlier that day had made me hear with my heart.

When I was finally able to let go, we sat down at the round, rattan table in our big, country kitchen. I asked Jul why she had waited so long to give me the whole truth. She began to explain the events that had kept her from sharing her deepest secret. As she spoke, I started to understand the pain in her scarred heart.

There was a childhood memory that had plagued her for years. One crushing line had been eating away at her confidence for over a decade.

It had started when Jul was nine or ten. At that time, her dad had had a girlfriend. Luckily she's no longer in his life. This woman was a living miracle. She seemed to be able to stay alive, even though her body lacked a heart. You see, as I told you, Jul is dyslexic. She struggled daily with her self-esteem. This woman had told her quite regularly, "You are stupid. No one will ever love you."

"Mom… I heard that line so often that I still wonder, even now, if it's true. You have no idea how often I've wondered if she was right: if there are just too many things about the *real* me that are unlovable." The look in her eyes screamed agony.

I just couldn't understand. "But honey, you know how much I love you. Why didn't you ever tell me about this? You've always been able to talk to me about anything — everything. Why not this?"

Jul tried to explain. "You didn't want to hear it, Mom. I tried, one day after an auction. I tried to tell you I was a boy. You totally shut me down."

I searched my memories. I had completely forgotten, or more likely blocked out that attempt.

And then there was the Oprah day. Jul said, with tears welling up again, "If I had tried one more time after those horrible attempts, and you still didn't listen, I wouldn't be able to try again. It would be over."

As I sat listening, I thanked God that she had found the strength to tell me. I couldn't believe the pain I had inflicted. Large tear drops rolled down my face, landing on my tightened chest.

How could I have been so stupid?

I guess fear can really make you a fool.

It wasn't only my refusal to listen that had silenced Jul, however. The horror stories of people like her had repeatedly run through her mind. Stories of people who had tried to be truthful, people who had been left totally alone by their loved ones.

Jul had thought a lot about someone she had become acquainted with online. "I've gotten to know a doctor who is a male-to-female transgender. I feel comfortable talking with her; I can ask her anything.

"Before transitioning, she went to therapy for *two years* trying to come to peace with her true self. She did *not* want to face what she was. She wanted to be normal. She's the father of two children, and she wanted to keep the life she'd made with her wife and kids, but she couldn't do it."

This woman's courage to be her true self had caused serious damage to her life. "It's awful, Mom. She's been disowned by her friends. Her kids blame her for ruining the marriage to their mom, and they say she's made a disaster of their lives. They've hated her for a year now. But you know what the worst part is? Because of her courage to change, her parents won't speak to her.

"Her life seems to have turned out the same as all those people on Oprah. I don't know how anyone can survive losing the people closest to them." A big tear ran down her cheek.

My own tears had stopped, but seeing Jul so emotional started them up again. Of course, this doctor's story would make her hesitate to try to tell me again.

"Well, I'm glad you told me now, honey. What made you decide to?"

She looked a little afraid to tell me. "You're not going to like this… Cally thought I was a boy. I'm her boyfriend, Mom. My name's… Kip."

She waited for a reaction, but there was no chance of me getting mad at this point. I just waited.

"I knew that this time I couldn't let it go on. I knew I had to tell her. But thinking about it felt like getting ready to slit my own wrists. I figured telling her the truth would probably kill the relationship. But, living this way was worse, so I forced myself. And… she didn't want to end things; I couldn't believe it, I was blown away."

This girl had accepted the real Jul. (Actually, she had accepted the real "Kip" — Jul's chosen male name.) Cally's love had given Kip some much needed courage.

I sat, amazed. "But, you've been seeing her for months. How could she not know?"

"I strapped down my breasts when I was living as Kip. I told her I didn't like being touched, but I didn't give her a reason why. I couldn't let her touch me… I mean, she'd feel the bandages. And what if her hands had, umm… wandered? What if Cally had, you know… felt between my legs? She'd have instantly known I wasn't a boy. So I set the rule — no touching."

I wanted to know more about the night Jul confessed. How had this girl accepted such crazy and difficult news so easily? "Tell me about last night, honey. What did you say?"

"I started by saying that I had something 'big' to tell her. But then I couldn't find the words. I guess she could see how upset it was making me; she tried to hug me. I had to stop her. I said something like…'No touching, Cally. After you hear the whole story, you probably won't want to touch me anyway.' I figured once she knew the truth, she wouldn't want to be with a freak."

She looked so sad when she said those words.

"Those thoughts made me wonder how I would ever get the words out. But I had to. Cally kept watching me; I had to say something."

I could imagine the tension that would have been building with each passing moment. "How did you finally say it?"

"I just blurted out, 'I'm a boy in a girl's body' and it was so weird, Mom, Cally looked relieved. She said she was just glad it wasn't that I was going to die or something like that."

The story made me smile.

"Then she said, 'That's it?! Is that all? Can I touch you now?' I thought I was going to go crazy. I got really loud." Jul's eyes got wide. "I said, 'WHAT?! I just told you the hardest thing I could ever tell you, and you say — That's it? Is that all?' WHAT?!' I couldn't believe it, Mom."

I knew Cally was a very touchy-feely person, and she said she desperately wanted to comfort Jul. Not being able to touch "Kip" that night had driven her crazy. The connection between them was strong enough for her to want to get through this problem as a couple.

Later Cally told me that as the long minutes passed while she waited for Kip to find his words, her mind played out frightening scenarios. She knew it was something significant by the tension that filled the room. Cally knew what a transgender person was. She figured it was either that or something similar, or that Jul had a life-threatening disease. Her fear was that, whatever it was, it would be followed by the words "I don't think we should see each other anymore." She said, "I was relieved that rather than hearing I was going to be discarded from the relationship, it was an issue that we could tackle together." She didn't want to lose Kip.

Jul was floored. That reaction had made her do some very deep soul searching. After spending the evening confessing, she had endured the six-hour bus ride back to college. On that long dark trip, she realized that the lies had lived long enough. Once home, she hadn't slept.

It was time to tell me, or end the pain.

She had spent the night in bed holding the biggest knife she owned.

Now you have to understand that Jul is *not* the suicidal type. The thought of her contemplating this idea was totally absurd to me. How could such a strong, bright, level-headed kid even think of suicide? How could she have hidden so much pain?

She explained to me that a huge percentage of transgender people ended their life at this critical turning point. What they face every day is excruciating, and there is a consensus that telling the members of their family is the hardest part of the whole process.

Jul described sitting in bed with the knife in her hands, weighing the pros and cons of telling me. She felt that if her mom, who accepted everyone, couldn't deal with this that there was no way the rest of the family would. And even though her new girlfriend seemed to be open-minded and wonderful, the relationship was a little too new to trust. They had only been dating for a few months, and it had been long distance, at that. What if it didn't last? She might end up alone.

She sat all night, trying to decide if she could muster the strength to try to tell me one more time.

Jul had been totally unprepared for Cally's response to her news. She was pretty surprised by my change of heart, for that matter. Maybe fate was trying to tell her that we shouldn't always try to figure out the end result. That doing the right thing is what really matters. It was a lesson that I hadn't learned yet.

By the end of the story, I was completely amazed. My tears had changed from horrifyingly ashamed and guilt ridden, to relieved and extremely grateful. This girl, Cally, may have saved my daughter's life.

No, my son's life.

Chapter 12

For the next few months, my emotions learned gymnastics. In my stomach, there was something much bigger than butterflies, and whatever it was, it was practicing cartwheels and back flips.

My relationship with Jul was back to how it always should have been — honest and unguarded. We were talking openly again. That filled me with gratitude, but at the same time, I juggled fear and selfishness. I felt like an attraction at a sideshow. I was the two-faced woman. Part of me felt pride in the incredible strength Jul had shown, yet part of me wanted to keep this difficult secret hidden.

What would people say? I felt sure that there would be many narrow-minded people who would ostracize us. How many would reject the realness of this misunderstood problem? My mind failed to locate a single positive memory on the topic — any story about a transgender that had a happy ending, a kind word about someone who had changed, anything to reinforce my spirit.

I would have to get tough.

We were going to have to learn to dodge the arrows that closed minds would shoot at us. I was trying to fake some confidence, but all my memories were ganging up to intimidate.

Then, on a blustery, winter night, that fear manifested itself in my kitchen.

Maybe the weather was trying to warn me that a storm was on its way straight for us. It appeared in the human form of one of my husband's closest buddies.

We were having a New Year's Eve celebration. Our kitchen was filled with a dozen or so of our good friends. None of them knew our secret yet. No one did.

The whole group sat around the table laughing and chatting. Luckily, Jul was not one of the people at that table.

Late that evening, after snacking on nibblies, and having the typical New Year's Eve beverages, the discussion turned to a colleague of one of our guests. He was referring to this colleague as "it." The way he said IT was horrible; he put such fiery, hot-blooded emphasis on the word. I found myself flinching every time he used it. His hatred for IT filled the room. You could see it in the sharp angles of his eyebrows, and the glare in his eyes as he spoke. You could hear the passionate hate as his voice grew louder and louder.

He told the story of this "thing" who he worked with. IT was a man who wanted a sex change. He was living as a woman. IT wore very short miniskirts to work. Our friend snarled how he didn't know how the "thing" even covered its penis in them!

I sat in shock thinking, *This can't be happening! I'm not ready for this!*

Our friend worked for an airline carrier, and the place was filled with men. He explained how IT would prance around trying to draw attention to itself. Of course, the attention IT got was undoubtedly negative. When colleagues would tease or ridicule this person, she would pull a poor-me line, saying, "Look at how they treat me!"

Our friend was disgusted by IT. He was furious with IT for parading his sexual deviance in their faces. The whole loathsome display IT performed daily was sickening. What did IT expect from them?

Every time he said the word IT, he scraped at a nerve that sent damaging electricity through my whole system. As I listened to him talk, the horror grew inside. The air in the room seemed to thin. I closed my eyes, and tried to take a few deep breaths. I tried to talk myself into thinking that this was just one person's opinion, struggling to remain calm.

My attempt to compose myself wasn't working. It was such a tender, open wound. If they had been talking about how many kids were careless enough to have sex without condoms, and my Jul had been trying to hide a teenage pregnancy, I would have been embarrassed and uneasy. I would have sat there, uncomfortably, trying to look normal, trying to hold it together and not cry. What I was experiencing was similar, but it went a whole lot deeper than that. I was down-right panicky. I wasn't ready to talk about this subject yet. It was too fresh, too delicate… too tricky.

I looked across the table at Will, desperately wanting him to put a stop to this. I could see him squirm at the mention of this new, touchy topic. He looked back at me. The embarrassment in his eyes said, "I'm sorry, but I don't know what to do." Will hates confrontation. I was sure he was at a complete loss as to what to say that night. That I could understand. I didn't know what to do either.

The angry comments kept coming: each one hitting with the force of a baseball bat to the stomach. I fought the urge to let the tears burst out, and run from the room. I fought the urge to jump across the table, and squeeze his neck until he couldn't speak another painful word. My emotions jumped from one end of the spectrum to the other. I guess it was a fight or flight thing.

I had to do *something*. My imagination was taking me to the worst places. I could picture people referring to my Jul as a thing and calling her IT.

I searched my brain for a way to somehow shut him up!

He just kept talking. He told us about how the Human Resources Department had brought all the guys except IT in to tell them to cool it. HR thought that IT was purposely trying to get negative reactions. They thought her choice of clothing was designed to push buttons: that she was attempting to lead the guys into doing something that would give her grounds for a sexual harassment or discrimination case against the company. HR figured she was trying to win money for the operations that lay ahead of her. She had been heard saying, "I want a sex change. That's why you guys don't like me," in her overly flamboyant style.

Everyone in the room knew our friend was a homophobe. IT probably knew it, too. She probably also knew that many people lump anyone sexually different into the same category — unacceptable. Homophobes would certainly have the buttons she was looking to push. If she *was* doing it on purpose, it was definitely working beautifully.

This part of the story gave me something to work with. Maybe I could make our friend see that it was just the personality traits, and chosen behaviors of this person that he hated. If I couldn't get through to him, maybe I could at least save some of the other people in the room from being infected by his warped views.

I wanted to attack. Instead, with scrappy determination, I just started asking him what exactly made him so furious. "Why do you detest her so much? Is it the fact that she's different, or is it the fact that she's trying to take advantage of the system? If she was a girl who was trying to entice a sexual harassment case for her own personal gain, would it be less offensive? I don't think it would be. It'd be just as bad." I tried to peel at the layers of hate.

It didn't seem to be working.

"Maybe it's her choice of clothing that makes people uncomfortable? If she wore appropriate work attire, you'd probably see her differently. You know, if she dressed like she should, there'd be no reason to hate her, right?"

I wanted him to see that he was generalizing about a group of people, but it wasn't transgenders that he hated; it was a unique individual — an individual who lacked scruples, discretion and compassion for others. A person who was living only to fulfill her selfish needs. I tried to show him that he hated her work ethic and attitude, he hated her personality — the fact that she was a transgender was an irrelevant detail in his rage.

He couldn't understand. He wouldn't admit, or even recognize, what I was trying to say. The closed mind of this friend was more terrifying than anything I had experienced in a long time.

It wasn't enough that I was dealing with this guy's phobias, but several others in the room thought his whole performance was funny. They didn't seem to notice the tears I blinked away periodically. They sat snickering, egging him on to tell more stories about IT, amused with the exaggerated enthusiasm the evening's alcohol consumption had encouraged out of him. I couldn't stop any of it. Couldn't they see in my face that this wasn't the least *fucking bit funny*!

As I neared the lashing-out point, a thought crossed my mind. *Just tell them! THAT will shut them up!*

But then we would all be left just sitting there awkwardly, not knowing what to say next. It would probably end the party. That didn't sound like a bad thing by then; the conversation had gone beyond saving, anyway. But I just couldn't do it. I couldn't do that to Jul. She hadn't told the people who were close to her yet. She would be so hurt to find out that *this* was the way the first people in town found out. It wasn't fair. And they didn't deserve this private knowledge that day.

My fears were sitting in front of me, directly across the table, and I was helpless. I sat there numbed, stunned with where the evening had taken me, feeling totally defeated.

I realized later that this friend was dealing with his own fears. Ignorance and apprehension are the forces that keep minds closed. I wondered how I was going to heal this fear in people.

At the time, however, I felt no sympathy for our friend. I had my own problems to deal with. I thought this scene in my kitchen was what my future would look like. A life filled with hate, prejudice and ridicule of my oldest child.

As the days passed, I played this scene repeatedly in my head. I wanted to find a way to fix the future.

How many people would sit in their kitchens making jokes at our expense? What other awful scenes were ahead of me?

Could I take the twisted conversations I would surely have to be part of? I was afraid of the dark. The dark, uncertain future.

Could I live like this? Jul planned to tell the world she was a man, but maybe she didn't realize that it didn't only affect her. There would be uncomfortable moments for all of the people who loved her.

Funny how I looked to therapy for so many things during my life... my first marriage, the hand under Joey's bed, Jul's teenage troubles, but during this time of turmoil it didn't even cross my mind. Dumping my pent-up feelings out onto a good therapist's couch couldn't have hurt.

I had no idea that there were support groups for parents like me. Meeting up with other parents, or talking to some type of therapist knowledgeable about these issues might have eased the stabbing pain that made taking a deep breath so difficult a lot of the time.

The least I could have done was read. Learning that I wasn't alone, and not to blame would have eased the panic. Material that helped me to see that it takes a huge amount of trust and respect for a trans teen to tell might have made me realize what a compliment my child had given me. Hearing the good news: that transition typically resolves mountains of stress for a transgender person, and that many go on to live happy and fulfilled lives may have helped me to see the whole process as a thing of hope, instead of a snowball of problems that grew with every turn.

And it might have put me in a better place to deal with the evening I'd faced.

But I didn't consider allowing someone to help me; it didn't even cross my mind.

The only solution I could think of lurked deep in the shadows of my head. I didn't develop the idea intentionally, but regardless... out it popped. Maybe there was a way that would allow Jul to be a man without this conflict. It wasn't a completely open and honest plan, but it was all I had, and maybe, with some luck, it just might work.

Chapter 13

In my mind, my plan seemed logical; a little less than honest — maybe, but logical.

I knew it was time to accept Jul for who she really was. She had the mind of a boy. She explained to me how scientists describe this phenomenon. During the first trimester of pregnancy, the body develops as one gender, but the brain develops as the other. It's simple, really — all babies, regardless of whether they are a boy fetus, or a girl fetus, start off indistinguishable. At six to eight weeks in the pregnancy, the fetus will release a surge of hormones in order to change it into a male or female body, beginning the growth of the appropriate reproductive organs. If all goes normally, the fetus will release another rush of hormones to develop the brain to match that gender. If something goes wrong... voila. You have a baby that appears typical, but is actually very different.

It's simply a birth defect, a developmental glitch. You can't change the brain, but you can change the body to make a match. When you think about it in such rational terms, it makes sense. I could understand that.

We could not change Jul's brain, but it was time to do something about mine. I would have to rearrange my way of thinking. I had no idea, however, how immensely stubborn one little, three-letter word could be. It seemed the word "she" was sticking around, no matter how hard I tried. I thought my biggest challenge would be calling Jul by a new name. Getting a steady handle on using "he" was the much bigger obstacle to overcome. That stupid, persistent, little, three-letter word just seemed to slip out whenever it wanted to. I thought I'd never get it chiseled out of my stubborn memory.

And then, there was the reprogramming of the twenty-year name habit. Not quite as big a challenge, but not a great deal smaller either. This is where my great plan came in.

Jul was obviously more comfortable in places that were diverse enough that a person could fade into the crowd. She planned to live in a large city when she graduated college. My plan was for her to use a gender-neutral name; then we could just avoid the whole controversial transgender subject in our small town, and she could have her new life in the city as a man.

Jul had been using a genderless name for her on-air shifts for months. When she did her radio show at school, she was known as Jay. It was almost like it was meant to be. If she changed her name to Jay, no one who knew her as a child needed to know she was transgendered at all. If someone who had known her asked me how Jul was doing, I could just say, "It's Jay now. It's her on-air name in radio and it just stuck." There'd be no painful explanations, trying to make people understand. Gossip and criticism could be totally avoided. It was just the thing!

Now all I had to do was sell Jul on the idea.

One winter weekend, when she was home to visit, I gave it a shot. We sat in the living room together. I laid out my sales package for her, with all its wonderful accessories and free extras.

"It's perfect, honey. Some people attach a real negative stigma to this sort of thing, you know that. If we call you Jay we can avoid all that. We won't have any uncomfortable moments trying to explain that you've always been a boy. That's tough for people to grasp. We won't have to face any gossip or prejudice when you're here. The transition will be a lot less complicated. And, it's a name you're used to using! It's perfect, really! What do you think?"

Jul sat listening, wearing a very confused look on her face. Her eyebrows lowered over her eyes, and she crossed her arms. Her body language headed in the opposite direction of what I had hoped. When I had practiced this scene in my mind, her reaction had been very different.

Jul quietly, but firmly said, "But Mom, my name is Kip."

"But, honey... my plan is so much less risky. There'd be no opportunity for people to attack or question. It's such a simple solution." Trying to diffuse fear, anger or prejudice simply did not need to happen.

Jul didn't seem to get it. She knew nothing of the horrendous "IT" conversation. I wondered if telling her about it would convince her. It probably would, but how much damage would it do at the same time? She didn't need confirmation that there were people that wouldn't understand. She might even somehow think that she had been the cause of my pain that night. And it wasn't her fault. My embarrassment, my fear, those were my issues. She had enough to deal with.

No, it was better to keep the IT memory stored away. Instead I tried to appeal to my daughter's... sorry, *my son's* caring nature. "Well, being Jay would make the transition a lot easier for me. Think about it... please, honey."

At the end of the weekend, as Jul got ready to head back to school, I asked her if there was a counselor there who she could see. Not that she seemed to be struggling with any one thing in particular. I just felt that she should have someone to turn to, if things got difficult. Maybe they could even discuss the name problem.

One of Jul's classmates had seen the school counselor, and told Jul that she was really good, so Jul made an appointment.

This woman was more than a bit surprised by her new client. When Jul shared her story, her comment had been, "I have *never* heard anything quite like this before!" To me, it cemented just how hard this concept was to grasp.

Experience would have been a plus. If Jul had talked to a professional who was knowledgeable about trans issues, it might even have spilled over and helped me. I felt so alone.

But the counselor was easy to talk to, and a good listener, and Jul enjoyed going there to vent. Before long, the conversation made its way to me, and *the plan*.

The whole Jay plan left Jul feeling confused. She didn't understand why it meant so much to me. She didn't see why it had to be such a big deal. She was irritated. She had kept it well hidden in front of me, but she was angry.

The counselor tried to help Jul understand what a hard time a parent might have with this transition. She tried to help her see that, in effect, I was losing Jul. It wasn't as bad as death, but there wasn't anything much closer for a parent. I had given Jul her name, and called her by it since the first young hours of her newborn life. I had spent twenty years enjoying a closeness that only a mother and daughter could understand. Jul, my daughter, would be gone, forever. It would be an indescribable adjustment. She told Jul that if using the name Jay made things easier for her mom, maybe she should consider it. Doing whatever made it less difficult for her mother was the right thing to do.

Jul didn't like it. She told me later that she'd felt it wasn't fair, but she thought, "Well, if it makes things easier, I guess I'll have to do it."

* * *

The next time Jul came home, HE was JAY.

And Jay brought Cally home to meet us. I am sure it was as surreal for her as it was for us. We were adjusting to the new name, but so was she. She had fallen in love with Kip.

And poor Jay... you could tell that he just wanted to skip ahead in time a year or two. You could see him cringe every time I accidentally slipped out a Jul here, and a she there. His eyes would close as he tried to control the embarrassment.

I felt like such a disappointment every time those stupid, little, three-letter words made an appearance. I would get it... it would just take some time and practice.

Despite the unusual circumstances, I was overwhelmed with happiness to have the two of them in my kitchen. My child was not going to have to feel the pain of abandonment that many transgender people experience. Our big kitchen was full of love for him.

It was a strange, but nice evening. I wondered what this girl thought of me. I had been so blind for such a long time. To her, I probably appeared selfish. To my knowledge, the only thing Cally knew about me was that Jay had considered suicide at the thought of sharing the truth with me. Good God, I needed a glass of wine.

I was undeniably very nervous, and I had good reason. After all, it was my first night with my new son, Jay. My fears that I would slip up with the new name and pronoun had materialized. Then, as I was preparing dinner, I realized that the frozen fondue meat I had bought the day before was freezer burnt.

Out to the store to get more at the last minute.

That wouldn't have rattled me on a normal day, but that night was my opportunity to make a better impression on my son's girlfriend, and it wasn't starting out well.

Then, to shake me up a bit more, Jay and Cally walked into the kitchen as I fussed, getting things ready to start our meal together. Jay stood behind Cally, his arms wrapped around her as if it were nothing.

I was instantly embarrassed. I tried to focus on the food, hoping they wouldn't notice. For years, I had attempted to prepare myself for the first time my daughter was openly affectionate with someone. It's an adjustment for any parent, I guess. But that moment caught me more off guard than I expected. I hadn't thought I'd have to deal with it so soon, and definitely not with this strange twist.

My wine glass seemed to empty itself. That first glass went down so quickly. I wasn't thinking about how alcohol sometimes hits me harder when I'm nervous. I was thinking about how I would make Cally see that I really wasn't a bad person; I was just a little… naïve. I had a second glass because the first just didn't seem to be working well enough. And maybe a third would finally make me feel less edgy. Plain and simple, I had too much wine, and when I have too much wine, I get silly. It did help break the ice, though.

We have memories of my silliness that night that will last forever. Sitting around the table, two couples — Jay and Cally, and Will and I, having a fondue, a get-to-know-you conversation and a few laughs (mostly at my expense).

If you've ever had a fondue, then you know that each person gets different colors of forks, so that you can keep track of which of the items cooking in the shared fondue pot are yours. Well, the story goes (according to the kids) that I read the riot act about who had which colors of forks. I stressed the importance of everyone paying strict attention to their fork colors when dipping their food into the hot oil, or when checking their bubbling nibblies. Then shortly after… yes, you guessed it, I took the wrong fork and stole Cally's meat!

Cally did not let me away with it; the girl was definitely a little spitfire. But it was all in good fun. I could see behind the devilish twinkle in her eye. She had a warmth I could feel.

As I cleaned up afterward, I giggled away to myself.

Cally looked at Will, and asked, "Is she always like this?"

Will just smiled in his easy-going way, and nodded slowly.

It turned out to be a nice evening. We enjoyed each other's company. But more importantly, you could see the strong connection between the two of them as they laughed. I liked the way they looked together. It looked comfortable and right. I was happy.

I was happy for Jay — definitely. Was it still an adjustment? Oh, yeah...

Joey: 2002-2005
Chapter 14

I couldn't stop thinking about it — that wonderful day that Joey and I spent together at the reptile zoo, and how amazing it was to see Joey overcome his fear of spiders. It was truly a perfect memory, and I wanted more.

I decided that a relaxing Sunday morning breakfast was the best time to pop the idea on Will.

Over the smell of ham, eggs and hash browns, I began to timidly tell my husband my idea.

"So, what do you think?"

Will looked back at me seriously. "I'm just afraid that, in six months, you're going to end up with a bunch of animals to feed and look after. What if he grows out of the idea?"

With Jul off to college, I needed a change in my life. "You know how I am, hon? I'm ready to learn something new. I'll make sure he understands the commitment that goes with this."

"Are you *sure* you want to do this?"

I could just picture Joey teaching a group of kids as they sat in a semi-circle on the floor, looking up at one of his little critters. "It'll be fun for me, and it'll be a great confidence booster for him. And really, anything that gets him away from those damn video games for a while has to be a good thing."

Will took a sip of coffee to wash down his mouthful of breakfast. "Well… it might teach him responsibility. And it's always good to have experience in business."

A little enthusiasm from Will was all it took to set me off. "It was *so* awesome to see him overcome his fear of spiders. I want to help people like that. God, that would be so cool!" I smiled and scrunched up my shoulders.

Will shook his head at me. "Well, it's got to be his investment, Jamie, and the upkeep will have to come out of the profits."

"I know, I know, I'll be good." I threw my arms around my husband's shoulders and planted a big kiss on his cheek.

We already had the rats, and Joey had a good bit of money saved. I knew he'd be eager to use it for a collection of interesting animals to share with people. It would give him the perfect excuse to get all the little critters he'd always wanted. With Will's blessing, I decided to share my idea with my son.

Joey's face lit right up. Trying to keep him from getting carried away, I gave him my spiel on how this idea wasn't something to take lightly. "If you want to try this, it'll be a real commitment; animals don't look after themselves. You'll have to learn a lot of facts on each animal we choose. And you'll have to buy food for the animals and pay for advertising out of the profits."

He nodded eagerly. He wasn't discouraged in the least.

So it was decided; we would give it a try. I just hoped I wasn't getting in over my head.

We began to look for interesting little beasts that were easy, and inexpensive to care for. A lizard was a must, according to Joey. We found a very small variety, his body not much bigger than your thumb. This Caledonian Crested Gecko had sticky pads to crawl up the side of his small aquarium, or your arm (or your face, if he decided to jump suddenly). He would lick peach baby food off your finger. Joey was right; the kids would love this little guy.

Next we picked an African Pigmy Hedgehog. I didn't know any children who had touched the prickly quills of a hedgehog, or the soft tummy underneath. It would probably be pretty exciting for kids.

Joey knew he wouldn't be able to get a snake. Will had *no* interest in overcoming that fear. But, to my son, there was one thing that was a priority. "We *have* to get a tarantula."

I looked at Will.

Will's face tensed. Then slowly he lifted his eyebrows. "Well... okay, but... if it ever gets loose, and I come across it, I will be squishing it with whatever I can get my hands on."

I giggled. We couldn't really argue with that; it was a compromise.

So we decided on a Rose Haired tarantula. That was what Joey and I had held, and we knew they were very docile. We named her Tara (the terrible). She was two and a half inches across and covered in hair.

With Tara, we were almost there. Including the rats, we had four fun species to show when we opened for business. Joey thought we needed a bigger variety of lizard. We settled on a species called Uromastyx. He was about eleven inches long, and covered in pre-historic looking pointed armor.

It was enough to get started. We studied our facts, noted any comical events that accompanied our learning curve with the animals, and named ourselves Joey's Furry Friends and Other Curious Critters.

We were ready.

I found a couple people at work who had a child celebrating a birthday and offered them free entertainment. Maybe not the most perfectly polished entertainment, but if the kid was an animal lover, they probably wouldn't notice.

The freebees we did offered us valuable learning. Not only did we find out how to show the animals, we also figured out how not to show them.

During our debut show, Joey sat on the floor with Sonic, the hedgehog, after he had met his first group of children. I had turned away, getting out the next critter, when Sonic suddenly decided he was *really* finished with the show.

Joey gently leaned into me and quietly said, "Mom, I have a bit of a problem."

The little bugger had run right up Joey's pant leg. It had happened so fast that I hadn't even noticed that Joey now had company in his pants. Unwelcome company, about the size of a man's fist. Hedgehogs backs are covered with quills; approximately seven thousand of them. They aren't as sharp as porcupine's: more like pointed toothpicks with extra sharp ends. They are, however, definitely sharp enough to make a predator, or a person, jump back if you are stuck by their points when they are raised.

Joey was certainly in a predicament. Every time he moved, Sonic would either raise his quills, or climb higher up the inside of Joey's pant leg, and he was dangerously close to the panic area already!

Luckily, Joey thought to stand up quickly, and Sonic had come tumbling out. No harm done. Hedgehogs roll very well.

After a couple more freebees, a few more lessons, and a very nice-sized newspaper article, things pretty much took care of themselves. This time, the word-of-mouth that spread so quickly in a small town was a wonderful thing. Before long, we were doing two or three shows a month in our town, the neighboring towns and even in the city the reptile zoo was from.

We enjoyed three years of business together. The experience definitely brought us closer together, and I think I learned as much as my son did from those three years. Unfortunately, the parties had to stop. We couldn't really continue past the third summer. By then, I was never sure if Joey would show up as Joey.

Chapter 15

During those three years of business, the number of cages in our home slowly grew. Every time Jay would come home from college, he would shake his head. There was always something new.

We had added an amazingly soft and quite crazy chinchilla, a third to our lizard family (a very large, Blue Tongued Skink), a Roccoco Toad, a second tarantula, and one of my favorites — a pair of hairless rats.

The new rats had very soft, wrinkly skin. One was grey, the other pink. The pink one almost looked like a cross between a newborn piglet and one of those funny little wrinkle dog puppies. The grey one's body reminded me of a miniature hippopotamus.

Hairless rats belong to the part of the animal kingdom that is so homely they are absolutely adorable. Well, at least to me they were, anyway.

The rats were always my favorites. We affectionately referred to them as "the girls."

When we had company, I'd get a kick out of going to get the hairless pair. For some reason, the absence of fur always seemed to startle people when I plunked them in their laps without warning.

My sister's husband had been pretty open-minded about our critters; his wife was an animal lover like us. But one day, when I dropped those soft little bundles of skin into his lap, there was an undeniable moment of terror. Just a moment. Then it was gone, and he laughed.

I think maybe Jay thought we were losing it, or more so, *I* was losing it. On one visit home from college he laughed as he told me the story of a dream he'd had.

He'd come home to visit, apparently years later, and found Will as a very old man, sitting at the kitchen table smoking a pipe. He asked where I was.

Will flicked his head, motioning toward the next room.

Jay looked in and saw me as a little old lady, standing in front of a cage, talking in my enthusiastic, mushy animal voice. The conversation went something like, "Hello there, little fella. Ahhh... look at you. How are you doin' today?" That sort of thing.

The cage was empty.

The room was filled with cages, all empty.

I think at least in Jay's subconscious mind, I had gone over the edge.

I really hadn't, though. The business was just doing well, and we wanted some variety since we were getting repeat customers. Joey's sixteenth birthday helped with that problem.

There wasn't much for sixteen year olds to do in our town. For his birthday, Joey had planned a pool party. But it was the end of May and in this Canadian climate, a pool party at the end of May in an unheated pool can feel like a polar bear swim. Contrary to popular belief, we don't live in igloos here or anything, but most years there is still a mini-iceberg floating in our pool until sometime in April and it takes a while for the water to warm up after it melts. That year had been an especially cool spring. The Fear Factor thing we dreamt up was an alternative to that freezing end of May swim. In the end, it had entertained Will and me just as much as the kids.

Joey had been skeptical. "Well, what would you make us do?"

"I'm not telling you that. You'll have to be as unprepared mentally as the rest of your friends. No unfair advantages allowed."

I could see he wasn't sure. He hesitated a minute, and then came out with, "Well, it better not be lame!"

I laughed. "Don't worry. It won't be lame." What I had planned was a mixture of fun and fright.

Joey studied my face. "Well... okay, go ahead."

It wasn't lame, for anyone. It turned out to be amazing fun, torturing teens without any guilt whatsoever, and having them eat it right up; I strongly recommend this type of party to parents.

The spring warmth was welcoming on the day of that party. We were on the driveway. Joey was in his element. He was proud of how the game was going; he wore it like armor. You could see the strength and fearlessness that surrounded him. The worry that his party would be "lame" was gone.

As we began the second challenge, their eyes followed the box I carried — a little container of feeder-crickets — to the table I'd set up earlier. I hadn't told them what this challenge would be. I hadn't even told them the name of it, because, of course, that would have given it away. I'd told them to stand behind the first line taped on the driveway, then I'd gone silent as I worked. I wanted the anticipation to bubble in them.

They were all shirtless at this point; their skinny early-adolescent torsos pale with the newness of spring. Their shirts had come off with the first challenge — *Frozen Fear*. I'd had T-shirts embroidered with Fear Factor, one for each of them, a memento, to take home and tell stories about. Rock hard embroidered shirts. Soaked wet, folded neatly, and frozen solid individually. It was a two-part challenge. They'd had thirty seconds to pull and press and force it open and pry it over their heads, then they had to wear it for another thirty. They'd squealed like ten-year-old girls during that event.

Fear Factor was to be a mixture of fun & phobias. The first game had been fun. But the second one — it justified the words on the souvenir shirts.

Joey had invited his good friend, Dan. "What are you going to make us do with those bugs?" Dan asked.

I avoided an answer on purpose. "Come check out the *size* of these things! I bought extra large this week, just for you guys."

I stepped back from the squirming mass of bugs. As they moved in closer to peer into the little box, I started my description of the challenge. "This one's called *Cricket Spit*."

I barely had the words out before Tim, one of Joey's buddies, started to vibrate. The poor kid wasn't as outgoing as the others.

"You need to pick a cricket... I suggest the one that looks the laziest to you, because when crickets are scared, they're active, and let me tell you, they're going to be scared! You take your cricket, pop it in your mouth, try to steady it if it panics, and spit it past this second line, over here. If you get it over the line, you get a point."

Tim just stared at me, shivering. "Oh shit, that's gross!"

One of the other boys yelled, "Do those things bite?" It had been a serious question, but it had a laugh attached to the end of it. Probably nerves. They were a bit nervous, but they were totally into it. All but maybe Tim, but even he fought courageously for every point.

After a couple hours of squealing, laughing, and cheering we arrived at the seventh and last challenge. Each boy had to roll the dice and eat whatever was sitting on the gross food wheel. The delicacies included oysters, a dog biscuit, escargots, a piece of jalapeno, a hunk of raw onion, bull's testicles (yes, real bull's testicles) and the kicker — a small, live, wriggling earth worm. Believe it or not, they liked this challenge so much, they did it twice. And luckily, no-one landed on the poor little worm.

At the end of their gross taste-tests it was time to award the runner-up prizes to the boys who had the fewest points. The runners up got silly things like new underwear in case I'd scared the crap out of them. The winner, and I was happy to see it was Nervous-Nelly Tim, got "Champion" brand sweat bands, which he wore proudly.

Everyone, including Will and I, had a wonderful time. It was such good fun, in fact, that we decided to offer it as part of the business. I knew I could come up with challenging events for a variety of ages; just the right amount of fun and fright, slip a curious critter into a challenge here and there and it would be perfect for customers with a taste for adventure.

I called the newspaper to tell them about this newly-offered addition to our business. The weekly paper arrived the next Friday night, and on the front cover was a full-page color photo of Tara, Joey's largest tarantula, spread out on his face. The caption read, "Our Town's Own Fearless Spider Man!" We started getting bookings right away.

This new feature seemed to appeal to all ages. I'd thought we would be doing mostly boys' birthdays. But as usual, when I thought I had life figured out, I was wrong. We were booked for events with boys, girls and a mixture of both. Fear Factor gigs became our most popular bookings. And I loved them.

I had no idea one of these parties would become the doorway into a frightening and dangerous world.

* * *

A year and a half after Joey's Fear Factor birthday — three years into our joint business adventure — on a sunny October evening, we prepared for a Friday night party in a neighboring town. It was for a ten year old's birthday celebration. When I arrived home from work, Joey was already there.

Perfect. We had just enough time to pack the car and be on our way.

We'd been hired to do a Fear Factor the year before for the celebration of this kid's ninth birthday. His face had shone with pride when he'd beaten all his family members; finishing the game with the highest score. He had decided right then that he would have us again the next year — this time to share the fun with his friends. His mom had told me that he had loved it so much, he had yammered on about that party to everyone he knew, and he had waited a whole year to show his friends how much fun it was.

I started giving Joey directions to get Tara into her travel box, and put Sonic, the hedgehog, into his. He seemed to have a funny look on his face, and every once in a while, he would hesitate when I gave him an instruction. There was obviously something on his mind.

We headed off, right on time. As we drove through town towards the highway, Joey hesitantly broke the silence. "There is something I need to tell you."

Damn. I knew that tone of voice. It meant he had something to tell me that I wasn't going to like. I quickly looked in his direction. "Is it going to upset me?"

He tilted his head to the side as if thinking about how to answer. He looked right at me, and said in earnest, "I'm not sure."

"Well, let's wait until after the party. I really need to be able to stay focused right now."

He accepted that for roughly a whole sixty seconds. Then, with a strange, uncomfortable, almost panicky look, blurted out, "No, I don't think I can wait. I really need to tell you something."

I pulled over to the side of the road, and looked at him impatiently.

He put his head down as if trying to hide from me a bit.

God... what now? What is it?

Secret Selves

 The moment he said it, I wished he hadn't.

 He looked at me, and in a quiet, sort of shy voice said, "You keep calling me Joey. People have been doing that all afternoon. I take it he's your son. I don't know who this Joey is, but my name's not Joey."

CHAPTER 16

When my son said, "I don't know who this Joey is, but my name's not Joey," I didn't know what to think.

What?! Your name's not Joey? What the hell?

I could tell he wasn't goofing around. His face was dead serious; he looked so concerned.

"Well... well, who *are* you then?"

He tilted his head down a bit and shrugged his shoulders. "I'm not sure."

What?! My hand came up to my face. As I looked at him, my palm rested on my chin, my fingers covered my mouth and nose.

My mind struggled. I think I just sat there for a minute. "When did this happen?"

"I've been around all afternoon."

How the heck had he gotten through the whole afternoon like this? "Did you go to school?"

"Yeah... Joey's friends helped me find his classes."

What the hell? It was too much.

It must be some sort of mental breakdown.

"How did you find your way home?"

"I had this weird dreamlike memory that Joey's house was under construction, and I sort of knew which direction to go. I recognized the house when I saw it. I have some memories of Joey's life, but they're all... really faint."

Every time he referred to Joey as if he were someone else, it sent a little shiver up my spine. He really thought he wasn't Joey.

As my confused mind tried to figure out what to do, we spent a couple of minutes in silence. Joey would have been impatient by then, wanting me to drive on. He hated waiting. This boy sat quietly, patiently letting me process the situation. He appeared nervous, that was for sure, but at the same time, he had a calmness or peacefulness to him that my son never possessed.

My brain stalled out for a second or two, and then went into overdrive. For once in my life, I didn't over-think the situation. I reacted like I image a firefighter, or a policeman would. There was a need for action, so I took action. Afterwards, when I thought about it, it seemed crazy to me, but apparently, in a crisis situation, that often happens. The nerves wait to kick in; they come after the fact.

I wanted to turn the car around, get home to safety as fast as I could, grab the phone, cancel the party and pray for this absurdity to leave. But I couldn't cancel this ten-year-old's birthday party at the last minute. I just couldn't. It would be like telling the poor kid there would be no Christmas that year.

We had the birthday cake, the loot bags and we were the entertainment. If we didn't arrive at that boy's house, he would have no tenth birthday. My mind formed a picture of his pitiful little face when his mom told him that we wouldn't be coming. I had seen that look of disappointment far too often when my two were growing up. I had needed to cheer them up, to ease their hurt over and over, after their dad had canceled plans with them at the last minute. Even though it shouldn't have been, it had felt like my responsibility to make them feel better. I couldn't do it to this poor kid and his mom.

What the hell am I going to do? I had no idea what I could do to help my son come back, so I guess I focused on the only thing I did have control of.

I had to think fast. The fact that we were barely on schedule probably saved me from becoming a full-out mess. There was no time to worry.

My eyes were cemented to this timid-looking boy sitting in the passenger seat beside me. He definitely didn't look dangerous;

that was one thing that was working in our favor. He looked shy and uncomfortable, but he was cooperative; I knew that much from how he had followed instructions when we loaded up the car. Afraid to hear the answer, I asked, "Do you know what we are heading out to do right now?"

"Nope, sorry — not a clue."

I took a deep breath. "We are going to do a Fear Factor Party. Does that ring any bells?"

"Nope."

How am I going to get through this party when Joey seems to have forgotten his whole friggin' life?

He didn't even look like Joey. Even when Joey was young, he'd always had a confident air. At seventeen, in those rebellious teenage years, it had done anything but subside. When I tried to give him advice about something ... anything, he would act as if he was uninterested.

But this boy was openly looking to me for a solution to this craziness. His confidence had been replaced with a shy, frightened manner, and he seemed to be hoping that I would be the hero who would rescue him from his fear. His eyes darted from the floor to me. He looked as though he was searching my face for answers. When our eyes met, he was somehow younger than seventeen.

As I turned to the steering wheel, trying to make my brain function, I heard, "You seem very nice."

I looked over at him, and tried to fake a smile. "Thank you. So do you." *God! What in the hell am I going to do?*

I knew I could handle the party myself. I had done one on my own and it had gone fine, but there was no way I was taking Joey home in this condition, and just dumping him on Will and leaving. I wasn't dropping him at the hospital either; I had a feeling that this anxious Joey #2 would be terrified if I did that. And my gut told me that the extra stress would make the situation worse.

Truthfully, I really don't think I could have walked away from him at that moment anyway.

There was really only one choice.

The first thing to do was to teach this seemingly void mind what a Fear Factor Party was. He sat listening, saying nothing.

I gave him the rundown and asked, "So… how do you feel about coming with me? You wouldn't have to do much: just sit and watch, and keep score. You *will* have to let me call you Joey, though."

He looked at me with such a childlike expression, it made my heart drip into a puddle on the car floor. After a long hesitation, he nervously said, "I'm scared."

This time my smile was genuine. The poor thing looked so frightened. "You don't need to be scared at all. You're gonna have a great time. These parties are a lot of fun. I think you'll really enjoy it."

Slowly, timidly he answered, "Well… okay. You make me feel comfortable, Jamie, more comfortable than anyone else I have met so far."

I couldn't believe it. My life had been a bit weird up to this point, but this… this was way over the top! The way he talked to me, as if we were total strangers.

But he was my son.

Yet somehow, at the same time, he seemed different, unfamiliar to me. He had a distinctive gentleness, where Joey was all rough and tumble. He seemed tender and soft-mannered compared to my son's tough exterior. Joey has a soft heart, but seldom lets it show like this boy did, and he rarely expresses his feelings. I think that struck me as one of the strangest parts of it all… to be sitting there with him telling me that I made him feel comfortable. It was too weird.

How can this be happening? Oh God… please don't let me come unglued now.

I just needed to hold myself together long enough to get through the damn party.

I remember my hands trembling on the steering wheel.

I forced myself to drive. We arrived five or ten minutes late. There was no time to waste; I just wanted to get it over with. I gave Joey #2 orders to unload the car, watching him nervously. I told the birthday boy and his mom that Joey "didn't feel like himself," and that he would just be keeping score.

Man... if they only knew.

I tried not to let myself think about what would happen if they found out the truth ...the embarrassment I would feel, the shame for trying to slip this by them.

God... am I doing the right thing?

The party turned out fine. It went well, considering the circumstances: weird, but well. At one point, as I was standing in front of the line-up of boys on the couch, I explained an event called Worm Circles. Each boy was challenged to move a good sized pile of wriggling earth worms from one circle to another, a couple feet away, in under thirty seconds... using only their face. If they succeeded, they got a point. Joey #2 was behind me sitting in an armchair. When the first competitor began his attempt, I felt a tap on my shoulder. Joey #2 wanted me to move over a bit so he could see. A naive, amused smile had replaced his nervous look.

Is it normal for a person's brain to just take a break like this? Geez, Jamie... of course it isn't normal!

With every event, he became more relaxed, and happy looking. As the last boy let our big hairy tarantula walk across his face, I began to feel a bit calmer too. We were almost there. Next I had to take care of the loot bags, and if that went well, we were home free.

This portion of the party took much less of my attention than the challenges did. As discreetly as possible, I kept Joey #2 in my line of sight.

As I placed an empty bag in each boy's hand, I gave a short speech about how important it is in life to be able to laugh at yourself. The first thing I dropped in their loot bag was a diaper for the "poor babies" who had fewer points than the winner. Seven boys groaned in unison. Then I stopped, and looking in Joey's direction said, "Wait a minute. Joey... did we pack the clean diapers or the dirty ones?"

Usually at this point, Joey would shrug his shoulders indicating that he couldn't remember. Joey #2 didn't seem to know what to do when I looked at him. He looked the same as all the other boys. Young, curious. He sat expressionless, smiling, waiting for whatever came next.

Each boy grabbed his diaper out of the bag and opened it, exposing a smudge of chocolate icing with an unwrapped miniature O'Henry bar squished into it. Along with laughter came the chiming of "Ew... gross."

Out of the corner of my eye, I watched as my son reacted the exact same as these ten-year-olds, just like it was the first time he had seen me do this. It was a trick we had previously pulled at least a dozen times.

Unbelievable! Distracted, but anxious to finish, I yanked my thoughts back to the boys. I went around the room, dropping in each bag candy called Nerds, Crabby Patties, then Airheads, and finally, some gummy tarantulas for them to practice with in case they ran into us again some day. Joey #2 grinned as he watched the boys react to their loot.

The last loser prize was a rubber chicken for each of the evening's "chickens." The boys howled in laughter as they realized the chickens were like a stress ball. When squeezed, an egg came out of the butt, and then disappeared back in when released: an effect that is apparently hilarious to ten-year-old boys. Joey #2 asked if I had an extra one for him to try. He had squished the egg out of these chickens dozens of times, but that day he looked fascinated, like it was an amazing magic trick he'd never seen before.

He smiled and giggled with a strange innocence as I gave some gummy hotdogs to the evening's "Hotdog," some Excel gum that I changed into You Excel and a nail on a leather chain because the winner was "tough as nails." The last winner's prize was a Joey's Furry Friends T-shirt. Joey looked down at his own shirt as if he was thinking… *hey, that's like the one I'm wearing.*

Never before was I so glad to see the end of a party. It was like I was carrying a bomb that could explode at any second, and I had no idea how I would clean up the mess if it did.

Safely back in the car, we headed straight for home. Joey #2 thought that that tree was beautiful, and that car was so nice and what a pretty town we lived in. He peppered me with questions about our lives all the way home. He wanted to see the grocery store where Joey worked, and was amazed by how big and beautiful it was when I drove past. It was a No Frills store; not particularly beautiful, but he was totally taken with everything as if he were in a new country on a different continent for the very first time.

When we arrived home, he asked me if he should unload the car.

Stalling sounded great to me. *While we're getting everything back to where it belongs, maybe I can figure out how the hell I'm going to explain this to Will. Poor Will. How am I going to give him this news?*

Joey #2 took care of that for me. He walked right up to my husband, and said with an outstretched hand, "You must be Will. Nice to meet you." He took Will's hand, shook it enthusiastically, and smiled warmly… then went up to Joey's bedroom to watch TV.

Will looked at me in confusion; his mouth was sort of hanging open. He said nothing. What does a person say to that? I tried my best to explain the evening to him, even though I didn't understand it much myself. It had been an insane night.

"What do you think we should do with him? I doubt if I'll be able to reach either of his doctors. I probably won't be able to talk to them until Monday."

Will shrugged his shoulders and shook his head slightly.

"If we take him to the hospital, they'll probably admit him. I know it sounds weird, but he's a pretty shy kid right now. I think he'd be terrified.

"Maybe we should just leave him. Maybe he'll wake up in the morning as Joey. If he doesn't, we'll just have to figure out what to do with him then."

Please God, make him wake up in the morning as my son.

JAY: 2004-2005
CHAPTER 17

Before that crazy Fear Factor night hit, the party business was a good distraction for me on the days I worried about how the inevitable hormone therapy would affect Jay when he was able to start it, and how dangerous the future surgeries would be when the time came. Or on the days that I worried about the reactions people would have when we began to share this news. Or the days that I worried that Jay might still not be happy with who he was after all the irreversible steps were taken. Agghh! God, I wished my brain had an off button!

As time passed, I knew I couldn't carry my new secret around in my pocket much longer. I had to take it out, show people, tell them about this crazy twist my life had taken.

How was I going to tell people that my daughter was going to become a man? I'd hardly told anyone. Will and Joey, and my sister, that was it.

I'd asked Joey how he felt about Jul's news. His reply had surprised me. "I wish Jul had been born a boy, so we wouldn't have had to go through so much crap. I know we would have been closer. We both would have been happier.

"I always felt like there was something between us, keeping us from having a really close relationship. I guess it was body envy. I was born with the right body. I finally understand."

I figured most people wouldn't adjust as well as Joey had. That fear made sharing our news more difficult. I'd managed to tell my sister about Jay, but I hadn't done a very polished job.

My sister is the closest person in the world to me, and I couldn't even push the truth out with her. It had taken me a couple of months to manage even the words, "Jul has a girlfriend." And that was all I could muster. The rest I left to her imagination. She, of course, assumed that Jul was a lesbian. That was how I needed things. Baby steps. Very small, very timid baby steps.

It had been just before Christmas, a few weeks before the "IT" conversation, when I'd managed that one little sentence with my sister. Mel had seemed a bit surprised that I'd openly shared this news with her, but other than that, she didn't seem too rattled by it. Mel's not a prejudiced person. She asked me if it was okay to share the news with her family. I told her I'd let her decide when the time was right to do that.

She chose Boxing Day. It's a big day for my family. We all get together to share a simple meal, and a color-themed gift exchange. We draw names to see who we'll buy a gift for — often a silly one. That year was orange.

I'll always remember that year because of the outfits. We were greeted at the door of my brother's house by a crowd dressed in various orange hunting attire. It was for effect. We aren't usually rednecks, honest. Boxing Day is meant for fun. The relaxed environment offers everyone time to catch up.

Mel thought she'd wait until after it was over to share our news. She had no idea that Jay had pulled her daughter, Amber, aside right in the middle of the houseful of family to whisper his news.

Amber was the first family member to know his real story, and she got all of two minutes to process it before being thrown back into mingling with the rest of the cousins, aunts, and uncles.

Mel couldn't hold what she knew longer than a few minutes into the drive home that Boxing Day. As she, her husband, Amber, and her brother Eddie, drove away from our Boxing Day celebration, Mel blurted out that Jul was a lesbian, and that she had a girlfriend.

Amber didn't say a word. She waited until they were home, and pulled Mel into a room where they could be alone. "Mom, Jul isn't a lesbian. She's a transgender… and she's planning to get a sex change."

Mel didn't question me. She suspected that I had omitted *that* little detail because I wasn't ready to talk about it yet. So she waited. It took me several long weeks to grow the courage to tell her the whole story.

In the beginning, my feelings of panic and embarrassment were the strongest. It's ironic that that's when a parent has the least support… dealing with a monumental parenting challenge like that all alone. Getting those awkward sentences out the first time with a person less invested in our lives, at a support group, or on a professional's couch, may have made the conversation with loved ones a little less terrifying. Practice makes perfect. But, in my cocoon, the growth was slow.

Now, months later, I still didn't know how to get the words out. My friends didn't know I had a new son… a new, twenty-year-old son, and I had no idea how to tell them.

*   *   *

One afternoon, I was going to lunch with a co-worker; she was a real sweetheart. A cute little thing, but more importantly, she was open-minded and understanding. I was almost positive she would not judge Jay. She was the perfect test-subject for the new, not so fierce courage I was pretending to have.

I had convinced myself that this was the day: I was going to say it. As we sat eating our lunch, I searched for the right moment to tell her. How could there be a "right moment" to blurt out something like this? And exactly how do you say it? "Hey Marie, you know my daughter Jul? Well, she's becoming a man." If there was a right moment, I couldn't find it.

Getting into the car to go back to work, my friend put the keys in the ignition. I rolled down the window in an attempt to be able to breathe. I was running out of time.

I took a deep breath and started my attempt with, "Marie, I want to tell you something."

She looked at me with an expression that told me she knew I was uncomfortable. She gently offered, "Sure."

My sentence was stuck. I opened my mouth but the words held back. I pushed out the beginning, "Jul wants to be…"

Okay, it was time to say it. The hesitation just seemed to be making the whole thing more dramatic. That wasn't what I had wanted. I'd wanted to say it as relaxed as possible. In my mind, saying it casually would make it less of a big deal… but it wouldn't come out.

I finally forced myself to say it…"a boy." It seemed to come out in a weepy whisper. And then the tears started.

Marie looked at me tenderly… her eyes welled up with big tears, and she fanned her face with her hand like it would send all the difficult feelings and emotions floating out of the window.

I had done it, an important step — admitting. Kind of makes it sound like some sort of "twelve-step" program, doesn't it? Denial, panic, disappointment, fear, embarrassment, admittance… I had made it through the beginning stages. It was a start. And Marie was definitely helping.

She filled the car with wonderful supportive words on the way back to work. I have no idea what they were. Not much registered; it really didn't matter. All that mattered was that she was accepting and caring, and she didn't judge. She made me think that maybe, just maybe, everything would be all right.

She gave me the courage to tell a few more friends, and guess what? Nothing terrible happened when I said the words. My heart seemed to pound slightly less ferociously each time I explained it.

Then one day, the unexpected happened. My best friends and I would go out for lunch every Friday, and it was Friday. We arrived at the sporty, bar-type restaurant, and ordered our choices. I hadn't noticed anything unusual when we arrived.

Suddenly, one of them pulled a gift bag from under the bench in the booth we were sitting at, and plunked it on the table.

I knew it wasn't anyone's birthday. *Why are they all looking at me?*

One of my friends gave the bag a shove toward me. I'm sure I looked completely confused as I asked, "What's this?"

They smiled gently. "It's for you. We just wanted to."

I opened the package to find a book called *Simple Abundance…A Daybook of Comfort and Joy*. "It's a book for healing, Jamie." And with it, a card filled with the most beautiful supportive words I had ever seen.

My thoughts exploded. It was unbelievable. I'd been so afraid that this secret would bring heartless labels, damaging biased opinions and anger, and all it had brought me so far was love.

I will be indebted to those three friends forever. That book did more for me, and for Jay, than any of them knew.

I found a peace when I read from it. It really was a book for healing.

But there was something else it did for me, as well. I thoroughly believe that everything happens for a reason. I soon understood the reason for my friends buying me this book.

After a few months of struggling with "he" and "Jay," I was finally starting to get the hang of those stubborn little words. It was like learning a new language. I really wanted to get it, but practice was the only way there. Slowly, the mistakes were happening less and less.

I was working on finally conquering the remnants of this challenge on a weekend that Jay and Cally were home visiting. On Sunday afternoon, I was sitting in my favorite spot, my rocking chair, reading *Simple Abundance*. Without warning, I was struck with a serious "Aha!" moment. You know, one of those moments when a light bulb floods your head with insightful light, and you think, "What the hell was I thinking?"

The following paragraph seemed to slap me in the back of the head:

Many women confuse self-esteem with self-confidence. For me, self-esteem is how we really feel about ourselves in the secret sanctuary of our soul. Do we love, accept, and approve of ourselves unconditionally? Do we believe that we are worthy of the love of others and the best that life has to offer.

And then I read the part that brought it through to home plate. *"The quality of our self-esteem is very deeply connected to the relationship with our first and most important critics: our parents. If they unconditionally loved, accepted, and approved of us, then we probably do too.*

Something in those words made everything clear to me. The concept of loving Jay openly had seemed too risky. By forcing him to be Jay, I was acting as narrow-minded as the people I had imagined I would have to deal with. A loud, nagging voice inside me shouted, THIS IS WRONG.

Reading that paragraph coaxed me to think about my relationship with my parents. *Had they loved me unconditionally?*

The thick, cloudy fog floated away from my sense of reason. As I sat in the warm sun that day, I felt as if I could finally see clearly.

I realized that we can learn from our mistakes, and that everything in life can be used as a lesson once we're willing to be taught. I knew what I had to do. I finally understood what I should have realized months ago. I picked up a pen and began to write.

Later that day, I drove Jay and Cally into the city where Cally went to school. I gave Jay a hug as we said goodbye, and before he could walk away, I tucked a card into his bag. I felt wonderful. In the card, I had written:

Honey, the reason I was not close to my mom is because I always felt that she was trying to force me to be someone I wasn't.

One reason I think I was so close to my dad is because he just let <u>me</u> be <u>me</u>. He didn't say much; he just loved me for who I am. I could see it in his eyes.

Jul... Jay... Kip — honey, I love you just the way you are! And I am so proud that you are standing up for yourself, and being who you really are!

It took me a long time to realize that that is the only way to really be happy. So why am I trying to force you to be Jay? I don't know. Sometimes I am stupid. But from now on, honey, you are Kip. I want you to be comfortable with who you are, and I want you to be truly happy.

Love Mom

I had accepted... really accepted. Now it was time to find out if my family could do the same.

Chapter 18

The famous author Ralph Waldo Emerson once said, "To be yourself in a world that is constantly trying to make you something else is the greatest accomplishment."

My Kip had accomplished so much in his mere twenty years!

And I, as an unsuspecting bystander, was growing as a person by leaps and bounds. I was beginning to learn that happiness is not a reflection of what others think of you; it comes from within. Did it matter if the odd person did not accept Kip for who he was? Of course not. What mattered was that I loved my first born child with all my heart. It felt great, and I was ready to tell the world — no matter what they thought!

…Except maybe my mother…

Was I really ready for that? She was eighty-one years old, still a devout Catholic and trained her whole life to think in very strict, very defined directions. Maybe it would just be easier on her if we didn't tackle the subject with her at all. Did she really need to know?

A nagging memory wore steadily at the back of my brain. The Catholic religion does not accept homosexuals. I had heard my mom say, while she wrinkled up her pudgy nose, that there was "something wrong" with people like that.

When she learned her granddaughter was attracted to women, would she feel there was "something wrong" with her? When people hear of a transgender person, they often say, "I didn't know he was gay!" It's an easy conclusion to jump to. An old-fashioned mindset would struggle with the difference between the two things.

Even if she *did* grasp the full extent of what Kip had endured, she would most definitely be tormented by what God would think. Was it fair to do that to a little old lady?

Kip and I tried to figure out if we would even be able to make her understand this outrageous phenomenon, let alone accept it.

When I had left my first husband, my dad had told me that she had cried for six months, as if grieving a death in the family. Learning Kip's story would have to hit her just as hard, maybe harder. My dad was no longer with us, so this time he wouldn't be able to help her through the difficult adjustment period.

Maybe we shouldn't tell her?

Finally, after months of stupidity, I booked an appointment with a counselor. We needed help.

I found a sexual therapist. It sounded like the closest thing to a specialist for this type of thing; at least it was the closest I could think of.

It wasn't.

This therapist hadn't had the opportunity to tackle a problem like ours before. But she was certainly willing to learn. She did her research, and then asked the questions that made our decision easy.

My mom still lived in our tiny hometown, but now in a retirement residence. What if she found out by hearing sordid, incorrect or exaggerated rumors? What if someone walked right up to her, and flat out said, "So I hear your granddaughter is becoming a man?"

The *what if's* were definitely more frightening than the idea of telling her. Kip and I decided together, after discussing all of our options with this counselor, that telling my mom the truth was really our only choice.

So, the task lay ahead of us — it was time to tell the *whole* family. We were just not sure exactly *how* we were going to swing it, but it was next on the agenda.

Kip has always had a creative mind. He had written a bit when he was a teenager, and was good at expressing himself on paper. It was the obvious solution — he could write a letter to our family.

That, of course, would require figuring out where to start!

How much should he say?

Would our family understand what this type of unusual birth defect was?

Would we become an embarrassment: the part of the family that is kept a secret? Many of them were as religious as my mom was. Would their generation be more open-minded about this, even though it might fall into somewhat of a gray area in their religious beliefs?

We had no way of knowing until the deed was done.

Joey had accepted Kip without batting an eye. Joey and I share a powerful conviction – we both feel passionately about the injustices of any prejudice. He thinks people should always be who they are, and that no one has the right to judge. He doesn't understand why people should even care.

We wondered if any of our family members shared these convictions. We could only hope.

Fortunately, we learned that we had, in the coming months, an event that solidified a deadline… and a desperately needed push. My niece was getting married. Kip firmly decided that if he was going to the wedding, he was going to wear a suit, and have Cally on his arm. He had to tell the family, and soon. He forced himself to tackle the topic, and put his story to paper.

The letter Kip wrote still makes me cry when I read it. To this day, I have kept the first copy I printed with a handwritten note on it to Will that says, "This is Kip's letter. What do you think?"

Will thought it was perfect.

When I read it, I sobbed like my heart had been broken for the first time. I hoped it would bring out the same love and compassion in everyone who read it. And it was time to find out!

One bright spring morning, Kip sat down at his computer, typed in fourteen addresses, copied me in and hit Send. His letter went directly to Will's family members, and to mine (all except my mom). The recipients ranged from age eighteen to seventy-six.

Later that day, as I sat at my desk, I would periodically hear the plink of a response to the letter as it showed up in my e-mail in-box. When the first one arrived, I wondered, *Should I open it? Maybe I should forward it home and wait?*

My emotions were fragile that day, and my nerves were worse. If I read them at work, I would probably cry, and embarrass myself. My desk was in a four-by-six foot cubicle in a room filled with many more of the same. There was very little privacy. Everyone knew everyone's business. Not everyone knew about *this* yet, though.

I wondered what I would say if they asked me what was wrong. But could I wait until the end of the day? No way!

I clicked on the first response and held my breath. It was from Kip's twenty-something male cousin who was writing from work. It started with, "Thanks for the e-mail. It means a lot to get a thoughtful message like that. I just wanted to send a quick note of support." It finished with his home phone number, and an invitation to talk or head over to his place at ANY time!

I survived it with only a slight mist in my eyes. I was going to be able to get through this. It was much better than waiting apprehensively through long hours until the end of the day — that was not even an option!

A short time later, a second reply arrived. It was from my sister-in-law. I swallowed hard. This one might not be so easy. Early in life, she had become a nun, and had served the Catholic church for many years. She had married my brother later in life, but was still a loyal follower. Recently, she had retired from her position as a director for the Bishops. I knew her to be a caring and intelligent lady, but I had no idea what her views on this would be. I placed my pointer over her reply, closed my eyes and clicked. This is what she wrote to Kip:

Dear Jul,

Thank You! Thank you for the courage and honesty that you're showing. Thank you for trusting us enough to share your life story with us. Thank you for being brave enough to pull yourself through the pain and doubts and confusion that you've suffered for so long. You've probably leapt over one of your biggest hurdles: acknowledging to yourself who you are. You'll be able to jump the others as they come along. The people who really love you will always love you, Jul. For some, it will be hard to adjust, perhaps. But they won't stop loving you. I hope you can feel my arms around you today, and that you know they will always be that way.

It 'might' be hard for Grandma to understand, but she won't stop loving you. She's lived a long life and is a wise woman. Telling her yourself is the best thing you can do. It will be tough, but after all you've been through, you can do it. And she'll see the person you are, the one she's loved all these years.

When I was young, I knew someone who became your typical rebellious hippie (the sixties!). She moved away with her boyfriend when she was sixteen, married him, eventually came back to Canada and lived in a commune for a while. You know what I remember best about this whole episode? How her parents, who were older than most people's, reacted throughout the whole time. They were the ones most accepting of her lifestyle, loved her more deeply, always had the door 'open' in case she needed to come home. They were the last ones I expected to be like that. I tell you this story, because we so often underrate the 'love-ability' of the people closest to us. And Grandma has lots of love-ability.

I'm sure you know now, Jul, if you didn't before, how great a mom you have. She will walk with you, and probably jump one or two hurdles with you along the way. What I hope is that you get the best advisors and healthcare assistance that's available. Make sure that you do! Continue to be strong and courageous. You'll have a long and tough road ahead. But like you said: one hurdle at a time.

With much love,
Betty

I finished the last line, tried to catch my breath, and put my head down for a minute. It looked like a gentle spring rain had started to fall on my keyboard.

I was so completely impressed. How had this woman known exactly all the right things to say? She had broken through that last bit of nagging fear that seemed like a stain I just couldn't quite get out. As she put it, "We so often underrate the 'love-ability' of the people closest to us." I had looked up to her before that day, and should have known how she would react.

Maybe she was right about Grandma? Each one of us possesses free will. We can love and help others, or we can hate and harm. I'd chosen to love and help. Maybe my mom would do the same.

Chapter 19

I thought about my sister-in-law's comment about Kip telling Grandma himself. I knew how hard it would be to get those difficult words out. I wondered how *I* would manage it, when someone asked how "Jul" was doing. I planned to keep a copy of the family letter in my purse. If I became choked up when trying to explain, I would simply say, "Good, but there is something that I'd like you to read." I'd take the letter out of my purse, hand it to them and walk away, feeling pride, and a settled satisfaction that some of my small town was about to experience a bit of the growth I could feel.

How I wished I could just do that with my mom. I pictured myself going to visit her, talking distractedly about the weather, and my job and then, with a burst of courage, dropping the letter in her lap as I kissed her goodbye. I would walk away lightly, as if a million pounds had floated up off my shoulders. But I knew the farther away I got, the more that weight would pick up speed as it descended back down to land squarely on my shoulders. I couldn't just leave her a bomb like that, and walk away — not with my mom. Of course, a mailed letter would be even worse. But still, picturing the look she would have on her face as Kip or I tried to explain *this* haunted my thoughts.

The day Kip and I headed over to the seniors' home where my mom lived, the afternoon was warm with the spring sun, but both of us shivered with the worry of the unknown. We parked the car in the small lot and walked toward the one-story building; quiet together in our nerves. The corridor leading to my mom's room seemed narrower than usual, and strangely deserted that day. I had wished it was longer, so I would have more time to somehow come up with just the right thing to say.

We arrived at the door of her room. I looked at Kip and raised my hand to knock. I hesitated. I didn't want to have this conversation. I forced myself to rap on the door a couple times, and then pushed myself in.

My mom greeted us with a loving smile as always, happy to have visitors on a quiet Saturday afternoon. I hated having to take her happy look away from her.

Kip and I sat down in her two visitors' chairs. Her room was small. Its contents — a single bed, three chairs, her dresser, desk and TV— filled it to its limit. I perched anxiously on the edge of her sky-blue easy chair, and stalled with some idle chatter about her health, Kip's studies and the weather.

Trying to talk about everyday things seemed to be winding up my nerves tighter and tighter. It couldn't wait any longer.

I began my timid explanation. "Mom, we have something very difficult to tell you about Jul." There, I had done it. I had stolen her contented look, and replaced it with one of fear. I quickly continued, "She isn't terminally ill, or anything like that, but it might be something you aren't going to be happy about."

Kip's heartfelt words offered our best hope of reaching my mom. I took The Letter out of the safety of my handbag. Her eyebrows lowered suspiciously over her eyes as she watched my hands, glancing quickly at Kip, trying to see if this news would be something she could recognize from across the room. I gingerly handed it to her, and softly said, "This is a letter Jul wrote for our family."

She held out her hand to receive it, her eyes questioning and hesitant, and then opened it and began to read. Kip and I locked eyes. This was it — absolutely the most difficult moment of truth.

He looked as frightened as I felt. For years during his childhood, Kip had spent his Sundays going to church with my

Secret Selves

mom. He knew her views matched those of the Catholic Church as far as sexual variance went. We were both dreading what we already knew — that she would be passionate that *this* was wrong.

I was sure she wouldn't be able to hide her repulsion. I didn't want my son to experience the heartbreak of his grandmother's rejection. I was there for support, though. No matter what happened, I was there for him.

I looked over at my mom. She was reading with intense concentration. I figured she was probably around half of the way through Kip's words.

Then it happened — our worst fear.

She looked up, and glared a fierce look I can only describe as *How Dare You* straight at Kip.

I didn't have to look at Kip to know his horror. I could feel it. Her piercing look emitted anger, and something that to me seemed to resemble disgust. She looked back down to the page, and Kip and I immediately looked at each another. We were both thinking the same thing — *Oh God!*

Then time stopped.

It couldn't have taken her more than a few minutes to finish reading, but those few minutes seemed to last a lifetime.

She finally set the letter down, and slowly stood up.

Oh God, what is she doing now?

She took a few awkward steps toward Kip, and held out her arms. When he stood, she put her arms around him, and tenderly said, "Honey, I hope you don't think we would ever stop loving you."

Those words are engrained in my memory for life. The tears rolled easily down my face. I had worried for months about this moment. I watched my mom as she stood hugging Kip tightly, and realized that people's "love-ability" could have amazing strength.

My mom slowly sat down. I attempted to explain that doctors described Kip's problem as something that happened in the first trimester of pregnancy. It was a type of developmental problem in the fetus where the brain forms as one gender, and the body as the other.

From that moment, my memory of that visit becomes a bit of a blur. I do remember my mom's eyebrows softening, though, as she told us that she had always thought this sort of thing was a life choice, and that maybe she had been wrong. The angry look in her eye had changed to compassion.

I was stunned. After a temporary moment of panic, my mom had received this difficult information with grace, and an open heart. I learned that she could, when necessary, have a mind much more open than I had given her credit for. I realized then that throughout my life, she had been trying to mold me into the type of person she thought was the "best" type. Maybe it wasn't a control tactic. She just wanted the best for me. She wanted the best for us. It was because she loved us. She could, however, accept us for who we really were when it came right down to it.

It is amazing how a few well-phrased words can have such power. This is the letter that helped me understand my mom; the letter that changed her thoughts forever:

Dear Grandma,

I find that writing this letter to you is one of the hardest things that I have done in my life up until now. I am going through something so hard right now that I don't really know what to think of anything. Please understand that my heart goes out to you all as you read this because I think that as you read this, you will feel what I felt writing it.

For the last year or so I have been in a battle with myself. The first six months of that fight I thought that for sure I was going to lose. I hit rock bottom in the fall of 2003, and didn't see a way of getting out. But I finally bit my lip and came to terms with myself and got help. I saw a counselor while I was away at school and she helped me to be able to talk about what I was going through and now I want to share that with you.

I am a transsexual. I don't know if this will be a surprise to you or not. I guess it really depends on how well you know me. On that note, I don't know if you really know what a transsexual is. If you don't, here is the best way I have heard it explained:

Transsexualism (or transgenderism) is defined as feeling a persistent discomfort about one's gender intense enough to cause them to seek to change sex. The best way to really understand this feeling is to imagine that tomorrow morning you woke up and found that during the night you had been changed into a member of the opposite sex. Your mind is the same. Your internal image of yourself as male or female is unchanged. However, your body has changed and you will have to live up to the expectations of that gender. If you can imagine that for just an instant, you can understand what it is like to be a transsexual. Transsexualism then is simply having internal gender identity of one sex and the body of another. Put another way, it's being a woman's mind trapped inside a male body or a man trapped in a female body.

I feel that I am a man. Since I was very young I felt trapped inside of the wrong body, and with this I have been living a double life. Inside I have always felt male, but since my outside was not that of a man I had to hide this deep down inside. As a child things were not so bad. But when I got a little older around the age of 12 or so things became so very hard to deal with. Living as a girl was so hard. It never felt right, and for years and years I went to bed at night praying that I would one day wake up from this living nightmare. At some points I honestly thought that death would be much better than the feelings I held inside. But I never wanted to die. I just wanted to feel right with my body.

Life until now has been one big act for me, and now I want out. I want a real life. I want to be happy since I have held so much pain and sadness inside for so long.

The hardest part of all of this is to tell people that you care about and love. I have never been as scared as I was the day that I told my mom about the choice that I wanted to make. Lucky for me, everyone that I have told so far has been great about this and very supportive of my decision. But my biggest fear in any of this is that I will lose the people I love and that they will turn their backs to me.

The change will take time to happen. It is not something you just do and will regret. You visit many doctors. You don't jump in and it's over, no turning back. You go through years of treatment to make sure that you are strong enough to deal with everything that will come. The doctors build you up emotionally before doing anything physically. So it will not just happen overnight.

I know that this is very hard, not only for me but for you as well. I know that you must have questions about this or concerns. Please call or email me about this at any time. There is no real way to end a letter like this. I know that I have left a lot of information out, but I didn't want to go into great detail right away. I thought that I would tell you the general information and if you want to know more you can contact my mom or me. Thank you for reading this. It means more to me than you can know just getting this out. I will leave you with a quote that I think is very fitting for this:

"One hurdle at a time."
With Love,
Jul (Aka Kip)

Kip and I left my mother's room after telling her our news, feeling partially as though we were in shock, barely able to believe her transformed reaction, and partially as if we'd been injected with a power source. If this was what it felt like to be totally honest about life, sign me up for honesty. I will never forget that feeling of relief, and contented amazement. It gave both of us strength.

The next obstacle to overcome somehow did not seem quite as high a hurdle. Still, it would take a bit of courage. Our next obstacle was the wedding.

Chapter 20

To Kip, the first and most important thing to consider about his cousin's wedding was whether the bride and groom wanted him there. The bride's response to the family letter had been loving and accepting.

But *this* was different — this was her wedding day.

It would be an adjustment for everyone in the family. Kip would be wearing a suit and tie. Cally would be his date. It was how it had to be.

First, though, he felt he *had* to get my niece's blessing.

He asked the question, in an e-mail, to both the bride and groom, and her parents. He said he understood completely if they felt it was too soon for such a big step, or just a little too weird a happening for such an important day in their lives.

He heard back from his aunt and uncle first. They seemed unsure.

I sensed a bit of anxiety in their reply. It wasn't anything specific they said; they just wanted to discuss the topic with the bride before replying. I couldn't blame them. It was quite a concept. Some of the family of the bride's mother, my sister-in-law, might ask where my daughter was. They had known me for years, and knew that I had one girl and one boy. It might add a little extra tension to an already stressful event. I couldn't help but think that maybe Kip and I had been given a small dose of reality.

Then Kip heard from the bride.

"Of course, we want you there! Of course, you'll be in a suit, and have Cally by your side! There's no other way. How could you think we didn't want you there!?! You will come, and be yourself as it should be!!"

It seemed like a small victory — a loved one fighting for Kip's rights. Each little victory added reinforcement to the feeling that we were doing the right thing: a feeling that had once felt entirely shaky. Each time we received support, it made talking about Kip's change with the next person a bit easier.

Kip loved his cousin for those words of encouragement. He had thought a lot about arriving at her wedding — his first time in a jacket and tie. His first time around the family as a man.

He had waited so long for this to happen, but he didn't want it at the expense of his cousin, the bride. It was her day. He worried that his changed appearance would somehow steal some of her thunder. Would his presence leave our family feeling a little distracted? He wondered if it was right for him to go at all.

Kip's practical side found the solution. He asked me if we could have a family barbeque before the wedding.

I thought his idea was perfect. It was a chance for the family to meet Cally…and for that matter, Kip. If there was going to be an initial adjustment for anyone, it would be far better to deal with it before the wedding.

Privately, I began to develop a little plan of my own. My imagination saw the day as a bit more than a barbeque.

My sister Melanie had been one of the first family members to read Kip's letter. Whenever life was difficult for me, she had always been there, and this time was no different. She had been a bit concerned about my stress level, and had offered to do whatever she could to help make things easier for me. I decided to take her up on her offer.

I called Mel, and explained Kip's reservations about the wedding, and his idea. I knew that, out of all my family and friends, Mel was the one person who wouldn't see my little addition as crazy. When I whispered my idea to her she was instantly on board, offering her home for the event.

Through the phone line, I heard Mel's voice get louder as her playful spirit kicked in. We definitely have the same quirky sense of humor. I didn't have to see her to know that there was now a twinkle in her eye. This would be a way of showing complete acceptance, but in a light-hearted, non-serious way. I felt that it was about time I got back to being me. This was how the old me would have tackled something new, with a smile on my face, and a positive attitude. This was going to be fun.

I sent out the invitations to all my family members. I mentioned that a gift was completely optional, but if they were so inclined, something small and inexpensive would add to the fun of the day. The theme of the party was to be kept strictly secret, though.

I sensed some of them thought that I might be just a little "off-my-rocker," but they accepted the invitation just the same. The message I wanted to send was obvious — we love you. This doesn't change that. It just doesn't matter.

Mel and I got busy prepping for the party. We shopped for light-hearted decorations and accessories; anything that would add a little something to the atmosphere.

The day before the party I went to Mel's house to help decorate. She had made a large sign that said, "Welcome, Kip!" and a second that said, "And you too, Cally!" We attached them to the wall above the couch that would be their seat of honor. That was, if Kip didn't run for it when he realized what we were up to. I wasn't worried, though; he wouldn't get far. There wasn't anywhere to go. Mel's house was in the middle of nowhere and I would be carrying the car keys.

I had a feeling that the next day would be a special one. If I could hold on to this attitude, the feeling I had that day, I knew happy memories would follow naturally. All I had to do was work a little harder on remembering not to worry about if we fit into society. What the neighbors were thinking about us just didn't matter. In the past, that concern to fit in was constantly getting in my way. That day, I felt that I had given it a firm shove out of my path.

The next morning, I headed to the city where Kip had moved after finishing college. I'd warned Cally earlier in the week about what lay ahead that day. She seemed to get a kick out of my quirky side. As I pulled into the parking lot to pick them up our eyes met for a moment. I quickly looked away. I needed to conceal my nervous excitement. Kip is a sharp one. I didn't want him to notice anything unusual. I'd hate myself if he became suspicious an hour before the party.

The trip to my sister's home was a sun-warmed drive, filled with music and comfortable chatter. There are times in life when everything seems right. Times when you can just feel you are doing the right thing. This was one of those times.

Our arrival at my sister's looked like the arrival at any other family gathering. A variety of cars lined the long, country laneway. As I stepped from the car, crunching onto the coarse gravel, I consciously tried to conceal my enthusiasm. I wondered if the effort was working.

As we stepped up to the door, I tried the handle. Locked. Perfect. I was hoping it would be. The doorbell would announce our arrival to everyone if they hadn't seen us drive up.

Kip looked at me, and asked, "Why would Aunt Melanie lock the door today?"

I hadn't prepared an answer for that one. I quickly tried to come up with a fib, but stumbled. "Um, she just got a new door knob. They're usually stiff at first. It's probably just stuck."

Kip studied my face. I could see doubt in his eyes.

Mel was quickly at the door, greeting us with a smiling face, and a sparkling look in her eye. We could hear everyone talking and laughing in the next room.

In the distinctive voice she uses when she is having fun, she said, "Hello, come on in!"

Kip felt almost as at home in my sister's house as he did in ours, so he led Cally into the living room. It only took a few steps for him to see the "Welcome, Kip!" sign flanked by blue, helium-filled balloons that said, "It's a Boy!" Blue streamers hung from the ceiling and beside the couch sat a small pile of presents wrapped in baby-shower paper.

He turned around, and glared at me.

I wouldn't say it was a distinctively angry look. His eyes didn't pierce me. He wasn't smiling either, though. The way his brow was tensed made his look seem serious, but there was definitely a faint (well, maybe a very faint) look of amusement in his eyes. His stare said, "I'm going to kill you... but I love you."

I sheepishly raised my eyebrows, the way you would when asking for forgiveness, and jokingly said, "Surprise."

Kip shook his head a few times. When he had wanted my acceptance, he hadn't been prepared for what went with it. He'd been expecting a bit of an awkward moment that day, but hadn't pictured this!

Kip was told to take his seat of honor, although "seat of horror" may have described it better. As he made his way through the room, my family asked him if he was going to introduce Cally.

I think the poor kid was speechless. Mel and I had done quite a job on the room. We had both ended up finding the same shower napkins. They had a picture of a cartoon-like stork on them and they were just silly enough. My sister, having inherited my dad's creative nature, decided we needed a six foot replica of that stork to hang on the wall.

When she'd shown me her huge stork with its smiling baby, peaking out of the blanket hanging from its beak, I'd come up with an idea to complement hers. I'd asked her if she had a good picture of Kip. She found one of him with her daughter Amber. We took it to her photo-copier and enlarged it. I carefully cut around Kip's head. I walked over to the proud stork, and held Kip's teenage face over top of the face of the baby. It was perfect, and it was hilarious.

As Kip walked toward the couch he got a glimpse of the stork, and the cake. It had been sent by his hairdresser. She knew his whole history. Although quite a devout Catholic, and a little worried about what God would think of all this, she wanted to show Kip her love. She'd sent a blue and white cross-shaped cake that said, "God Bless You." On the table beside it sat a centerpiece Mel had made out of assorted workshop tools and sandpaper. Kip looked back at me as he and Cally took his seat, still shaking his head.

I sat down close to them, smiling like a cat that had just devoured a huge canary, proud of myself, and satisfied. I had a thoughtful, brave son, and I was lucky enough to have a family who recognized that, and understood my peculiar sense of fun.

When it came time for Kip to open his presents, he found assorted gifts of acceptance. He opened a hammer, a tie, a cigar, a movie about farts, and a GQ magazine (Gentlemen's Quarterly). My mom had brought her acceptance in the form of a very masculine cologne set. Mel and I teased each other that we had gotten the best gift, each of us sure of ourselves, and eager for Kip to end the debate. I wouldn't tell what I had gotten Kip, but my sister said whatever it was, her gift would top it.

Kip untied the razor I had added to his gift as decoration. I had gotten him a striped, button-up-the-front shirt that I later saw him wear again and again. It was the type of shirt that he always wanted to wear as a teenager. When he had, we had quarreled about it. I hadn't wanted my teenage daughter wearing men's shirts. This gift said, "No more quarreling."

Then he picked up the second gift in the package — the one that tickled my fancy. The one I had been waiting weeks to give him. He opened it to expose gleaming, electric nose hair clippers. I looked at Mel.

Had I won? What did that look mean? She was smirking a bit, but I couldn't tell what that meant. She wasn't admitting defeat. She wasn't doing anything.

Kip picked up the gift from her. He opened it, looked back and forth at the two of us, and shook his head again.

Sitting in his hand was the exact same nose hair clippers, same make, same model!

We were forced to call it a draw, making me and my sister look even sillier than we had already made ourselves look. So much for the bantering over who was the more clever shopper.

Still shaking his head, Kip picked up the last gift. Inside was a T-shirt, and on it a large picture of a remote control. Everyone chuckled as he held it up, so we could read the caption. Underneath the remote was written "It's a guy thing."

Of course, there was no point in letting him off the hook at this point. Together we chorused, "Speech! Speech!"

Kip stumbled over his words, doing his best to thank everyone for coming, and making the day "special." Even through his embarrassed expression though, you could not miss his appreciation and relief.

Melanie rescued him by calling everyone to lunch.

As the afternoon grew short, people began to leave my sister's. My mom gave me a hug goodbye, and squeezed tight. I stood at the door thanking everyone, hoping that they could see the gratitude that I so badly wanted to express. Saying the words, and giving them a hug, just didn't seem like enough. They had given us a beautiful memory — one of love, humor and a room full of open hearts.

Before leaving, I pulled Kip aside to take a picture of him hamming it up beside his six foot stork. He gave me a hug, and told me that he loved me... then he added, with a devilish smile, that I could count on him to eventually get even for this... someday!

Chapter 21

It's funny. Sometimes, our minds seem to trap us in our fears. I saw it all the time with the Joey's Furry Friends parties — people afraid of friendly, affectionate rats. Silly. But we can't help it. Our fears aren't always justified, but there they are, just the same.

I remember when I first thought of the coming wedding. I felt uncomfortable with the idea of being out in public alongside Kip wearing a suit. But by the end of our "It's a Boy" party, the wedding didn't seem nearly as big a hurdle to overcome.

Actually, it didn't end up being much of a hurdle at all. The reception hall was a large space filled with tables of ten. Across from us, Kip and Cally sat talking and laughing with Joey, their cousins and their dates. From where I sat, one table over, Kip looked very natural in his jacket and tie. I enjoyed watching him and Cally when they were on the dance floor.

I don't know why it surprised me, but one song gave me a bit of a jolt at first. In the middle of a conversation with the others at my table, I looked up to see Kip twirl his Grandma around the dance floor to a waltz, smiling. There was a time that I would never have been able to picture that scene in my imagination. Yet, there it was. It gave me such a feeling of peace.

The only "moment" that I know of was handled beautifully. A sister of the bride's mom was talking to Melanie, and asked if my kids had come to the wedding. My sister replied that they had, but wasn't quick enough to move the conversation to a new topic in time to prevent what followed — more questions about where my kids were sitting, and how old they were now.

After my two boys were pointed out to her, the bride's aunt developed a puzzled look. She quickly said, "I thought Jamie had a girl, and a boy?"

My sister answered flatly, "No, two boys."

The aunt did not let the topic die. "But I thought her oldest was a girl?"

Mel stood her ground, and simply replied, "No, two boys."

I learned something that day. My sister, who was completely comfortable with Kip's change by then, knew this was not the place to talk about it. It's my nature to explain the whole truth in detail when asked a question. I seem to have this compulsive need to share. In the past, there have been times when it has been a good quality; there are times when it has been a complete curse. That day I learned that it's not always necessary to share every detail of everything with everyone. There's a time and place for that; the wedding reception wasn't either.

Mel gave Kip his wish. He hadn't wanted to steal any attention from his cousin, the bride. And to our knowledge, he didn't. To everyone at the wedding, he was just another young man enjoying a family celebration.

* * *

As my summer holidays neared, I realized that I had spent roughly seven months learning to adjust to having a second son. But, with the exception of a few close friends, my colleagues at work still thought nothing had changed in my life. I wondered if I should keep it that way, or bring my news into the open.

My workplace employed roughly two hundred people; their backgrounds, and range in education, made for quite a varied mix. Many of the employees were born and raised in my small hometown. Since Kip had worked for my employer in the IT department that summer back when he was in college, most of my colleagues knew him as Jul.

I was sure this new tasty morsel of gossip would make its way to my workplace. There might even already have been talk about me or Kip. If there had, I hadn't heard it, but I was quite sure, that the rumor mill, if not already pumping out stories, would be in full swing before too long.

My best option, in my mind, was to put the fire out before the sparks had a chance to take hold. I didn't want to have to deal with darting eyes and whispers abruptly stopping every time I entered a room. This was not a juicy snippet. This was my life. I wanted people to understand. They needed to get the real story — not some embellished version that took on a new twist every time it was enthusiastically passed on.

Of course, I knew I couldn't prevent the gossip completely, but I could certainly do something to diffuse it. If my story was common knowledge, it wouldn't be nearly as much fun to whisper about. It was my best bet — just be honest, and put it out there.

I really didn't know how to share this news with my colleagues, though. It wasn't as if I could just pick up the intercom, and make an announcement over the paging system. "Your attention, please. This is Jamie, and I would just like everyone to know that my daughter is now my son." Can you imagine?

The best thing I could think of was to use what had already worked — the letter. Kip's letter had helped both my family and Will's to understand. Maybe it would do the same for my co-workers.

Being the little chicken that I am at times, I decided the perfect time to share it was the last day of work before our company began its summer holidays. The two weeks off everyone enjoyed would give them time to let the news sink in, and I could hide while it did!

Timing would be crucial. If I dropped it off too soon, I was sure to have to face some of the recipients before the end of the day, and I didn't think I could. I was feeling unsure about the whole thing, and I was afraid that if someone said the wrong thing, or actually, even the right thing, that I would burst into a teary mess.

But if I waited too long, they may not have gotten it in time to read it before they started their summer break. Some of them would probably even leave early, which would really complicate things.

I waited until sometime around midday. Trying to hit all the different departments, so that the news would get around, I put a copy of the letter in a couple of dozen of my colleagues' mailboxes, along with a short note of explanation from me. Then, I sent an e-mail asking each of them to please pick up their mail before they left that day.

As I hit the send button, my hand shook just a little. My experiences had been positive until this stage. Was this the turning point? Was this when judgment would rear its ugly head? Maybe I was wrong about putting this news out there? Maybe this would just get the gossip off to a running start? Too late now. It was done.

My timing seemed logical to me, but my logic was flawed. I'd expected people to process this information for a while. Instead, I received a reply e-mail within minutes. Actually, most of my colleagues took the time to respond before we left work that day.

They reacted as people do — in every way, shape and form. Some came right over to give me a warm hug. A few came to thank me for sharing such personal information with them. Some e-mailed back beautiful words of encouragement. Others said nothing; I guess they couldn't find the right words. The reactions I did get were supportive.

That year, I started my holiday in a somewhat emotional, shaky state. I don't know what it is, but when people show me compassion, I tend to soften into mush, like ice cream in the hot sun.

In the end, I was glad it had worked out that way. It was behind me, and when I went back to work, it would be a fresh start. Something told me that the support I'd been given would give me courage to talk about it more openly.

Actually, I was surprised at how supportive everyone had been. I'd been pretty much wrong about everyone we had shared Kip's secret with. Even Earl's reaction had been different than I'd expected.

Both Kip and I had been nervous about what his dad would say when Kip told him. Earl thought "Jul" was gay, and he didn't like it one bit. He had tried to tell Jul she shouldn't be gay a few times, acting as if it were a choice. Kip and I figured that when Earl heard the real situation, he would hit the ceiling, go through the roof, possibly even break through the earth's atmospheric barrier!

Kip says he was totally astonished when Earl replied, "You like girls... you want a penis... now *that* makes sense to me!"

I couldn't help it; that line made me laugh. You just never know what people are going to think, or say. No point in trying to figure it out. I would just go back to work, and deal with whatever came at me.

When my holidays were over, it seemed like business as usual. There were probably a few rumors, but nothing I noticed. If there were, it had been worth it. It was important for me to let people know that I had accepted the fact that my son needed my support, and that I was going to give it to him. When I talked about him from that day forward, it would be using his new male name.

I slowly started throwing the name Kip into conversations, each time holding my breath, waiting for someone to say, "Who's Kip?"

I wondered how much the confused look on their face would rattle me. Amazingly enough, I didn't ever have to find out; it didn't happen. I had planned to reply, "My oldest son," and leave it at that.

My fear had been that a distorted version of Kip's story would spread rapidly through my workplace. My openness had apparently seemed to put out that fire, but maybe a little too well. Every once in a while someone would ask, "How's Jul doing?" To my surprise, the story hadn't reached everyone who knew me.

The first time it happened caught me totally off guard. I choked out, "Fine," and just kept on going, in an embarrassed panic.

Of course, as soon as I walked away, I knew that I had handled the situation badly.

The next time I heard that question, I was better prepared. I answered with the same, "Fine," but added in a positive tone, "I have something for you to read, though."

That family letter was my savior time after time. If people could not understand a letter like that, with such heartfelt words and emotion, then they weren't people I needed in my life.

People still bring up the letter once in a while. I have a friend now who worked in the same company when I shared the letter that day — but I didn't know her as well then. At the time, she says that she thought to herself, "Why is she airing her dirty laundry to everyone at work?"

That comment made me smile. People are all so different. Honesty is usually instinctive to me; it surprises me when people think it a bit strange.

That friend now looks back, and thinks my actions did exactly what I had wanted them to do. She had been taught to keep her personal life separate from her work life: that talking about private things at work would only give people cause to gossip. She now thinks that I did the right thing, and remembers seeing signs of that right off the bat. Someone had brought up the subject of the "News" with her. It ended up turning into a discussion that brought the truth to the surface instead of feeling like a juicy secret. Where there are no secrets, there is less room for gossip.

I enjoyed the rest of that summer feeling good about the fact that I didn't have to hide my son's new life. It was just in the nick of time, too, because, if things went as planned, I wouldn't be able to hide it much longer. Kip was ready to start his physical transformation.

Chapter 22

Every autumn brings colorful change. The trees show themselves in all their dazzling brilliance. My dad loved our autumn, seeing the maple leaves change from green to ocher, pumpkin orange and then, finally, flaming red. He'd used countless rolls of film capturing their wonderful transformations so that he could reproduce them on canvas. The process of developing those images into art was a fascinating thing to watch. We hoped that the fall of 2005 would bring a new transformation for us to witness. Kip was ready to show his true colors.

To begin his physical transition from female to male, he had to meet with a specialist who would give the necessary approval. In Canada, you must first obtain a referral from a counselor who has gotten to know you. The counselor we had spent time with that spring, when we were making the decision whether to share our secret with my mother, had given Kip his referral.

She hadn't offered much in the way of information about the process, though. She had admitted that even though she specialized in sexual therapy, it was the first time she had met someone who identified strongly enough with the opposite gender to seek a change.

After submitting her referral, Kip had been made to suffer five months of wait time until the appointment.

Finally, it was time to see one of the only psychiatrists in the large nearby city considered qualified to determine if Kip was actually a transgender or not.

It seemed ridiculous to me. Wouldn't Kip be the best person to decide that?

Apparently not. I learned that there are times when a transition is denied. Sometimes a person who is gay is unable to accept his own homosexuality, and seeks to "change" in order to make his life bearable. Other people are denied because of certain psychiatric disorders like schizophrenia. An extreme example of an inappropriate reason for a person to transition would be in order to hide from the law. Kip would have to answer dozens and dozens of very personal questions for the specialist to determine if he did in fact have Gender Identity Disorder.

I asked Kip if he wanted some company that day. His eyes grew big as he nodded and answered, "Oh yeah!"

Sitting in the tiny waiting room, a million questions rolled through my thoughts. How many sessions would it take to make this diagnosis? What prying questions was this guy going to ask us? When would Kip start to change? What would we do if Kip *wasn't* diagnosed as a transgender? And that damn nagging question I despised every time it popped into my head — what if, after all the transformation steps were finished, Kip was *still* miserable when he looked in the mirror. My brain wouldn't quit. God, I needed that off button again!

Suddenly, the door to the psychiatrist's office opened.

The doctor said goodbye to the patient who had been in before us and turned his attention to us. He was a tall, dark haired, olive skinned man who gave off a *very* intimidating vibe. He introduced himself without smiling, and shook our hands.

The man made me instantly squeamish. He had the air of a nearing retirement, fed-up-with-the-world Supreme Court judge. I didn't feel comfortable asking, but I blurted out the question anyway, "Is it okay if I come in with Kip?"

With a strange look I didn't understand, he looked over at Kip and asked, "Is that okay with you?"

Kip nodded as he answered, "Yes."

The doctor's eye brows lowered. "Are you sure you want your mother to hear this? The questions I'll be asking you require you to speak frankly and the answers may be difficult in front of a parent. Can you be completely honest with her in the room?"

Kip looked at me, a smidge more fear on his face. He looked back to the doctor, but all he could force was a nod.

When Dr. T saw Kip's nod, he turned and, without another word, walked into his office.

We entered a large room, filled with dark, heavy furniture, and row after row of books. The doctor sat down behind a desk that fit his serious look. There were two chairs in front of it. He motioned for Kip to sit down.

I reached for the other chair. In a detached, uncaring voice, I heard the doctor say, "That is your chair over there."

I looked in the direction his finger was pointing. There was a chair in the corner of the room, roughly twelve feet away from where Kip would be sitting.

You've got to be kidding.

I looked back at the doctor. His face remained expressionless. He said nothing. The man had the warmth of an iceberg. His message was clear — sit over there, and be quiet. I got the distinct feeling that if I offered any verbal support, I would be asked to leave. I felt helpless, and I was beginning to dislike this stranger already.

He started by telling Kip that he would be asking a lot of questions, and that Kip needed to answer as honestly as he could. He held a piece of paper in one hand, looked down at it every once in a while, and, with his other hand, took notes on another document.

He started his cold questioning with, "When did you first know you were in the wrong body?"

Kip said he was intimidated by him from the get-go. The answer to the question was easy, but he struggled with it. He told me later he was thinking to himself, "What the heck is going on?" He'd known something was wrong from the time he was around four. He remembered a day in junior kindergarten. The class was separated for a game; the girls were put on one side of the room, and the boys on the other. Kip had thought to himself, "What am I doing on this side? Shouldn't I be over there with the rest of the boys?"

But now as he was asked this question, his answer was coming out as, "Well, uh, umm, I guess, umm, I mean, I think I was about four." He was having a hard time meeting the eyes of this man who looked annoyed at having to be here listening to another patient complain.

Kip said he had been thinking, "Okay, I'm going to go hide in the corner with my mom now."

The monotone questions continued fast and hard:

"Are you 'into' men or women?

What do you think of your body?

How does that make you feel?

Do you ever wear skirts or dresses?

Have you told any of your friends?

How will you tell your family?

Will you go through with both surgeries?

There will be a minimum cost of thirty or forty thousand dollars. How will you pay for this?

Have you ever dated a boy?

How did that make you feel?

Have you ever had intercourse?

Have you ever had a girlfriend?

How did that make you feel?

Do you have a girlfriend now?

How long have you been seeing her?

How does she feel about you 'changing'?"

Kip described how strong his relationship with Cally was, and how she said she would be there beside him through it all.

I thought there was an important detail that Kip wasn't mentioning. *Should I say something? Will I be kicked out of the room if I do?*

I took a deep breath, and decided to chance it. I blurted out, "When they met, Cally thought Kip was a boy."

I was shot with an icy, penetrating stare. It said, "Speak again, and you are gone."

The message was unmistakable. My gut had been right, and my initial dislike for this doctor was growing.

God, did he have to be so cold? Did he not know what I was going through? He'd studied psychology. Didn't it cross his mind that I might be in a bit of a tender state right now? He obviously didn't care about anything but getting through his list of goddamned questions.

He ploughed right on through. "How is your relationship with your dad?"

Earl, was a sensitive subject on the best of days. A series of constant broken promises had done serious damage to their relationship. Not to mention the fact that Earl had a Dr. Jekyll / Mr. Hyde type personality. If in a good mood, he would be jovial and silly, unable to talk seriously about anything. But, if it was an off moment, he would be hot-headed and unapproachable. And you were never sure when his mood would switch over. Spending time with him could be a frustrating or intimidating experience, depending on the day. I knew those feelings; I'd been there for years.

The added fact that he regularly made Kip feel inadequate, with his constant criticism and condescending comments, had made Kip struggle to have respect for him. Kip had stopped putting up with it when he was still Jul, at the age of twelve. The two of them had been playing basketball.

I'd received a phone call from Earl that day, asking me to come over, and talk some sense into her. He told me how they had been playing basketball, and described how he'd given Jul a bit of a shove, sending her to the concrete. He had held out his hand to help Jul up. At that moment, Jul seemed to have decided that her dad had "pushed" her one too many times.

Jul looked up at her dad, and met his eyes. Holding the eye contact with calm intensity, she had said, "Fuck off."

Jul's dad, in shock, looked at her, and demanded in his well-practiced, intimidating way, "What did you just say to me?"

Jul still unwavering, answered, "I said 'Fuck off,'" with conviction.

The basketball game was over... and the relationship not far behind. That day had ended years of Jul living half of the time with her dad, half of the time with me. From that point, she only visited her dad once in a while. Their relationship had been a tight-rope walk ever since.

It became so difficult to even visit that Jul began to see a counselor. This psychologist had told Jul that her dad sounded like an adult-child, and that even though she was only in her early teens, she would have to assume the role of "parent" in the relationship. Jul was told to use her best judgment, and end the visit whenever her dad did something inappropriate.

He gave specific examples of things Jul's dad had done that required action. If her dad belittled her at a family dinner, or in front of company, it was time to end the visit. If her dad used guilt to try to pressure her into moving back by telling Jul that she had ruined his life, she was to get up and leave. When Jul stood up to him, one of her dad's favorite lines had been, "Oh, are you going to go hide under your mom's skirt now?" Jul would simply have to say, "Yes" and walk away. It would be up to her to teach her dad where the "lines" were, and that crossing them was unacceptable.

That day, years later, as Kip answered questions about his relationship with his dad, tears began to roll down his face. The doctor, still showing less emotion than a Siamese cat, and once again looking annoyed asked, "Why are you crying right now?"

As Kip tried to describe how he felt there was an absence of genuine love from his father, he shifted uncomfortably in his chair. He choked on his words, trying to hold himself firm in front of this man who had the exact same intimidating presence that had driven a wedge between Kip and his dad.

The few feet between us seemed to grow into a mile.

Why do I have to sit so far away?

Kip couldn't feel my support from here. I wanted to put my hand on his leg, so that he would know he was not alone. It was killing me to sit back and watch.

Breathe your way through this, Jamie. Kip's so strong. He'll be okay. You'll just have to be as strong as he is.

I looked at the doctor. He looked like he was going to start drumming his fingers on the desk at any second. My dislike was turning into hate at a quick pace.

After approximately thirty minutes of this insensitivity, the questions stopped. "That's all for today. You'll have to come to my office on a regular basis for quite a while. You will have to be monitored while you live as a man. Transition can be a highly traumatic process. I'm going to book you for the same time next week, unless that's a problem. And if you must cancel, I will need 48 hours notice or you will be billed for my time."

Then he stopped talking.

I knew Kip was thinking the same thing I was. I was fed up with sitting in my little chair and behaving. I asked the obvious question that he *had* to know was on our minds. From across the room, I said, "How long will it take for you to make a diagnosis?"

With a sly look of satisfaction, the doctor replied, "I knew after being with you for five minutes."

Okay, it was official — I hated this man! I wanted to tell him that he was rude, and an arrogant son of a bitch, but... Kip needed him. This hateful man would have to give the referral to the next doctor: the doctor who would start Kip's hormone therapy.

I bit my tongue, and tried to think positively. This next hurdle would be the exciting one!

Joey: Summer 2005
Chapter 23

The next summer, the summer we were waiting for Kip's hormone therapy to start, was not a good one for Joey. We had a rough few months before that crazy night when Joey forgot who "Joey" was. From what any of us can tell, April twelfth was the day that triggered the strangeness that led to that unusual Fear Factor party six months later, when my son sat with me in the car and said, "I don't know who this Joey is, but my name is not Joey."

That spring, Will and I spent every free second working towards opening an antique/gift shop in the front of our house. We hoped to open in October but had to renovate the outside and inside of our home first. After work on April twelfth, I'd been rushing around running errands, trying to chip away at our ever growing to-do list. I came home to find Joey on his knees on the floor of our kitchen.

The boy had the face of a doomed man sitting in an electric chair. He looked drained of energy, void of hope. His face made me freeze for a second, and wonder, *Oh crap, what's going on?*

I didn't see her right away. As I got a little closer the smell was the first thing to hit me. In front of Joe lay Sandy. She was sprawled out in a pool of urine and vomit. Her eyes were zipping back and forth, back and forth, very quickly, obviously uncontrollably. It was an eerie sight. The dog looked as if she were possessed by some evil spirit. I searched Joey's face, lost for words. His pleading eyes said, "I didn't know what to do."

My tone was soft. "What happened, honey?"

Suddenly, Sandy, hearing my voice, realized I was home, and tried pitifully to stand, her eyes still darting back and forth. She managed to get two unsteady front limbs somewhat out in front of her, only for them to slip out, and land her back down in her horrible pool of fluids. The effort activated more vomiting.

Okay. Now I get his horrified expression.

Joey's never been able to watch animals suffer. I knew Will wasn't home yet. That had left him to go through this with her, alone.

I tried to find something useful to say.

Nothing.

I looked down at him, and asked again, "What happened?"

Joey's eyes rested on our pet as she lay in agony. "I don't know. This is how I found her."

I looked at her lying on the floor, and wondered if this was the end. She was fifteen. That's a pretty good life for a lab-husky mix. But she was a huge part of the family, and no one was ready to let her go. I watched as Joey patted her back, trying to comfort her as she lay dry heaving and whimpering.

"I'm calling Will. We need to get her to the vet."

With a strange expression Joey asked, "Don't you think we should call Kip too, and tell him… you know, just in case… he needs to be ready?"

I wasn't ready to accept that it was the end. I needed to do something. I tenderly answered, "Maybe, but we'll get her to the vet first."

The vet's diagnosis was Old Dog Vestibular Disease. Sandy's world was spinning. If you've ever had too much to drink, and had the "spins" when you lay down, then you know how our dog was feeling. It's a horrible, miserable feeling, and it was the cause of the vomiting and inability to walk. But, as long as we could keep her hydrated, it would probably pass in a couple of weeks. The vet said we should prepare ourselves however; most times it's

Secret Selves

the beginning of the end. From what the doctor had witnessed, six months was the average remaining life span once this happened.

All of us felt that our family would soon be less one member, but amazingly enough, in a month she was playing like a pup again. She seemed like her old self, except for her now permanently tilted head: a constant reminder to us that her days were numbered.

Joey had to see that reminder every time he looked at her.

*   *   *

As with any spring, there are days when the weather isn't great. I was glad I'd made a pot of soup the night before. The rain made for a perfect soup day. Will had turned the bread maker on so the kitchen smelled of that warm, yeasty goodness when I got home. I took the soup out of the fridge and started it warming.

A short while later I knocked on the door of Joey's room. "Dinner's ready, honey."

His voice sounded drained. "I'm not hungry."

Skipping dinner wasn't an option in our house. When it was ready, the kids came and ate what was on the table.

"What's wrong? Are you sick?"

"No, just tired."

He seemed tired a lot lately. It was beginning to worry me. "Can I open the door?"

"Uh-huh."

I turned the door handle to find him in bed. It wasn't even six o'clock. "Why are you so tired?"

"I don't know. The workload is way too much right now. And there's no point telling the teachers; they give us no respect, they won't listen. It's really getting to me."

"Do you need some help with your school work?"

His mood seemed to instantly flip from frustrated to angry. "No, Mom. Geez! I just need some *sleep*."

"Well, come down and eat something. You'll sleep better on a full stomach."

I went back down to the kitchen and dished out bowls of homemade soup. Will sliced his loaf of warm bread.

Joey thumped down the stairs and stopped to watch Sandy walk by. She liked to pace around the kitchen when we were cooking. His face took on a sad quality. "Is her head gonna be tilted like that for the rest of her life?"

"I don't know. She's an old lady now. At least she's playing, and pacing like normal again. Here... we're having hamburger soup." I handed him a bowl. It was one of his favorites.

He sat down with his dinner but just looked at it, and said nothing.

"Will made bread. You want some?"

"Yeah, I guess. I'm really not hungry."

I looked at my husband and shook my head just enough so that Will could see but Joey couldn't. Will knew exactly what I meant. We'd talked about Joey's spirits. Usually when Will made bread, Joey would want to cut into it the minute the bread maker beeped. That day he had no interest whatsoever.

He seemed down most of the time, and he was sleeping a lot more than usual. When his mood was up, it seemed that the least little thing could sadden or anger him, like a switch had been flicked.

Depression was weighing heavily on my mind. There were people on both sides of his family tree who suffered from it. After the close call with Kip, I couldn't face Joey going down that road, but I didn't quite know how to talk to him about it. It was a sensitive topic to tackle, so I simply asked, "You seem a little down lately, honey. Do you want me to make you an appointment with a counselor — just someone to talk to?"

He squished his face like I was crazy. "No, Mom. I don't think it's bad enough for *that*. I think I'm just getting worn out; I really need summer holidays."

What could I do? I couldn't force him to go. He was at that age where he knew everything. I knew it would have to be his idea, or he would fight the help.

"Well, it's an open-ended offer. If the time comes when you think it's a good idea, let me know and I'll set it up."

In the meantime, I privately vowed to keep a close eye on him and do what I could. I used to be able to count on our parties to lift his spirits.

"Hey, we got a booking for a Fear Factor next Saturday. I think Uncle Rich will be able to get us some bull's ball by then." Mel's husband was a meat inspector. Joey always liked the reaction bull's testicles got when we were able to get them.

"Hmm." He sat there expressionless, looking at his soup.

There'd been a time when a new booking made him smile, but lately, he didn't seem enthusiastic about it at all. He had fun when he got there most of the time, but he was finding it hard to even muster the energy to force himself to go.

* * *

As spring got into full swing and Joey neared his seventeenth birthday, the month of May turned gorgeous. The evenings seemed perfect with their warm sunshine. In the late afternoon, it poured through the kitchen window, filling the room with massaging fingers of light. I stood at the counter one night, frying vegetables for a stir-fry. The air was thick with one of my favorite fragrances: the punchy smell of onions cooking.

Joey clomped down the stairs and hovered in the kitchen. He bent down and gave Sandy's head a tussle, then he just stood there.

This was *not* a typical Joey activity. He was always in his room before dinner, and wouldn't surface until called. I'd usually have to yell up at him a few times.

Okay, Joey... what's up?

I waited for him to start the conversation, but nothing was coming. It was usually up to me to start things. All right. "How was your day, Joe?"

"Umm... actually, something weird happened to me today."

I casually looked over at him, and continued to stir the vegetables. He was obviously hesitant. "Oh yeah, what's that?"

He lowered his head a bit. "I'm not really sure how to explain it."

His voice didn't have that quality that would set the alarm bells ringing for me. Actually, I didn't understand the tone. He sounded more intrigued, or maybe a bit concerned or confused, but not overly stressed. It didn't sound like a tone I should worry about, so I decided not to push; he would tell me when he was ready.

He bent back down and patted Sandy again.

After a long hesitation, he said, "It was really weird. I... umm... I was in Science class, and... across the room... I saw another me."

Okay, you have my attention now, kid. But I had no words, so I just looked at him.

"He was wearing my favorite sweater, but his hair was different. His face looked just like mine. It was so weird. I started to walk toward him, but... as I got close, he faded away."

My face was frozen. My brain wouldn't work; it seemed stuck.

What the hell am I supposed to do with this story?

Joey stood watching me. He looked like he was waiting for me to come up with some cool explanation for it. That in itself told me he was concerned. He was usually such a know-it-all.

I wanted an explanation, too. I wanted to go back to an ordinary evening of making dinner, but I struggled to come up with something. "Are you sure you didn't fall asleep? Maybe it was a dream?"

He rolled his eyes, and shook his head. "Mom... I was *wide* awake the whole time."

I had nothing.

I'd never heard of anything like this before. I didn't know what to think. Schizophrenia tried to crawl into my thoughts, but I quickly shoved *that* away. It couldn't be *that*. "Well... how far away was it, maybe it was someone who looked like you?"

He tilted his head to the side and gave me that 'You don't know what you're talking about' look, and said, "Mom, it was me. I'm *sure*."

What would cause his brain to make him think he saw himself across the room? What was going on in there?

One thing I did know for sure... it was time for Joey to talk to someone.

And surprisingly, he didn't argue when I suggested it was time to see a professional. Seeing this "other Joey" across the room had shaken him enough to knock away his usual armor. His guard was down — way down.

His willingness to let me make him an appointment proved he understood exactly how serious the situation was. I've always been a firm believer in getting help when I need it. I'd been to a counselor probably a dozen times over the years. I'd shown Kip the benefits of talking things out with someone impartial, but Joey... although I'd suggested counseling when he found life difficult, at seventeen he'd never let me arrange even one appointment for him. Well, that is, unless you count the time when he was four and the doctor told me to lock him in his room, but he hadn't been a willing participant in that.

The only other time he'd seen a counselor during his childhood was when his elementary school had arranged it. He'd become the class clown; I'd hoped it was just one of those stages. The therapist wondered if there was more to his acting out than the fact that he was enjoying making his classmates howl with laughter.

Joey said that the sessions with that therapist had been a total waste of time, and he'd decided right then that counseling wasn't for him. His willingness to see someone now spoke volumes.

Chapter 24

As the summer began, and we waited for the day of Joey's appointment to come, it seemed as if he was almost eager to go. It was just a feeling I had; he'd never tell me things like that, but I think he really needed an explanation for seeing himself across the room.

I only met his counselor briefly; I wasn't invited in for the sessions. He looked to be around fifty-something, and reminded me of an aging hippy from the sixties.

After two hour long appointments, he called to give me his diagnosis. "I think that this problem has come from Joey's very creative imagination. I don't think there is a serious underlying condition, so there isn't much I can do for him. I do have an idea, however. I've given him a list of books on paranormal activity; he seems really interested in that sort of thing. I think it would do him good to explore the subject. It'd be good for him to transfer his attention from himself to another interest."

Jesus. You've got to be kidding me.

This guy had made this informed decision after two short sessions. I don't know how he felt he knew enough about Joey to suggest *this* treatment.

His solution was reading about the paranormal? The only time Joey read was when it was required at school. How would a therapy of reading work for a non-reader?

Joey was not impressed either — he said the guy was useless, and nicknamed him "The Antichrist of Therapy." The boy often has an interesting way of putting things.

This counselor had one thing right — he wasn't going to be able to help Joey. That was for damn sure. I was angry, and I wasn't wasting another minute with this twit.

I had to find someone else.

Joey's next appointment was with a young psychologist. He'd been recommended by our family doctor. When I called to book the appointment, he told us when and where to meet him.

The sun was shining beautifully that day. We arrived before he did. While we waited, Joey tried to teach me the art of hacky sack. I made a pathetic attempt to bounce the little bean-filled bag off my foot more than twice in a row. "One... two... damn it!"

Joey made it look easy. I counted out loud as he reached very close to twenty consecutive bounces, like it was nothing.

With a curious expression, this young doctor asked, "You must be Jamie and Joey?"

We stretched out our hands and shook. "Nice to meet you," I offered.

He still looked curious. "What are you two doing?"

Ummm, isn't it obvious? "Playing hacky sack." I waited for an acknowledgment. "Haven't you ever seen hacky sack before?"

"No, but it looks like fun."

The term hacky sack means nothing to him? He's a young guy. Did he spend his whole youth with his nose in a book?

I hoped so. He might need all the knowledge he had for this session.

He smiled warmly and said, "Well, let's get right at it. As I said on the phone, this appointment will be a little longer than usual; I'll need to take a personal history of Joey. You can sit in this room, Jamie. We'll come and get you if we need you," and he led my son into a private room.

I settled in with the book I'd brought. This might take a while.

After an hour and a half, I was invited into the room. The doctor's pleasant, compassionate face put me at ease. He encouraged me to sit down. "Joey and I have had a good chat. We talked about everything: school, hobbies, family life."

He hesitated for a second and then got right to the heart of things. "It's this 'other Joey' that troubles me. I've never worked with that sort of thing. I don't feel qualified to proceed from this point. Just to be safe, I'm going to make an appointment with someone more specialized. I want Joey checked for schizophrenia."

Schizophrenia? Oh my God. Goose bumps instantly covered my arms.

"Isn't schizophrenia a hereditary thing? How could he be schizophrenic? There isn't anything like that in either family."

"It isn't always hereditary." He stopped talking and waited for me to reply.

There's no way. It couldn't be.

The doctor was talking again. I forced myself to listen.

"I asked Joey if he ever hears voices. He says he does. Now, these voices don't give him instructions — that would be very concerning — but the presence of *any* voices, coupled with the fact that Joey has seen himself across the room, well, I think it's enough to warrant a specialist's opinion."

I couldn't think of a word to say.

This young doctor could see he'd shaken me. He gently smiled, "We just need to rule out schizophrenia before any other therapy can be considered."

Normally, I'm quick to smile back, but not that day. That day my gaze rested on the floor as I sat expressionless. This was too much.

I couldn't possibly have one transgender and one schizophrenic, could I?

Kip had just started hormone therapy. Things were finally starting to seem normal. I wanted both my boys' lives to be smooth again. Now this.

The car drove itself home that night. My mind was a thousand miles away, suspended in a heavy fog. How could one doctor think it was Joey's imagination, and another suspect schizophrenia? It didn't make sense. How could this be happening?

Maybe it wasn't happening. The doctor had said they "needed to rule out schizophrenia." There *must* be another explanation. I had to keep it together. I had to think positively. Whatever it was, I'd get through it.

When we arrived home, I saw Will's car in the driveway. *Poor Will. How am I going to tell him this?*

When we'd met, I'd wondered if Will had planned on having a family. I thought at the time that I had my hands pretty full with my two kids. It was killing me not knowing how many he saw himself having, once he found the right girl.

When I'd asked him, he'd replied, "I've never really seen myself with a family. I always thought I was more the 'DINK' type — you know… double income, no kids."

I was confused by that. "But… what are you doing with me, then?"

"Well, Jamie, I didn't plan this, you know. It just happened… and… I love you."

Imagine not really planning to have kids at all, and ending up with my two? What must go through his head some days! The poor guy had gotten more than he'd bargained for when he married me.

Joey and I entered the empty kitchen. He went right upstairs, probably to a play video game, and get his mind off this rotten mystery. As usual, I couldn't tell if he was upset or bothered by the idea that he might be schizophrenic. Most of the time, Joey's emotions are kept well hidden. But how could he not be bothered by it? He'd been quiet on the drive home. It was Friday night, the end of the week, and he must have been tired, especially after an hour or so of prying personal questions. It must have been painful for him, admitting that he heard voices, and was seeing things.

And the uncertainty of the future had probably contributed to his silence. Even if he didn't completely understand the implications of schizophrenia, he must have been thinking that if that was the diagnosis, he would become a complete misfit. I didn't blame him for wanting to be alone, and de-stress with a video game.

I looked to the back of the kitchen. The door to the backyard was open. Will was probably out on the deck

Pushing the screen door open, I saw my husband reading the newspaper, enjoying the early summer sunshine. It was such a beautiful evening, that time of night when the sun is going down and the leaves, grass and flowers all seem to pop with color in the twilight. I hated to have to ruin it with the conversation I was about to start.

Will looked up from his newspaper, and smiled. "How'd it go?"

I plunked down in the deck chair beside him. "Not the greatest." I had a hard time pushing the next words out. "Tonight's doctor is sending him to a specialist. He wants to rule out schizophrenia."

Will's eyebrows lifted, his eyes widened and his mouth dropped open just a bit. He didn't say anything. He didn't have to. I knew what he was thinking. We were sharing a moment of *"this can't be happening."* I was sure of that.

* * *

Thankfully, we didn't have to wait too long to see Doctor Number Three. I think I would have gone a little crazy if I'd had to.

She looked to be in her late thirties or early forties, and had a pleasant way about her. She let me stay in the room for her first session with Joey. As she read off a list of questions, it reminded me of sitting in a room with Kip the year before, as he answered questions in order to diagnose Gender Identity Disorder. I somehow doubted Joey and I would be leaving this appointment with the same feeling of elation that Kip and I had felt. We'd been hoping for a diagnosis that day; today we were dreading one.

The doctor asked Joey question after question, every once in a while turning to me for clarification, or to ask about our family history. She explained that there was no single symptom, or lab test, that would lead to a definite diagnosis. She would have to use his family medical history, emotional history and a full understanding of the current symptoms to reach her conclusion. It was amazing how many questions you could answer in an hour.

Joey's first appointment with Doctor Number Three turned out to be his last. She didn't think he was schizophrenic.

Thank God. Thank God. Thank God.

Schizophrenia is a complicated condition, but from what I could understand, although he had symptoms that were similar, the pattern of signs, and the combination of symptoms weren't just right to diagnose that particular illness. What a relief. It's a condition that is chronic, severe and disabling, and it would have been a struggle his whole life.

I was surprised to get an answer so quickly, though. I'd expected several appointments before getting the desperate yes or no result.

Thank God for small mercies.

It wasn't quite a feeling of elation, however. The doctor told us that she didn't think he suffered from bipolar disorder either, so Joey and I left that appointment still without answers.

We were told that Joey, having just turned seventeen, not exactly a child, but still fitting into the legal category, was being referred to a child psychiatrist.

The doctors were starting to sound like some strange 'flavor of the month' club. Dr. M was Doctor Number Four. We'll call him Mint Chocolate Chip.

He was in his forties, medium in height, dark haired, olive skinned and all business. He took very thorough notes on our family. At one point, as he did, he asked what Kip's full name was.

I answered, "Earl" Phillip. Kip's dad, Earl, had said that he would pay the fee for Kip to legally change his name *if* Kip would agree to put Earl as his first name.

Dr. M had written Joey's full given name only minutes before, and had obviously remembered that it was "Earl" Joseph. He lifted his head, looked at me and asked in his serious tone, "Is there a reason why they both have Earl for their first name?"

I locked eyes with him. "An intelligent reason?" I shook my head. "No."

A little sarcastic smirk slipped. "Well… I think we will leave *that* for another day." It was the only time I can ever remember seeing Dr. M smile.

His questions continued. When the past was exhausted, he began to ask behavior questions. I was impressed with his thoroughness.

After only a few visits, my fears were no longer suspicions: Joey was diagnosed with major depression. It required medication and therapy with Doctor Number Five. He would continue seeing Dr. M, who would be in control of his meds, but he would also begin weekly visits with Dr. D, to talk.

Dr D, also in her forties, had a friendly, caring manner that warmed me to her instantly. This woman was born to talk with teens about their problems; you could feel how much she cared. And she had a gentleness, a way of making you trust her almost immediately. Joey admitted he wasn't sure if it was helping, but he did enjoy going for their talks.

I wasn't sure if it was helping either. We'd been traveling to the city for two appointments every week for a couple of months, and if anything, Joey seemed to be developing a problem with anger. He'd told me that he had started experiencing inexplicable rage towards strangers. He would notice someone walking on the side of the road as we drove by, and think, "I want to hurt you." He hated the feelings, but had no idea why they were happening or how to fix them. He felt helpless.

This news was almost enough to push me over the edge. My soft-hearted protector of the underdog wanted to hurt someone?

He'd spent his whole life defending people from the injustices of the world. He wasn't a violent person; he was caring and sensitive. At seventeen, he'd never been in a fist fight. How could he want to hurt strangers? Someone can't change that drastically in a matter of months, can they? There had to be something serious to this. I made him promise to tell his doctors about his feelings.

Maybe it was part of working through his problems? I wasn't sure, but it didn't seem right. I didn't get the opportunity to ask. I wasn't invited in during appointments with either doctor. It was private now — between patient and therapist. My place was in the waiting room. I just sat, anxiously waiting, praying that he was improving.

When at home, I kept an eye on him as much as I could, in case something happened that I thought I should share with his doctors. Boy, did I come up with something.

After school one day, I passed by Joey's room. The door was part way open so I backed up and stuck my head in. "Hi, Joe."

I noticed that his forearm had a couple of spots that looked raw and blood-red. I couldn't see it well from where I was. "What happened to your arm?"

Moving his body so that his arm was no longer in sight, he answered, "Nothing."

I stepped in to get a closer look. "It looks red. Let me see."

He left it behind his body. "It's nothing."

I knew from his voice it wasn't nothing. "Joe..."

His eyes were on the floor. "Okay, I burned myself."

I still couldn't see his arm, but it didn't compute. "What do you mean... burned yourself? How? Whadya do? Let me see; maybe I should put something on it."

He hesitated, then moved his arm into my sight.

Three perfect cigarette holes. They were deep, and in their freshness, oozing.

Oh my God.

Three little circles of raw flesh.

What had he said? I burned myself? Had he done this to himself? Had he done it on purpose?

I blinked back tears. Goose bumps covered my body. "What did you do?"

He put his head down and just sat there, looking at the floor.

I quietly choked out, "Did you do this to yourself, honey?"

He didn't move.

I held back a sob. "Why?"

He looked at me and said, "I don't know... I guess I needed to get my mind off things."

I couldn't talk. I was really fighting to hold back the tears. In a shaky voice I managed to get out, "But why?"

Strangely calm, but with what seemed a painful sadness, he answered, "It's better I hurt me than someone else."

I didn't think I could stand it, my son in so much pain, and I couldn't do a thing to help him. Nothing was working. The medication, the therapy... they didn't seem to be getting him anywhere.

The stress was overwhelming. I wanted to hug him so badly. But physical contact was not allowed with Joey. It wasn't cool. I wasn't sure if that was normal teenage behavior, or part of this intense anger he was developing, but I wanted to break the distance. I really needed a hug that day. I stood there not knowing what to say, what to do, so I went downstairs to think.

I moved around the kitchen making dinner in slow motion, tears running down my face. It was September, and it had been a rough spring and summer.

We had rearranged our home to get ready for the opening of our new business in the front part of our house. It seemed as though there was too much work, and too little time. Move Joey's bedroom. Strip wallpaper, paint. Move our bedroom. Have plans drawn for the addition of a workshop, and wrap-around porch. Old bedroom becomes living room. Strip wallpaper, fix drywall, paint, add hardwood floor, move gas fireplace. Get estimates for addition to house. Shop for siding, porch rails, gingerbread trim, garage door. Living room becomes store. Add track lighting. Go to national giftware show. Pick suppliers, order stock. Move antiques into store. And on and on and on.

Between the worrying about my son, the renovations, setting up the business, working full time, running the party business, and dealing with all the doctors, I was totally exhausted. My system seemed to have reached its limit at that moment.

My movements became automatic: making meatloaf seemed like a desperate attempt for a bit of normal.

I couldn't stop the tears, though. They slipped out from above my lower lashes, rolled down my face, and dripped onto the floor.

What am I going to do?

I had placed all my confidence in the doctors. They were supposed to be helping him by now. That old feeling, like it was all up to me, was starting to push on my shoulders again. Did we need another friggin' new doctor?

After a sleepless night, I called his psychiatrist. In the message I left, I asked if there was anything I should do.

In the meantime, I had to do something: anything. Research was all I could think of. The results calmed my nerves a bit.

Self injury does not usually lead to suicidal behavior — I was flooded with relief. That had been my biggest concern. But it was hard to understand.

The articles explained that sometimes self injury is a way for people in extreme pain to keep from killing themselves. They release unbearable feelings and pressures through self harm. It can be used as a method of coping, an attempt to relieve emotional distress when other means have failed. Even though the relief is temporary, it sometimes gives a short rest from whatever intense feelings are occupying the mind.

And then the line that made me blink back tears again — many people who suffer from self-inflicted violence have had, in their history, some sort of physical, emotional or sexual abuse.

As I read, an image kept popping up in my mind: the picture of my son pressing a lit cigarette down deep into his own arm. It made me cringe horribly. I wondered what could have caused him to get to this point. Whatever it was, it was probably also the cause of Joey #2 replacing my son the next month, on that crazy October evening.

Kip: 2005- 2006
Chapter 25

As Kip and I walked away from the psychiatrist's office after the first difficult appointment with the gender identity specialist, Kip looked at me, wrinkled his brow and said, "What just happened there?"

I shrugged my shoulders, and let out one of those sighs — the kind that slide out after you finish something like an intimidating job interview that, in the end, turned out miraculously well. "I think you were just diagnosed with Gender Identity Disorder."

We smiled at each other and the tension of the appointment began to fade. We'd always enjoyed being together, but that day was special. I think we both felt as if together, we had conquered some odd battle that we had been thrown into unfairly. But we had won. And even though a lot of my questions remained unanswered, something indescribable felt very right. I wore a permanent, contented little grin that afternoon. Kip just kept shaking his head in disbelief.

I knew how anxious he was to get his transition started. Besides the pain he had suffered living so many years in the wrong body already, there were other motivations for Kip to change his appearance.

The city he had moved to was only a forty-five minute drive from home, and the university Cally attended was home to some of Kip's old high school acquaintances.

To Kip, the campus was a very dangerous place. Although he wore men's clothing, had a very masculine haircut, and strapped down his chest to live as Kip, he still owned the face of Jul. The clothes he wore, for that matter, weren't all that different from what he had worn throughout high school. And his hair had always been short. It was cut a little differently perhaps, but it still framed the face of Jul.

Until he was able to start hormone therapy, he watched carefully when he was on campus. There was one girl in particular who would bring his heart to a dead stop on sight. Kip had known her in high school, and knew her to be… well, somewhat boisterous.

He envisioned this girl recognizing him, and loudly making a scene, shouting some sort of greeting like, "Hi Jul, what are you doing here? How do you know Cally?"

The thought of his cover being blown in public, in front of all of Cally's friends, was paralyzing. He knew this girl was not the type of person to keep his secret; discretion was not her strongest suit. She might be just tickled to scoop up this bit of juicy gossip and scatter it throughout the dorm rooms. She lived on the floor just below Cally, and the worst part of it was… they shared the same kitchen.

When Kip saw her, he would feel instant panic. It was like seeing a hungry mountain lion in the hallway, and being forced to attempt to sneak by unseen, to prevent being eaten.

When he was greeted by someone who had met him through Cally, they saw just that, Cally's boy friend. Cally's "boy" friend. He would cringe as he imagined the shocked looks and disgusted stares as the people who had always known him to be one hundred percent male found out his painful truth. He couldn't bear thinking about the shame he would feel, or about how embarrassed Cally would be because of him.

Cally had tried to convince him that she didn't care if they knew; but that fact was irrelevant. Kip cared deeply. He was sick of the teasing and judgment and couldn't face it any longer. He wanted the world to see him as a man. He desperately wanted his looks to change, to match how he felt inside.

If he could get the process of hormone therapy started, the manly stubble that would help disguise his past would begin to appear. The hormones would change his bone structure just enough to make him look a bit different. His facial features and hair line would shift to give him the more masculine look that he craved. His voice would become deeper.

I wanted my son to have what we all take for granted: to feel natural in his body, in his face. I wanted him to no longer wonder who was looking at him and questioning which role he fit into in society, because he looked androgynous. It had been almost a decade since he had resembled someone who could even remotely be called girly, except of course on those special occasions when I forced it: my wedding day, his Catholic confirmation, any type of dressy celebration.

I had improved since then. I was gradually whittling away that concern with fitting him into society's opinion of the norm, and I was stressing less over what people thought of us, but there was still a small part of the mom in me who would miss Jul's face.

* * *

Baby Jul had a beautiful face. I'd peer down at her and love the sweet little thing looking up at me from her crib. Her perfect full lips. The Gerber Baby cheeks that were always chubbed up, rounding out her oval face in a big, eager grin. The little button nose. Her squeezable little chin.

It was the face of my perfect little angel.

How much would the hormones change the young adult version of it?

How much would I miss it? I couldn't imagine not seeing it any more.

It wasn't the first time I'd experienced the fear of losing her quiet, natural beauty, though. She had been five the first time.

I was home, sick, when the shrill sound of the phone woke me. A car accident. A serious head injury. Danger of internal bleeding in the brain. I was needed at the children's hospital immediately. Earl was at another hospital, complaining of severe back pain. They'd contact me whenever his tests were complete.

The person on the other end of the phone cautioned me not to drive; she said I was talking as if I was in shock.

I was.

The scene I arrived to at the hospital instantly slapped me out of my numbed state.

First I heard her voice. It was an aggressive, tortured demand, loud enough for me to hear it before I even entered the busy emergency room. "I want my mom. I WANT MY MOM!"

If that familiar voice hadn't been coming from the little thing stretched out on the gurney, I wouldn't have had my heart shredded to a million bits when my eyes rested on her. I wouldn't have known my little kindergartener.

Her face was swollen horribly flat. Tiny little fragments of glass, and some not-so-tiny, were embedded everywhere. As I walked toward her, I watched as the hospital staff bent her arms, and her wrists, and her fingers in an attempt to locate broken bones, Jul fighting every second of it, her panic increasing. At the top of her ability, she chanted, "I WANT MY MOM! I WANT MY MOM!"

I stood over her in disbelief. She didn't know I was there. Her eyes were swollen shut.

I took her little hand in mine and cooed, "Mommy's here, honey. It's okay, Mommy's here."

I only have fragments of memories about that first day, the first out of a week I spent sleeping in a chair beside her hospital bed. But I do remember one question that, somewhere during the craziness of that first day, selfishly passed through my mind. *Oh, her beautiful little face. What's it going to look like when it heals?*

What a trivial, stupid thing to worry about then. My daughter had survived a massive head trauma. I still had my child; that was the important part. But parents get so attached to the face they've looked upon and loved.

Maybe that car accident was a lesson given to me years earlier in preparation for the loss of my daughter's face. I had been a kindergartener then too, I guess; a beginner in the years of parenting classes ahead. I didn't know then that the body was merely the packaging of the soul I loved.

It can be wrapped in lovely paper, tied up with a beautiful, matching ribbon, or it can be sitting plainly in a simple, wooden box. It's still the same soul inside, and it's what's inside that is the valuable part.

* * *

As I waited for the call saying that the appointment for the first shot of testosterone had been scheduled, I began my goodbye to Jul's face. I was grateful that I was at least learning to be a little less absorbed with outside appearances. I might still feel a little twinge when the time came and the changes started, but I was ready to confront letting go. I would learn to love the new face as it came. Underneath it would still be the same spirit, heart, and soul.

To Kip, however, the day of that first shot of testosterone could not come soon enough.

There would be yet another wait, however. We knew that, in the eyes of the medical professionals, any diagnosed transgender must tackle telling family and loved ones before hormone therapy begins. Kip had cleared that hurdle, but there was one requirement he hadn't quite accomplished: prior to beginning the hormone therapy or scheduling surgery, a transgender is required to live as a member of the desired sex for a period of at least one year.

This period may even be stretched longer if the psychotherapist has concerns about the transsexual person's emotional readiness. The wait is for the patient's benefit. Any difficult task would only be made much worse with powerful foreign hormones surging through his or her system. The tough stuff has to be dealt with before the hormone war begins.

But Kip was ready. He had faced the scary, emotional parts of his battle. It seemed cruel to me, after conquering so much, to be made to wait, and wait, and wait.

There *was* a positive side to things, though. While answering the long list of questions on his first visit, Kip had explained to Dr. T that he had been living as a guy for many months. He was hopeful that those months would count. It was the first thing he planned to talk about at his next visit with his doctor.

During the next few months of appointments, Kip made it his personal mission to impress this seemingly unreachable physician.

At the doctor's request, he brought in the letter that he had written to family members. Dr. T loved it. He asked if it could be used to show other patients: people who were struggling in this area of their journey. He also wanted to use it for student training; Dr T was not only a psychotherapist, but also a psychology professor.

Kip said he had thought to himself, "Hell yes, if it gets me points with you, you can show the whole damn world!"

The doctor genuinely seemed intrigued with how well-adjusted Kip was, explaining that a lot of his patients found the events Kip had been through to be traumatic experiences. Kip was definitely winning him over. This man, who seemed like a living ice sculpture the day we met him, began to call my son his Poster Boy.

The next bit of information that came out of the doctor's mouth that day made Kip's jaw drop. "I don't see any need to make you wait the full year to begin hormone therapy. I think you're ready."

Kip said he almost wet his pants with excitement when he heard that line. He couldn't wait to get out of there to phone me with the news.

My skin covered with goose bumps as I listened to his animated, enthusiastic voice. The thought of the injections still made me slightly shaky, but I was learning to let go of my old habits, and see the future with an open mind. Relationships give us so much opportunity to learn… and unlearn. I was learning to love in a new way. It gave me a surprising new strength. Strength can come from such unexpected places.

I think Kip was feeling a change in himself and his life, too. On the day he called with the news, the excitement in his voice was almost palpable. "There must be some crazy astrological reason for life to suddenly seem to cooperate."

Had the effects of all the mirrors he'd broken, and umbrellas he'd opened indoors, finally worn off? It seemed too good to be true!

Probably because it was.

It was up to Dr. T to refer Kip to the next specialist, this time in the field of gender transition. Each time Kip had an appointment with Dr. T, he asked if he'd been scheduled in to begin hormone therapy. There was always an excuse.

Finally, Dr. T told Kip that he'd been put on the new patient waiting list, and that it shouldn't be too much longer.

* * *

Kip continued to see Dr. T regularly.

"How do you feel about coming to the university with me? I think a question and answer period with you would benefit my students."

"Sure." Kip thought doing a favor for Dr. T couldn't hurt. He was still waiting on an appointment with the hormone specialist. If Kip did something nice for Dr. T, maybe he would return the favor and push a little.

Aside from that, though, there was another good reason for him to say yes. To me, the whole thing sounded a bit like Show and Tell, but Kip saw the opportunity as a way of opening young people's minds. Maybe this generation would be the one to shatter the stigma attached to those who didn't fit into society's opinion of the norm. If there was something he could do to help, he would be right there.

On the day of Show and Tell, Kip sat down with Dr. T's students. He was surprised when he realized that they had been given absolutely no background history on him; they knew nothing about why he was there. Dr. T asked Kip to tell them his reason for visiting. As he did, the students sat with shocked looks for a few moments, and then started hammering him with personal questions.

"When could he first remember wanting to be a boy, and had he ever been 'girly'?"

"Was he ever suicidal?"

"How had his family reacted to the news?"

"What did it feel like to tell them?"

"When had it become really hard to live life in the wrong body?"

Kip's teenage years were definitely the hardest for him. As he tried to find the words to describe his horrible high school days, he could see their reactions change. He talked about how just getting up to go to school every day was incredibly hard. He hated himself during those years. He hated how people looked at him, as if he didn't belong. He hated being treated like a girl. He hated facing himself in the mirror every day. He hated shopping for clothes, and having his mom try to talk him into shopping in the ladies section *every single time.*

As he finished talking about those tormented times, he realized that all the girls in the room were in tears. One young guy sat stunned, his face softened, not knowing what to say.

Kip was surprised that they empathized so deeply. There were so many caring people in that room. All but one. There's one in every crowd.

A male student began a steady stream of questions. They went something like this:

Student: How do you know you are not gay?

Kip: Because I just know.

Student: But how do you know?

Kip: Well, I tried that and it didn't work.

Student: But how do you know it didn't work?

Kip: I just know.

Student: But how do you know for sure?

Kip (getting angry now): How do you know that *you* are not gay?

Student: Well, I just know.

Kip: Well, there you go, huh!

Having continued far too long this way, Dr. T must have seen that the conversation was going nowhere, and interjected, "Okay, on that note, let's move on!"

The other students continued their questioning.

To Kip, it seemed that they had started to reflect deeply on his life. They seemed to think carefully before asking their next questions. They wondered how long he had been living as a man, and if he had a girlfriend. They wanted to know what effect this problem had on his relationship with Cally. They asked what the testosterone would do to him. They wondered what the hardest parts of living life as a man were, when he still didn't have everything "done" yet.

When the questions were exhausted, the students told Kip that they had never thought about anything like his story before. They felt badly for him, and the things he had been forced to deal with. As he got out of his chair to leave, one of the girls got up, and gave him a warm hug.

Connecting with these students, and being moved by them himself, helped Kip get through the next few months of wait time, but his patience was waning. He began to wonder if Dr. T was intentionally keeping him around to get as much *use* out of his Poster Boy as he could. I wondered the same thing. There was something fishy to the whole thing.

Kip would call after an appointment and, with an irritated growl, say, "I'm still not booked in with the hormone guy." Then after eight months of waiting, depression set in.

I wondered why Dr. T had led Kip to believe that his hormone treatments were right around the corner if there had still been close to a year of wait time. Something didn't fit. I wondered if Kip's suspicions were right.

Whatever the reason for this delay, one thing was for sure — it was time to take this brutish bull by the balls!

Chapter 26

Depression did not agree with Kip. He'd come too far not to fight his way into the winner's circle at this point. He went to his next doctor's appointment with the same determination he'd shown during the day of my shocking Monday morning phone call at work. He needed hormone therapy, and he needed it now!

Dr. T either saw the change in Kip, and respected his confidence, or could hear the genuine need in his voice.

To Kip's amazement, the phone rang the next morning to confirm his first appointment with the transition specialist. His hormone therapy would begin in less than a month.

He called me to share the news. "My first shot is scheduled, Mom!" It was finally his turn to let out one of those sighs. A deep one followed his excited announcement.

The wait was finally coming to an end.

* * *

At twenty-two, Kip still had the same spirit and determination he'd shown when he'd teetered out onto the ice in his embarrassing pink sweater to learn power skating. And his love for hockey had grown over the years. He and Cally would go to a game every now and then.

One day, on their way out, at the end of the game, as they descended the stairs towards the exit, they passed by an older man. The stadium was crowded as usual, and he and Kip brushed each other as they passed.

For whatever reason, this guy took offense and decided to show Kip who was boss. He deliberately gave Kip a good shove, sending him back down several steps.

Kip looked up in surprise to see the man glaring at him confrontationally. Kip's instinct, for some strange new reason, had been to punch.

He fought the urge by having a little internal conversation with himself. "Okay, Kip, don't do it. Don't punch him. Control yourself. You don't want to beat up some scrawny old man because of that. They might never let you come to another hockey game here again!"

Cally knew there was more than one power struggle going on. She could tell that the new Kip and the old Kip were going at it inside his head. She remembers how she could literally feel Kip's rage, something that she wasn't used to dealing with. She took his arm, and tugged lightly, saying, "Okay, let's go home now."

A Hulk moment — one of the changes brought on by hormone therapy.

If Kip had run into this guy in the hockey stadium before testosterone, his reaction would have been a completely different — "Geez, buddy, get yourself some therapy!" He'd always had a naturally assertive nature, but that had definitely been stepped up a notch or two. He said the things that used to roll off him like nothing now made him crazy. Assertion had become aggression.

Luckily, this sort of event was not the norm. Ninety percent of the time, Kip's personality changed for the better. He seemed more self-confident, more at ease with the world, and in general, just happier.

Hormone therapy was like a gift to Kip. The surge of powerful testosterone brought continuous results. For a day or two after each injected shot, he struggled to control the strong emotional currents that charged through his body. But the benefits, he felt, were well worth it. He could see his body changing.

There was one physical change that I didn't even notice — probably because Kip had kept himself well covered the whole time he'd lived as Jul. It was a change that he'd waited on for years.

It's a trait that most women don't have to contend with. Very few try to achieve it. You can see evidence of mine in photos from the time I was six. I never felt they were a "blessing" — though it was the one trait of mine Kip would have loved to inherit. I've been "blessed" with impressive pipes — you know, large bicep muscles. I'm not really sure where they came from, or why they've hung around my whole life, but I've got 'em, and Kip wanted 'em.

He was grateful to learn that with testosterone comes muscle. Muscle gain went from being a frustrating struggle to something natural and rewarding. He began to experiment a little with weights. After a short period of time, his reaction had been, "Oh yeah! This is awesome!" He wasn't the weight room type, so he didn't end up with busting-out biceps, but at least he felt like he had the arms of a guy.

He began to see patchy facial hair, and not-so-patchy leg hair. He kept hoping to see the growth of hair begin on his chest — a valuable future ally that would help cover his scars after chest surgery. Unfortunately, except for a pencil-sized line down the centre of his chest, all his hair growth seemed to be from the waist down. Even each of his toe knuckles grew a fuzzy little tuft. He kept hoping his chest was next. It wasn't. "But hey," he said, "that's life for ya."

The most unexpected physical development came with a small financial burden… Kip had inherited my long, slender neck. After a few months of testosterone, he needed to wear a dress shirt to a special event. As he put the shirt on, he was surprised to find that he couldn't get the top button done up. No problem; he'd just go shopping for a new shirt, one neck size up.

A few more months went by before the need to wear a dress shirt presented itself again. When it did, Kip reached for his new shirt. The top button was just short of reaching the button hole.

A couple neck sizes later, Kip finally relaxed. His neck had stopped growing (for the time being anyway). Not only was it costly, he'd been a little concerned he would end up looking like a sumo wrestler, but only from the shoulders up.

His facial characteristics transformed, as well. His forehead worked its way backward, as the hairline framing it receded, and took on squarer, sharper lines.

I noticed something else about his forehead. The bone structure just underneath his eyebrows seemed to change. I could see something that sort of reminded me of a Neanderthal. Now, I'm not saying that the more male hormones Kip received, the more Neanderthal-like he became, but really, don't laugh, it was there. It wasn't a pronounced thing; it was subtle, but his forehead was different, and in a very distinctive male way.

The other changes in his face were subtle too. There was definitely something about his cheekbones. They appeared to recede a bit or shift position. His jaw seemed to change, as well. It took on a more squared look. Actually, his whole face seemed somehow squarer than before. He even developed a new, unfamiliar space between his two front teeth — something he did not appreciate; his teeth had been one of the only things he had liked about himself — but it was a small price to pay. As his jaw grew, so did the space between his teeth.

The changes didn't happen overnight, however. In fact, they were so gradual that I didn't even notice them at first. It wasn't until Cally sent me an old photo beside a recent one that I could see the full effect of the injections.

It's strange; I'd been so worried about how much I'd miss Jul's face. But I'd grown to love my new son's face as it emerged, without even realizing it.

I was trying to explain this to a friend one day. I told her about the time Jul had been in that car accident when she was five. I commented that now, in the end, that face I was so afraid to lose is gone. It has changed completely. Everything is different.

But Kip isn't a face, or a name, or a gender. Kip is a person. And it's Kip, not the "he or she" that I love to death. His soul is still the same. His face wasn't really a loss. I think about the parents who don't learn to accept. How can they let their relationship with their children die? Or worse yet, how do they survive their child's suicide? That's loss.

The story made my friend think about a woman in the U.S. who had had her face ripped off by a chimpanzee gone berserk. She had been interviewed by Oprah. While watching the show, my friend realized that "after the initial shock of seeing her mangled face, it became nothing, because her spirit was still there, full of pluck and courage. The outer packaging melted away to nothing."

That woman's story says it all.

Seeing a person with our eyes brings such limited results. When we see with our hearts, looking inside, past the surface, underneath what society dwells on, we see so much more. *What* we are isn't the most important thing: it's *who* we are. My son had helped me learn that lesson. The physical changes were not important. My son's "pluck and courage" were going strong. He made me proud.

Kip's changes were not just physical, though. Almost instantly, his energy level skyrocketed, and increasing at just as significant a rate was his sex drive. I'm sorry, I can't tell you too much about that. There are some subjects a mom just doesn't ask too many questions about.

Secret Selves

*   *   *

It was funny. I used to be so worried that Kip would finally get the hormone therapy he wanted so badly, and still not be happy. I'd done all my worrying for nothing. Kip was much happier — it was obvious that his change had been the right thing to do.

My family must have recognized this as well because on a beautiful, sunny afternoon Kip, Cally, Joey, Will, and I headed to my sister's for another BBQ. It was to be a small gathering organized for us to catch up with Kip's visiting cousin, Eddie. When we arrived, we saw another cousin already there with his wife and baby. Kip instantly became suspicious. He'd thought to himself, *Why didn't anyone mention that Percy and his family were coming?*

As more relatives arrived, Kip's suspicions grew. He thought, *Uh-oh, what are they up to now?* The whole family had once again gathered at my sister's home.

After dinner, Eddie, the outgoing one in the family, stood up sporting a Master of Ceremonies look. He cleared his throat.

Kip thought, *Oh God!* Memories of the "It's a Boy" party hovered in the corner of his mind. Artistic people can sometimes be quite odd. He knew that, and he also knew that my family was full of them.

Kip held his breath as Eddie began to talk. He announced that the evening had been planned to honor Kip.

Kip stared at Eddie.

I'd been prepared for his standard, embarrassed look. I'd seen it hundreds of times. What I saw was anything but standard. There were two extremely large veins making a rather sizable V in the middle of Kip's forehead.

I swear I could see them pulsing up and down. They were huge! I thought, *Holy crap, can someone rupture a blood vessel from embarrassment?* I knew he'd gotten a hormone shot the day before, and that it typically made his emotions double, but it literally looked as if that whole injection was sitting right there, stuck in the veins in his forehead!

I fought to pull my eyes down, away from this weird vein poppage. I couldn't do it. Every time I tried, my eyes would creep up until those bulging veins were back in view. They made him look angry.

Eddie then announced in his comedic way that the family felt that Kip should be able to take his shirt off to go swimming, or sun bathing, or just because he wanted to! He had organized a collection to help Kip get closer to having his chest reconstructed. He then handed Kip an envelope.

Kip looked at the envelope. He couldn't even bring himself to open it. Nothing came out of his mouth right away — probably because he didn't have a clue what to say.

That was completely obvious when he did open his mouth.

His first quiet sentence was, "Why do I keep coming back here?"

I chuckled a little, uncomfortably, and felt relieved as I heard a couple of others do the same. From the look on Kip's face, I figured I knew exactly what he was feeling next: regret. We've all had moments like that — reactive speaking before brain engagement.

After a few moments of silence, his thank you started. He awkwardly tried to describe how completely unexpected the evening had been, and how much he appreciated their generosity. It was a clumsy thank you.

I hoped he'd made it clear how much he appreciated the evening.

I know ladies, you thought that men just didn't *want* to talk. Well, it seems to be more than that. It seems to be an actual inability to express thoughts verbally at times. Maybe it's testosterone related? For Kip, after beginning hormone therapy, communicating seemed to become an unfamiliar struggle. The words didn't come as easily, he used more fillers like "um", "well", "ah"… and he blurted out dumb things from time to time. That day had been one of those times. He said as soon as he'd blurted out — "Why do I keep coming back here?" — he thought, *Oh God, why did I say that? I love it here. I didn't mean it in a bad way, but that's definitely how it sounded. God, I sound so ungrateful!*

I hoped his forehead veins hadn't distracted everyone and skewed the feelings he was trying to convey. I asked him later if he'd been mad, he'd sure looked that way.

He replied, "No, I know those veins make me look like I'm mad; people have told me that, but I wasn't. Those veins seem to show up no matter what I'm feeling — happy, excited, anything. Geez, it can be really hot outside, and they decide to say hello. They seem to have a mind of their own, but I wasn't mad. Overwhelmed," he said, nodding his head, "and of course, embarrassed, but definitely not mad."

Whether my family understood the extent of his gratitude or not, I don't know. What I do know is that they seemed to grasp the importance of Kip's need to have a flat chest, and their love had given him the finances to get him a third of the way to that dream.

Joey: Fall 2005 to Spring 2006
Chapter 27

On the morning after that Fear Factor party when Joey #2 first presented himself, I sat at the kitchen table alone, drinking a cup of coffee. I wondered how crazy the day ahead of me would be. I still had no idea what I would do if my son came down the stairs as Joey #2. I had hoped my subconscious would figure it out as I slept. No such luck.

If it was Joey #2 who emerged from the bedroom that morning, we would probably have to head for a hospital in the city. I could try to contact one of Joey's two doctors by phone, but I was pretty sure that it would bring the same end result — being admitted. Maybe the hospital wasn't necessary; I didn't know. I had no idea what the "right thing" was in a situation like this. I really needed to talk to someone to get my head around it.

My concentration was broken by footsteps coming down the stairs. I looked up to see Joey enter the kitchen. His face held a look of uncertainty or uneasiness.

Fear squeezed my heart. I hesitantly forced out, "Joey, is that you?"

He had his head down a bit, as if embarrassed. His eyes lifted to meet mine. "Yeah... it's me."

My eyes closed for a moment in relief. *Thank you, God.* I felt almost weak with the release of tension. Opening my eyes, I looked at my son and asked, "Do you remember what happened last night?"

His answer was one single nod.

"You were saying you weren't Joey."

"Yeah, I know."

"What do you remember?"

"It's all foggy, sort of like remembering a dream. I have bits and pieces of last night, but there are big holes all through yesterday. Actually, most of it's missing." He was silent for a moment, then offered, "I don't know if I should go to work today."

In less than three hours, he was expected at the grocery store where he stocked shelves.

Well, we were in total agreement there. I didn't like to think about what would happen if there was an encore of last night while he was at work. Not to mention that I definitely wanted to keep an eye on him for the rest of the weekend. "You're right. Call in sick, and take it easy. I want you to stick around here today. Okay?"

I sat at the kitchen table, and tried to relax. I wondered if this Saturday morning was the calm after the storm... or the calm before the storm. How much more of this could I handle? I really wasn't sure. It wouldn't do any good to worry, though. I had to stay positive, and do my best to make the right choices. The next scheduled doctor's appointment was with Dr. M on Monday. With a little luck, we would make it through the weekend with the boy I had raised for seventeen years, instead of a nervous, timid stranger. We could tackle this problem on Monday.

The weekend passed by. I checked on Joey every once in a while. Each time, he assured me it was him, I took a deep breath and thought to myself — *There, see! He's okay. He will be just fine.*

Monday rolled around without any more strangeness. We drove toward the city, listening to music on the way. Normally, I would be singing along, but that day I was quiet. I wondered what

Dr. M's reaction would be to our Friday night story. I privately prayed that it wouldn't create the need for another new doctor.

Halfway to the city I felt a pair of eyes. I looked over to see Joey watching me; an unusual, but strangely affectionate expression on his face. He smiled.

I smiled back. *Okay, Joe, what is that look for?*

I turned from him to the road. He was still watching me. I could feel it. I looked over at him again, waiting for him to say what he was thinking. That look on his face was throwing me off. He looked relaxed and content, like he would have on a day from his childhood when we'd just spent the afternoon together — maybe playing foosball, going to a movie or playing a game of mini-putt. It was as if, at that moment, all the tension of the summer, all the anger, was gone.

Quietly, with obvious affection, he said, "I've missed you."

I stumbled. "What do you mean?"

Still wearing that innocent, satisfied expression, he said, "It feels like it's been a long time. Where's Jul?"

What?! He just said Jul?

Joey hadn't called Kip Jul in two years. Out of all of us, he'd been the one who had adjusted the best. When Kip had shared his secret with Joey (even before sharing it with me) he had realized why Kip had seemed so angry with him at times. It was because Kip had been jealous of Joey; he had wanted Joey's body. The knowledge of this painful jealousy, coupled with the strong belief that people should be able to be who they are, always, seemed to make the transition easy for Joey. He rarely slipped up with the name change, even in the beginning. But today, he didn't seem to notice his glaring mistake.

I hesitantly asked, "Pardon?"

He repeated, "Where's Jul?" in a loving voice.

There was *no way* Joey would say Jul twice in a row. He would cringe like I did after the first mistake, and make the necessary correction. So what was going on now? I looked over at him again. He continued to look at me fondly, smiling like he hadn't seen me in years.

Holy fuck! Here we go again.

Something told me not to make a big deal out of it. Apparently, his mind was on holidays again. That's all it could be. So I answered, "At work."

"How are Wiggles and Kissy?"

He was referring to our aging cats. "Joe... Kissy's gone."

A gloomy look washed over his face. "Oh," he said, and sat silent for a second. Then he added, "I miss them, too." His head tilted down in sadness. His expression changed to fear almost immediately.

I repeatedly glanced from the road to Joey, wondering what was going on. He looked totally freaked out.

With eyes as wide as two full moons, he sat looking at his hands, holding them out in front of him. He looked up at me, and said, "Why are my hands so big?"

Jesus. What kind of question is that? There's no intelligent answer for that. "Because you're seventeen, honey."

His confused reply was simply, "I am? How?"

I took a deep breath. "Don't you remember?"

I looked over at him for his reply.

It was the strangest thing. Although he looked the same as always, at the same time, he didn't. His appearance was somehow younger. His features had taken on an innocence. The look on his face was so sweet.

Instead of an answer, I heard more panic in his voice. "Oh... my body's big, too! What's happening, Mommy? What's going on?"

He hadn't called me Mommy in years. "I'm not sure, honey, but we're on our way to see a doctor. He'll know, and he'll explain it to us. Don't worry, everything will be all right."

We certainly have more than the Friday night story to talk to Dr. M about.

I wondered if everything *would* be all right. As I've already said, at seventeen, Joey was a typical teenager who knew *everything*, and seemed to feel that his parents knew nothing. This boy in front of me was nowhere near seventeen, and openly needed my help. His eyes pleaded for answers. I had to fight to keep my composure. I'd gotten used to Joey keeping his feelings safely protected from sight. This new, fragile appearance made my heart pain. I wanted to help... but how?

He sat staring at his hands, obviously dumbstruck at the appearance of himself. Then he looked over at me, and eked out, "Mommy, I'm really scared."

I cooed reassurances. "It's okay, honey. It's all right. Everything is going to be fine." Inside I was thinking that it was the strangest thing I had ever seen or heard. From his voice and his language, if I hadn't been able to see him, I would have guessed him to be somewhere around seven or eight-years-old. When I was able to force my eyes back to the road, it was like I was listening to an old recording of him.

But as shaken as I felt, he appeared even worse. I took the steering wheel with my left hand, offered him my right, and said, "Do you want to hold my hand until we get there?" I was amazed at this automatic response from me. It didn't make sense for me to ask my seventeen-year-old if he wanted to hold my hand. It was just that he really didn't seem that old.

He smiled sweetly, and put his hand in mine. I hoped that holding my hand was helping him, because it was making me feel totally rattled. I had offered my hand to calm him, but it had done the opposite for me.

Even though we were close, talked openly together about most topics, and got along well, hugs and kisses were not cool in Joey's world - that was clear. He was at a time in his life where he kept to himself; body contact was something he avoided. I sat, trying to remember the last time he had willingly given me a hug. It must have been at least four years. Sometimes, when he could see I really needed one, he would offer it but you could easily see his discomfort for however many seconds it lasted.

As he sat holding my hand, a bad movie scene came to mind: one where people are stolen by aliens, and replaced with beings that don't quite know how to imitate the people who would normally be in their host bodies. We were in *Invasion of the Body Snatchers* and he was a pod person. This boy beside me was definitely not my teenage son. I took deep breaths, trying to remain calm. *You're almost there, Jamie. Hold it together. Concentrate on the traffic.*

Although reeling with apprehension, another less intense feeling was there, as well. I couldn't help but notice how nice the warmth of his hand felt, as if I were experiencing a memory I could actually feel. But mixed with this feeling of longing for a simpler day was dread. Why was this happening? What would cause his brain to suddenly jump back ten years?

I was in heavier traffic now, making my way through the city toward the psychiatric hospital and Dr. M. Joey suddenly looked very curious. His eyes widened as he said, "Mommy, can I see my face?"

It struck me strange that he didn't just instinctively look in the mirror under his visor. Probably a good thing: I wondered what the sight of his face would do to him. The look of his hands had made him so nervous. His face might send him into a total panic attack. I needed to delay.

Struggling to keep my voice natural, I said, "We're almost there, honey. There are mirrors in the washrooms at the doctor's office."

Although a bit disappointed with my answer, he seemed to settle a little.

I pulled into the hospital parking lot, and squeezed my car into one of the few empty spots. As we got out, and crossed the pavement toward the big brick hospital, I kept a close watch over him. His movements were childlike, more peppy and animated than that of a teenager.

We entered Dr. M's waiting area. At one side were the restrooms. The sight of the stick man on the men's room door brought excitement to Joey's face. "Can I go to the bathroom, Mommy?"

"Okay," I said, "but come right back." I was surprised at how I couldn't help answering him as if he were young again. It was all too weird. As I sat down in one of the stiff waiting room chairs, I desperately prayed that the doctor was on schedule.

Joey came out of the restroom without his glasses. He needed them to see across the room. They were the first thing he reached for when he got up in the morning. Today he walked toward me without them.

I held back more amazed apprehension, and said, "Joey, where are your glasses?"

He didn't answer. He simply patted his pocket to tell me they were safe inside.

I was totally mesmerized. Before his teen years, Joey had constantly taken his glasses off, and put them in his pocket. Keeping them on his face had been a constant battle. He had broken so many pairs that way, I'd lost count. Today, it was as if, somehow, my son was walking toward me as a young boy again. How in the world would we deal with this if it happened again, and he was suddenly ten years younger when he was not with Will or me? What if it happened at school?!

My fascinated stare was interrupted by the nurse's voice. "The doctor is ready for you."

Dr. M looked up from his papers as we entered, his face curious at my presence in the room.

"Uh... hi. I hope it's okay if I join you. We have a bit of a... situation."

Dr. M looked back at us, saying nothing. Joey and I sat down in the two upholstered chairs in the tiny office.

"It started on Friday. Joey was at school, and somehow... forgot who he was. He had really faint memories of his life, but thought he was someone else. When I asked him who he was, he said he didn't know. It lasted until the next morning, then he woke up normal. He was fine after that, until halfway here, in the car. Now he seems to think he's young again." I struggled in the end, saying finally, "His personality seems to be... umm, fragmenting."

Dr. M looked at Joey intently. He began to ask questions.

Out of the corner of my eye, I saw Joey go limp. Both of us watched as his body slumped, his arms dangled at his sides, his head bent forward, chin to chest, as if totally and deeply asleep, sitting up.

After about half a minute, he slowly looked up and blinked nervously, aware that he was being stared at by both of us. He looked from me to Dr. M, and back to me, with questions behind his eyes.

Dr. M took a deep breath. "Do you remember what just happened?"

As he answered, I knew my teenage son was back. "What do you mean? I remember being in the car, driving here." He'd only lost forty-five minutes this time, but he'd lost them completely.

The discussion that followed was one of options. If Joey was admitted, he would get a new doctor. Dr. M only met with outpatients. Although his office was physically attached to the hospital, he was not part of the staff. Joey would have to begin treatment with a doctor who worked in the psychiatric hospital.

A new doctor — that sounded like torture. We'd been through five already; starting over seemed to signify that all those appointments had been wasted.

Dr. M continued to explain that he wasn't sure that being admitted was completely necessary at this point. We would definitely need to increase our visits to try to get a handle on what was going on. He had his nurse check for available time slots.

The only problem with this plan was if something happened that scared me enough to consider it "an emergency." If I needed to bring him to the hospital while under Dr. M's treatment, I would have to take him to the emergency department of the children's hospital because this one didn't have an emergency admittance option. At the children's hospital, he would be treated by *their* psychiatrist, while waiting to be transferred when a bed became available. The whole process often took a couple weeks.

Both choices sounded lousy to me. I could either take him home, and continue to work with the doctors who knew him, but risk having him shuffled around like a piece of meat if something went wrong, or we could admit him to the psychiatric hospital right now.

Dr. M looked at Joey. "Do you think you're okay to go home?" he asked.

Joey's eyes shifted nervously between me and Dr. M. "I don't know. I guess so."

I turned to look at Joey. I was about to ask if that was what he wanted. Before I could get the question out, his body went limp again. His head fell down to his chest, and his arms went lifeless.

I looked at Dr M. I had hoped he would offer some insight, or words of comfort. Instead he looked back at me with lifted eyebrows, appearing as confused as I was.

Slowly, Joey lifted his head. His facial expression was different again. This time, he had an air of total confidence. His features crinkled into a creepy little smile. In a strange, arrogant manner, he said, "What's going on?" and he tilted his head slightly to one side as if amused.

Dr. M answered with, "We are trying to decide if you need to go into hospital or not."

With an intimidating stare, Joey slowly exhaled, "Hmmm… I see." Then he looked at me, his eyebrows lowered, his eyes intense and glaring.

I was scared. It might sound strange, but this person beside me did not feel one bit like Joey. I had gone from worried to confused to completely rattled, and now felt like I was nearing panic all within the inside of an hour, without any relief in between.

Dr. M's eyes remained fixed on Joey. "I'm not sure whether to put him in or not. I need a second opinion. There's a doctor on the hospital staff who may have some insight. I'll call him." He dialed the phone and sat waiting as it rang, watching Joey carefully.

Joey looked at him, and smiled his wry little grin again. Then he turned his attention back to me. He leaned in and whispered, "Get out of here, Jamie," his eyes piercing me.

My blood pressure shot through the roof. His intimidating, forceful stare actually made me want to get out of there. I didn't think I could handle much more.

Dr. M was talking now, asking questions to someone. I heard him say, "I was wondering if he should go into hospital until he has better control."

Joey looked away from me for a minute, and with an amused smile said, "Oh, don't worry. It's me that is in total control here." He gave a low, grating snicker that sent a shiver right through me. He looked back at me again; his head tilted down so his offensive stare looked even more intimidating. He said confidently, "Run,

Jamie, run. Get out of here. If someone gets hurt, I don't want it to be you." His calmness was frightening.

My eyes shifted to Dr. M. The tears I had been fighting became too massive to hold back. A wet trail quickly lined each of my cheeks.

I couldn't think.

What had happened to my Joey? I looked back at him, unable to believe this was happening, but quickly turned away. Looking at him sent fear through my system. It was too much. I couldn't look at this sinister person. A small sob slipped out.

Joey's voice got a little louder this time "Run, Jamie, run." Anger trembled in his voice.

The next voice I heard was Dr. M's. "Never mind. Send someone over to take him... *I'm* putting him in."

CHAPTER 28

After learning that Joey would be admitted, I sat alone in my car feeling like the supporting actress in some strange psychological thriller. Before that day, I'd thought I knew the meaning of the word surreal. Some of my previous experiences may have been close, but nothing like this. I sat quietly, stunned by the events of the day. After a time, I realized I was just sitting there... in the parking lot. My mind was off in some faraway place that I can't recall now.

What I do remember is giving myself a little pep talk. The nurse had told me to go home and pick up Joey's overnight things. It would give his caregivers enough time to get him to his room, and show him around. I was to go back and meet the staff at the hospital in a couple hours.

Luckily, Will was home when I arrived to pack Joey's bag. I needed one of his signature hugs: maybe an extra long one this time. Walking right over to him, I put my arms around his neck and melted into his body.

He could feel me tremble. "Are you okay?"

"No... not really."

"Do you want me to drive you back into the city?"

Oh God, yes. I had no idea what I was about to face back at the hospital. What goes on in a place like that? "That would be awesome, hon." I was so grateful. I wondered how I had managed to drive at all that day, given the fog I was in. Behind the wheel was definitely not the safest place for me to be.

Once back in the city, we followed the directions given by Dr. M, and drove behind the main hospital to the buildings where youth were treated. We were to look for a place called Algonquin Cottage.

The look of the "cottage" did not help to rid me of the feeling that I was trapped in a movie of the week. Algonquin Cottage was a perfectly round house. (Well, according to Joe and Will, it was actually octagonal, but somehow my memory has smoothed out the edges.) It and two other identical replicas lined the back of the hospital property, hidden from sight all the months we'd been coming. They were the strangest looking buildings I'd ever seen. The dull sky, and threatening rain, added to the eeriness. I was in a bad dream that just wouldn't end. *Please God, let me wake up... please.*

We parked the car, and walked towards these odd, round places. We found the one with a small plaque beside the door that read "Algonquin Cottage." Under the name was a listing of visiting hours: Wednesday from 7 p.m. to 9 p.m., and on weekends. I stood there, dumbstruck, as the realization hit. If he had to stay, I could only see my son on weekends and Wednesday evenings. I felt as if I would start to tremble again at any second.

I forced myself to rap on the door, its thick steel hurting my knuckles as I knocked. After a short wait, a teenage boy opened the door. He was thin and gangly, and he just stood there, looking at me. Finally, smiling, he said, "Hi." That was it. Nothing more. He just looked.

Uncomfortable, awkward seconds ticked by. He stood watching us, waiting, like we were two traveling salesmen, and we should be introducing ourselves and starting into some sort of spiel. I didn't know what to say. I didn't even know who I was supposed to be asking for. The only thing my brain could come up with was, "Hi, I'm Joey's mom. He just came here today."

Suddenly, a woman came rushing over. "I'm sorry, things are crazy at the moment. My name's Norma. I'm the chief nurse tonight. Please come in."

She was in her fifties, stocky, and had a very strict and serious look about her. She carried herself with confidence, giving me a feeling that if something was "crazy," as she put it, she would be able to straighten it out.

We followed her down the stairs from the door into a centre room containing a pool table. Around it, wedge shaped rooms radiated out from this middle, open common area. The ceiling of each wedge was painted in a different color, emphasizing the strange feel of the place. There was an office, a kitchen, a laundry room, a TV room, and what looked like a craft area with a large worktable. Here and there, a teenager was moving about.

Norma led us into one of the rooms, where Joey sat on the couch watching television. I could tell my son was back. He looked like Joey again, but the more convincing thing was that he felt like Joey. I'm not sure how to explain it. The frightening person who had been taken from Dr. M's office earlier had an intensity that was now gone.

Norma turned toward Joey. "Why don't you take your parents upstairs to show them your room, and get settled in with your things? After that, we'll have a meeting."

Upstairs, surrounding another common area, were eight bedrooms and two bathrooms: one that said "Boys", one that said "Girls." Joey led us into a bedroom two doors over from the boy's bathroom. "This is it."

It was a sterile looking space, nothing personal, just a bed, made up with sheets and a blanket. Beside it was a desk and chair.

"Will, why don't you head back out and bring in his things?" We'd been told to bring anything that would help him adjust to his new surroundings. Like me, Joey sleeps with a fan year round. Will left the room and went to get the fan, and his comforter and pillows from home.

Joey closed the door. He looked at me, his face clouded with tension. I could see and hear the panic. "Mom, I just can't stay here." As the beginning of tears lined the edges of his eyes, he blinked them away. "This place is crazy. If I stay here, there's no way I'll get better."

I felt so frustrated. He looked so scared. My own tears wanted to spill out, but I knew he needed my strength. "Let's go meet with them, honey. We'll see what's going to happen."

We found Norma doing paperwork in a little office on the main floor. Most of the meeting consisted of an explanation of what Joey could expect from the next several hours. He could not legally leave the building without seeing the doctor assigned to his case. They had tried to get him an appointment for that evening, but had been unsuccessful. He would have to spend the night, but in the morning, if the doctor gave her approval, Joey could go home.

His nerves seemed to settle a little with that.

"It's only one night, honey. You can make it through one night."

He looked like he was beginning to calm. Our nervous systems seemed to be connected that day. As I saw the tension start to leave his body, my own mess of nerves began to untangle.

Norma wasted no time. She looked like she wanted to get back to her paperwork. "Since it isn't a visiting night, you can have a short visit, get Joey settled in and then I'll ask you to head back home and let him rest. He's been given something to help him relax." It was a polite way of telling us we'd have to leave. "The doctor will call you in the morning."

The drive home was a quiet trip. An unfamiliar loneliness washed over me. I needed a drink, a strong one. I tried to convince myself it was only for one night, but the ominous truth lurked around every corner my thought patterns took. If I were a doctor, and had read Joey's file describing the sinister character he had become earlier that day, I certainly wouldn't let him go home.

After a good strong drink, and almost a full bottle of wine, we crawled into bed. The day had been charged with emotion, and I was physically and mentally exhausted. I slept, although fitfully.

* * *

The new day brought hope. Hope that Joey would be back in school before the week was over. Hope that I would soon be dropping my son at work again, watching him walk towards the other boys. Hope that the worst was over.

Will planned to start work later than usual that morning. He busied himself making an omelet for breakfast, stalling in case the phone call came early enough for him to offer support.

When the phone rang, I jumped. The second ring made me cringe. The shrillness crawled over my skin. I looked over at him. I wanted to answer, but was afraid of the words I was sure would come from the other end.

I forced myself to pick up the phone. Gripping the receiver in my hand, I heard the voice of Dr. H for the first time. "Hello Mrs. Johnson. I've had a good, long chat with Joey. He was cooperative and open with me, but regretfully… he will have to stay. The events of the last few days warrant a period of observation. Could you please bring him enough clothes for a while, and some of his favorite things: snack foods, games, anything that will lift his spirits, and make him feel at home."

She hadn't said to bring enough clothes for a few days. She had said a while. It had a very menacing ring to it. My hope that this strange course of events wasn't serious, and that my son would be home with us soon was fading fast, and I was desperate to hold on to a little of it. "Do you know what's wrong with him?"

"I need some time to observe him, and talk with him before I can be sure."

I hung up the phone and sat down at the kitchen table.

Will looked at me from across the room. "Do they know what's wrong with him?"

I shrugged. "She's not sure yet. I'm supposed to bring his things. She wants to observe him for a while."

"You want me to drive you in?"

I took a long, slow breath. "No. I'll be fine. I know you have things you need to do today." And I really did feel that I would be okay. I knew deep down that Joey was in the right place. He was safe, and the staff at the hospital offered his best chance to overcome whatever was going on with him.

I collected everything I could think of that would make Joey more comfortable. I found his favorite Jim Carrey movies - *Ace Ventura, Pet Detective* and *Liar Liar*. I wanted to picture him in the Algonquin Cottage TV room, laughing. I needed to have faith that I would hear him laugh again, and with a bit of luck, before long. I packed the cereal he liked, the chocolate chip granola bars he ate by the handful, a case of Coke, and his favorite frozen foods. Maybe his comfort foods would help him cope with his new surroundings.

It was mid-afternoon when I arrived at the cottage. The gray day matched how I was feeling; a mixture of numbed reluctance and dulled acceptance. Feeling lifeless, I banged on the steel of the door.

Perk up, Jamie, for Joey's sake.

Over the summer, I'd tried to stay positive: focusing on getting my son the help he needed. That morning I was still trying to reach for that positive outlook. But I was wearing down. There was no way my son was just going through normal teenage stresses. I mean, God, at the beginning of the summer when I had first found him a counselor, I sure hadn't pictured myself bringing Joey enough clothes and belongings to stay at a home like this, and definitely not for *a while*. And the look of this crazy round house, filled with…well, you know… kids, kids with serious issues, made it all that much more difficult.

Norma came towards the door with a set of keys in her hand. This time, the door was locked. She opened it, and waved me in. "Come in, Jamie. Sorry about this. Things aren't going so well today. Joey's upset about having to stay. We lock the door when we're afraid that one of the kids will try to leave: standard procedure when one of them is feeling agitated."

I swallowed hard. That lock tainted the casual atmosphere that had been present the day before. And Joey was the one who was responsible for it.

We descended the stairs to find Joey shooting pool. He looked a little tense, but calmer than I had expected. He nodded hello.

Norma walked straight to him. "Your Mom is here with your things, Joe. Find room for your food in the fridge and bottom cupboards, and be sure to write your name on everything."

Joey walked the few feet it took to get into the kitchen with his head down, and then, looking me straight in the eye, said, "Come over here, Mom… I need to talk to you." He walked over to the table, and sat down. He wasted no time. "Mom, you HAVE to get me out of here!" From a distance, I could hear a small dog barking.

I looked in his pleading eyes. *This* was what I had expected. I slowly began, "Honey, it's not my decision to make anymore."

He cut me off. "There *must* be something you can do. I just can't stay here. I can't! You think I'm crazy now? If I stay here, I don't know what will happen. Talk to them Mom… please." His voice was desperate, his pitch heightening with panic.

He was chipping away at my heart as if he had the skilled hand of an sculptor with his chisel. I didn't want to leave him behind. I wanted more than anything to take him home, to ease his pain. But there was nothing I could do. "The doctor needs to talk to you a little before she can release you, Joe. She needs to give the okay for you to come home. It's not up to me."

He started again, "You don't seem to understand, Mom. I *can't* stay here. I'm going crazy. You have to get me out. You have to try. God, at least try!" His eyes pleaded.

In the background, that annoying little dog was at it again. There is something about the sound of a high-pitched bark that eats at my nerves when I'm stressed. It really wasn't helping.

I didn't have the strength to argue with him. "Okay, let's go talk to Norma."

Together we left the kitchen. There was no sign of Norma in the large common area. I stuck my head through the open door of the office, and saw her. I asked for a moment of her time, and entered the small room. Joey hung back. He stood just outside the open door, cracking his knuckles nervously.

"Norma, is there any way I can take Joey home? I can bring him in for observation as an outpatient. I'll bring him as often as you want." I wasn't sure how we would swing that promise, but I would make it happen if it would make this panic go away. "He's really upset. I've never seen him like this. He says he's sure that staying will make him worse."

Norma looked at me calmly. Her expression seemed almost uncaring. It was clear that she was unmoved by my appeal. She'd obviously heard this story before, probably many times. She looked right into my eyes, and said, "I'm sorry, Jamie, only the doctor can release him."

I tried our only hope. "Can I speak with the doctor?"

She lowered her head to go back to what she was working on. "She has left for the day. She'll see him tomorrow."

I knew the conversation was over. But then another question popped into my head. "How long do you think Joey will be here?"

She looked up again. "That will depend on his progress, *and* how cooperative he is. Actually, if he's cooperative, he can even go home on the weekend. We work on a point system here. The more a teen does to make our environment a pleasant one for everyone, the more privileges he or she is given. The doctor will keep you informed of his progress."

I thought this news might help Joey calm down a bit. If he could relax and pull himself together, he could come home for the weekend.

My last question was one I never should have asked. Without considering the fallout, I said, "How long is the average stay here?"

"Six to eight weeks," she replied, and went back to her work.

My mouth went dry. *What?* I had been expecting one or two weeks... *six to eight weeks? Oh my God.* My throat was closing. The tears were headed out fast. *Gulp them back, Jamie. Gulp them back. Hold it together.*

I stumbled out of the office, stunned. I plunked down in a chair beside the office door directly in front of the pool table. Joey was pacing back and forth, wringing his hands.

My mouth hung open. *Six to eight weeks!*

Suddenly, I became aware of the barking again. Off to one side of the room was the skinny teenage boy who had answered the door the day before. *He* was the annoying little dog that I kept hearing. He was watching Joey pace, obviously stimulated and intrigued by the panicky look on Joey's face. He sounded exactly like a little dog. His high-pitched bark made me wince every time. That sound drove Joey's panic home. *How could I leave him in this place for six to eight weeks?*

Then I heard Joey again. Terror had completely taken over his voice. In a loud, desperate plea he said, "Mom, do something! I *have* to get out of here. I can't be held responsible for what happens if you leave me here. I can't stay. I CAN'T STAY. This fucking place will kill me!"

I looked up as he stood over me, his face scarlet with passion. I closed my eyes. I opened them, shook my head, and choked out, "Honey, there's nothing I can do. You can talk to the doctor tomorrow."

He yelled back, "Tomorrow? Tomorrow? I will be totally insane by tomorrow." He was in hysterics now. Loud and forceful, he shouted, "If you leave me here, something terrible will happen. I might hurt someone. I can't stay here. Mom, you can't leave me here. If I stay, I WILL hurt someone. I know I will. Do you want *that* on your conscience?"

I bent forward in my chair. My head fell into my hands. I had reached my limit. Nothing would come out of my mouth. Tears ran freely. I rocked back and forth in my chair slightly, head in hands as he shouted, not knowing what on earth to do. I sobbed a huge, body-heaving sob, gasping for breath.

Then I felt a hand rest softly on my shoulder. I looked up to see Norma. Her demeanor had totally changed. With the kindest expression I'd ever seen, she gently said, "Jamie, this is too much. You don't have to hear this. It's time for you to go home." She spoke with a warmth I would never have imagined her to have. She took her hand off my shoulder, took my arm and gently lifted me out of the chair.

There was instantly another staff member between Joey and me, a young man, preventing Joey from stopping me. I let Norma guide me to the stairs. I felt completely numb, like I'd been drugged.

Joey broke free from the young man blocking him, and ran towards me. The guy dashed after him, but heard Norma say, "It's okay. Let him go."

I was on the first step when I turned around. Joey threw his arms around me, and sobbed into my shoulder. He clung to me as if he would never see me again. Through his sobs, I heard him say, "Oh Mom, I am so, so sorry... I'm so sorry... I'm so sorry."

I couldn't speak. We just stood there holding each other, and crying.

We stayed that way for several minutes, letting the pain fade. Then I heard in a soft voice, "I'm so sorry, Mom. I didn't mean it. I love you."

My voice thickened with emotion as I murmured, "It's okay, honey... I know. I love you, too."

Chapter 29

Walking away from the hospital that day was the hardest, and most painful, thing I'd ever done. I sat in the car, feeling lonely as never before. The huge flood of tears came hard and fast. I let it all out then. I had no choice, really. The agony of watching my son spiral into a worse and worse place, and not being able to help. The wondering if I had done anything to contribute to it. The nervous worry from the withdrawal of his physical contact. It had all been pent up too long already. I needed to put it aside, to stay strong, so I let it out.

When the sobs slowed, and the tears let up enough for me to make my way, I tackled the drive home. As I drove, I told myself that I shouldn't take personally the arrows Joey had shot at me that day. They were not really aimed at me. I'd been an interchangeable pawn. They would have been pointed at anyone he felt might have had some power to save him from being alone in that difficult place. His anger was a defense mechanism... or maybe a subconscious attempt at manipulation. It was a desperate act. I think deep down, I knew that. I was his only hope of getting out of there.

But I knew he had to stay. As horrible as it seemed, that place was where he needed to be. I think at the core of my heart I knew that, but I still couldn't help feeling as if I was, in a way, abandoning my son.

By the time I got home, my heart was sore and tired. The tears had stopped. They had run their course. In their place, shaking had settled in. I did my best to describe what had happened to Will. He did the only logical thing. He took me in his arms, and held me for a while.

Afterwards, I just sat at the kitchen table shaking. I couldn't control the trembling — I didn't remember that ever happening for so long before. I guess I was in a mild state of shock.

Will reassured me it was for the best. As far as we could tell, Joey was in the safest place he could be.

I knew Will was right. There was something serious lurking behind all this drama. And there seemed a real sadness underneath Joey's anger: the anger was just a protective coating. The doctors were his best hope. But I couldn't stop my mind from wandering. What if Joey wasn't okay after six to eight weeks? What would happen then? Would my son spend his life in a hospital? What if he really did end up hurting someone? Would they take him off to jail? The trembling was coming in spasms.

How could I help him? I was so exhausted. I felt like I was given some incredibly difficult task without an instruction manual. A manual should be delivered to parents along with each individual child. I really could have used one.

*   *   *

Now, when I think back to that month of October, I wonder how I did it. The day Joey was admitted, it was only three weeks to the opening day of our store. We were on schedule, but just barely. The renovation to the outside of the house wasn't finished. The store was partially set up, but not even close to ready. Every other day, a delivery came. Each time the courier landed a collection of boxes on our door step, we had to check the order off, price it, and find a way to display it. I know now that it saved me from landing in the hospital myself. I had no choice but to focus. The timing, although unbelievable then, was a good thing; it took my mind off the worrying.

In between visits on Wednesdays and weekends, when I wasn't at work, I let the store consume me. I tried to fill every corner of it with the antiques we had collected over the years. I made Chocolate Bouquets, Happy Hour Gift Towers, Spa Baskets, Baby Baskets — anything to keep my mind occupied. I searched for the right spot for all the little gifts, gourmet food and baskets, trying not to ruin the country feel of the shop. It saved me from my thoughts.

Soon, Joey's doctor explained what his condition was. We sat in a small office at the cottage beside Algonquin.

"It's called Dissociative Identity Disorder. You probably know it by its former name: Multiple Personality Disorder."

You would think that that diagnosis would have come as a hard knock to me. Actually, you'd think it would have sent me flat on my ass, but it didn't. It was the only thing I could think of that hadn't been ruled out. I guess I'd been somewhat mentally prepared for it.

"It's thought to be the mind's way of enduring, and psychologically surviving, horrendous experiences. Can you tell me anything about his childhood that would have been significantly difficult for him?"

"Umm, I left his dad when he was three. And he had a sister growing up, Jul, that... is his brother now. His name is Kip." The last part came out choppy. I didn't know what else to say.

"How did Joey adapt to his new brother?"

This part was easy to talk about. "Actually, Joey adjusted better than anyone. He believes everyone should be able to be who they are. There's a teacher where he goes to school that used to teach Jul and asked Joey how she was. His answer was, 'She's my brother now. His name is Kip and he's doing fine.'"

"Well, that doesn't sound like the key. And, although we'll ask him about the divorce, that in itself doesn't sound traumatic enough to cause this disorder. It usually develops when people are put under intense stress. It's common in terrorist victims. Natural disaster survivors sometimes suffer from it, too. When it develops in teens who haven't recently suffered any over-the-top stress, it's usually because they have buried a severe and prolonged childhood trauma that occurred at a sensitive stage in their development. There's a good chance that Joey coped with something in his childhood by disconnecting himself from what was going on."

It couldn't be. How could I have missed that?

The doctor filled the awkward silence. "What do you do when you are in a horrible situation? Well, if you can… you leave, or create a boundary, so that whatever's happening doesn't happen to you. That's what a child tries to do. When horror happens repeatedly, the part of the child's consciousness that is 'left behind' to deal with the abusive episodes becomes stronger and more defined, until it splits from the main personality altogether."

Horror? Jesus!

"Has he been through something out of the ordinary recently, even in the last few months? Something really stressful?"

It took me a few minutes to speak. "Umm… well, he found our dog lying in a pool of urine and vomit. She looked like she was dying. He really loves that dog. He was alone with her like that for quite a while."

The doctor put her fist up and rested her chin on it. "Hmmm… I suppose that could have been the trigger that brought his alters back, they're a coping mechanism."

I'd had no idea that my son's brain had been reacting as strongly as it had that day. On the outside, he'd looked like any broken-hearted teen would, wanting to help ease the pain of the pet he loved. I didn't know his emotions were intense enough to cause this.

But... at least we had something to work with — it had a name now. There must be a treatment.

"What can you do to help him?"

The doctor looked almost apologetic. "Unfortunately, there isn't a miracle drug. There really isn't any medication, per say, for this condition. He'll continue on antidepressants. The appearance of these alternate personalities... they're definitely stress-related... but that's all we can do with chemicals. We'll try to find what caused this to happen, search through his childhood, and help him work through those memories. We'll make him stronger so he can deal with stress better. That should help a lot."

I have a "Sybil." Dear Lord.

I needed to know more about this unthinkable condition. I needed to read. What I learned was fascinating. It's amazing how complex our brains are. When this happens, the different personalities that develop may hold different moods. One may have been created to hold the pain from being traumatized. Another personality may hold the rage that seemed unacceptable for the child to express at the time. Later in life a terribly difficult experience will sometimes bring the dormant alters back to the surface.

While researching, I also learned that some psychiatrists are skeptical of a DID diagnosis. It didn't surprise me. Doctors are trained in science, and scientists need to prove things to believe in them. It's often extremely difficult to prove or disprove recovered early memories, but with un-recovered memories... it's impossible.

Luckily, all the doctors Joey had been in contact with took his condition very seriously. *I certainly didn't doubt the realness of what was happening.* My son desperately wanted out of Algonquin Cottage. He wanted to come home. If he was controlling the situation, or whatever these skeptical doctors suggested, why would he continue the "show" when he knew full well it would keep him in that horrible place? It just didn't add up. This was real.

I wondered what had happened in his youth to cause this, what dreadful burden was Joey carrying? I'd specifically moved back to my small hometown in an attempt to keep my children safe. I shook my head at that thought.

Who had done what to my Joey?

Kip had told me that one of their dad's girlfriends (the one who had told Kip he was stupid, and that no one would ever love him) had done some very mean things to them. Kip said that when their dad was away, she would lock them in the basement, so she wouldn't have to spend time with them. Joey had no memory of that. Was it because he was only around five or six when it happened or was it because he had blocked it out? Was this woman capable of worse? He seemed to have very little memory of any of the years she'd been around.

Then there was the girlfriend before that one. She had made a hole in the crotch of each of her pajama bottoms, and as she and Earl sat watching TV every evening, she would "get herself ready for him," so that she would be raring to go at a moment's notice. Why had Earl told me that? That, in itself, is one hell of a good question, isn't it? Maybe he hoped it would make me feel jealous. It didn't. I did find it horrifyingly disturbing, though, when I thought back to those months. But not nearly as disturbing as wondering if that girl had been interested in more than just grown up men. *Jesus!*

Then there was the "sleeping over" problem. Somewhere in Joey's childhood his ability to sleep over at a friend's house had ended. He would pack his overnight bag, and head out happily, but, like clockwork, at bedtime, he would call home pleading for us to pick him up. Had something as innocent as a sleepover morphed into something unthinkable?

Did I need to relive every questionable moment of his childhood?

The research I'd done suggested repetitive abuse. That couldn't have happened from the odd sleep over. Really... if you think about it, something could have happened anywhere: while with a babysitter, at school, in a playground. Who knows? You see stories of that sort of thing every time you pick up the paper. People hide childhood abuse inflicted by teachers, other students, relatives, even priests, all the time, holding it somewhere deep inside until they are emotionally mature enough to talk about it. The concept was terrifying to think about. The haunting scenarios were endless.

Every child has a monster in his or her head. Mine had been under the bed; I couldn't dangle my feet over the edge for years, but Joey... my God, Joey had had a real monster. My eyes filled with tears every time that thought forced its way into my head. Could I have prevented whatever had happened? Somehow?

The key to healing was to retrieve those memories.

The doctors spent their time trying to locate experiences in Joey's missing childhood days, experiences that would have caused him to break into pieces. If they found them, they could work him through the memories. They also spent time teaching him stress-coping tools, so that life could be more manageable. Hopefully, the better he dealt with the mess life seems to throw from time to time, the less we would see the alters.

Yes... unfortunately, I said alters; plural — there were five of them.

I never again saw the younger, childlike version of Joey who had traveled in the car with me on the way to the hospital the day he was admitted. If I'd been able to choose, I would have welcomed him compared to a couple of the regulars. They had names at this point. Names were necessary to record and track their appearances.

The boy that I had witnessed first, on the day of the Fear Factor party, said his name was Troah. He seemed to be the most dominant. Well, maybe dominant is the wrong word. He was the one who appeared the most often (thankfully). He was shy, very cooperative and intelligent. He loved to learn — about anything. There was a peacefulness to him. He was pleasant, and usually wore a bashful smile on his face... and a bracelet. Troah's bracelet was a handmade woven one, the kind you would see in a native craft store or at a souvenir stand in Mexico. I'm not sure where it came from. Joey never wore a bracelet.

We also often saw Jay. He was a typical rebellious teen who didn't put up with anything from anyone. He did things his way, and he would tell you straight up that that was the way it was going to be. I could recognize him by the more mischievous or cynical smirk on his face, and the devil in his eyes.

I didn't see the others as often. One called himself Inner Strength. His name said it all. He would be around whenever something was difficult. I couldn't tell the difference between him and Joey until he spoke; then the strength and passion in his voice gave him away.

Mr. Giggles was the one I saw the least often. He had a weird sense of humor. I found him to be like a creepy clown, but he seemed to be somewhat of a peacemaker between the others. There were times when Joey could hear the alters communicating in his head, and when things got heated, Mr. Giggles was able to ease the tension.

The last alter was usually the cause of that tension. His name was The Darkness. He'd been the alter who got Joey admitted, him and his frightening "Run, Jamie, run." I couldn't see a difference between his look and Joey, except for something in his eyes. They were different from Joey's eyes. They were cold. I always knew when he was around; I could feel it. He was a very angry soul. You could almost reach out and touch the rage. I was always uneasy when he presented. Luckily, he was not around very often.

On days I went to visit my son, on my way into the city, as I neared Algonquin Cottage, I would find my thoughts repeating... *please let it be Joey, please let it be Joey.* That prayer was even stronger on the night of our first outing together. When I arrived, and saw it was Joey, I realized I'd been holding my breath. I smiled at my son.

It was such a relief when we got out of that strange round house. And Joey seemed different, as though living away from home had opened his eyes a bit. He truly appreciated my being there, taking him to a movie. He really missed being home. As they say, you don't realize what you have until it's gone. Hopefully he would be allowed to come home for weekends soon, but not yet.

I was so relieved that Joey was himself that night. I don't know what I would have done if he'd been one of the others when I'd shown up. I wasn't sure if I was comfortable with the idea of being out when he was like that. There was no way I would have taken The Darkness out. But it was okay; he was Joey. We chose a movie that appealed to us both, a comedy. We picked up some snacks, and settled in.

I had to work at enjoying the show, staying focused on the story, and I did enjoy it, but maybe not quite as much as I normally would. I was happy to be there with him, but I couldn't help feeling fidgety. Nervous. One of the alters could come out at any time. I really didn't want to have to face The Darkness ever again.

Hearing Joey laugh at the movie helped me to relax into my seat a bit.

About halfway through, things began to feel like they used to: the two of us out enjoying a good laugh. The movie we'd picked was cute; it was turning into a nice evening.

With about twenty minutes left, I saw movement out of the corner of my eye. I looked over at Joey. His head was down. When he raised it, he looked around, and said, "Where are we?"

My heart sank. I missed my son. I wanted to spend the *whole* evening with him, and I was pretty sure it was over. It was like a damned merry-go-round. I never knew when or where it would stop.

I leaned in towards him, and whispered, "Follow me." We went out into the hallway. I hesitated a second…"Joey?"

"No, Troah."

Damn it. I knew the answer, but asked it anyway. "You don't know where we are, do you?"

"No, what is this place?" he replied with lively curiosity.

I slid down the wall into a sitting position. "It's a movie theatre. Do you remember the movie we were watching?"

"No, I don't. Sorry, Jamie."

It was time to take him back. We'd had a little break, but it was time to go back. I wondered if I would ever get used to this, the alters popping up, seemingly out of nowhere.

And I couldn't help but pray, *Please God, don't make me have to get used to this!*

Chapter 30

Joey's first weekend home was, coincidentally, the weekend we opened the store. On Saturday morning, late October, while I drove into the city to pick Joey up at the cottage, Will opened our doors for the first time. I felt torn. This store had been our dream for roughly ten years. We'd spent months and months getting ready to open, and I really wanted to be there.

But Joey was more important. I guess I could have asked his dad to go and get him, but their father/son bond was pretty broken down at that point. Forgotten promises and degrading comments had created a distance between them.

Until the previous spring, the spring when Joey's trouble began, he had still made an effort to spend every other weekend at Earl's house. That had changed when Earl had taken yet another one of his southern vacations. You may have detected a slightly bitter tone there. Well, it's just that Earl went south three or four times each year. Whenever I let myself think about it, his self-indulgence really ticks me off, especially when he had never offered even one hundred dollars a month in child support. His favorite line was, "If the kids want to live with you, then you feed them."

During this particular sunny escape, Earl had left a key to his house with one of his new employees — someone he didn't know very well. Of course, Joey had a key, too. When Earl returned, and found that something valuable had gone missing while he was away, he accused Joey of stealing.

Joey was furious. Not only did his dad accuse him of being a thief, but he wouldn't listen when Joey explained that he wouldn't do something like that. Right then, Joey stopped his weekend visits. It had been one of the contributors to his stress the last summer. It was why I felt that the responsibility to pick him up was mine. I wanted Joey to be as relaxed as possible on his first weekend home. I wanted to protect him from any "Earl moments."

That Saturday was a strange day. I was on edge when we first arrived home. I was still uncomfortable with the possibility of alters popping up out of nowhere; I didn't know them well enough yet to know what to expect from them.

Joey went right up to his room as always to play video games or watch TV.

I slid open the door that divided our kitchen from the store, and walked in. "Did you have anybody?"

Will smiled softly. "Yeah, a few people. You didn't miss any real excitement, though."

I looked around to check my displays; moved a footed carnival bowl this way, adjusted the position of an old washboard.

After that, I really didn't know what to do with myself. It felt so strange to have Joey home again. I guess it was just the newness of everything, opening the store and having my son (who wasn't always my son) at home.

By mid-afternoon, my nerves were settling. Every time I talked with Joey, and he was Joey, I relaxed a bit more. Thankfully, I didn't see any of the alters that weekend. It was a nice couple of days — a peaceful break from the drama of the cottage.

I had thought that taking Joey back on Sunday afternoon would be an emotional ride for both of us, but he didn't seem overly upset to be going back. He wasn't anxious to be there again, but it didn't stir up the panic it had in the beginning. He'd made friends by then, and had found that he had the ability to put people who had problems at ease. The other kids liked to open up to him; they told him he was easy to talk to, and he found that he enjoyed helping people. I marveled at how being in this difficult place had taught him something important about himself. He possessed a gift that he hadn't known he had.

Gradually, the weeks passed with Joey coming home on weekends. His dad would visit him the odd Wednesday or Friday night. I think that hour or so was a bit uncomfortable for both of them, but at least the man was trying. Kip was living in the same city as the hospital so he would go by once in a while with one of Joey's favorite treats. Joey was always happy to see Kip. They'd had their moments when growing up, that was for sure, but their bond seemed to be strengthening.

During those weeks, Joey spent a considerable amount of time with professionals. The social workers and doctors dug for clues. They asked him about Earl, Kip, Will, me, everyone and everything they could think of, trying to find a way to shine light on the roots of his problem.

The idea of Earl being a problem for Joey's subconscious mind made sense to me. I had lived through his bullying. For years, I'd felt as if nothing I did was good enough for him. But I could walk away, he was only my husband; not so easy for a son to walk away from his dad. I didn't think that that type of emotional abuse could cause something like this. I didn't blame Earl for Joey's problem, but I sure wanted to at times — him or one of his girlfriends.

Other times, I hoped it wasn't something that had happened at Earl's house. When I thought back, I felt guilt about letting the kids spend so much time with their dad. Maybe I should have fought it in court? I was never sure how many shady people were sharing their time. I didn't suspect Earl of doing anything seedy, but some of his friends made me squirm.

But I had made an effort to be fair. I mean, he *was* their father, and to be honest, I appreciated some time to myself. Now, the thought of that "me-time" made me feel sick. I felt that if something *had* happened there, it was partially my fault. Moms can't seem to help but blame themselves, I guess, but boy, did I hope it was irrational blame.

At times, Joey was sure that Kip had been the main cause of the pain that drove him towards his disorder. He remembers being little, and wondering why his sister would embarrass him in front of people... why she seemed constantly fired-up mad at him. In his words, "All I knew was — she was my sister and she absolutely hated me."

I guess Kip took his jealousy of Joey's body out on him at times. To me it just looked like a sister trying to deal with her pain-in-the-butt brother. And Joey was good at pushing buttons. The combination had been explosive at times. That coupled with Joey's highly sensitive nature... who knows? That's what the doctors were for — to figure it all out.

Joey's team continued their search for weeks. If there was a specific pattern of events that had caused what he was going through, and they could find it, they might be able to help him face it. If they were lucky, they could help him let go of it. If there was something in his past that had hurt him enough to do this to him, they said that working through it might be enough to let him heal.

Throughout my life, I'd heard over and over that "time heals" — not always. The deepest parts of our minds are not always subject to the usual laws of time. Maybe the power of wounds can even increase with time, in some cases.

Whatever the cause was, the professionals were having a hard time putting their finger on anything significant. Then again, I thought, *if* the cause of this condition was memories that were painful enough to block out, then they where painful enough to be afraid of. If they hadn't convinced Joey that the benefits of facing those memories outweighed the risks, then maybe his subconscious was more comfortable leaving them right where they were... buried.

I was trying to smother a thought of my own those days. Maybe the turmoil of living in a house turned upside down had been the final straw in a stressful adolescence. They had said that this disorder was "usually" caused by traumatic childhood events. What, besides trauma, could cause it? I was afraid to ask. One thing I did know, there was definitely a side of Joey that was annoyed with the role of the importance the store had taken in my life. *That* had come out in a meeting at the hospital.

I'd been invited to an update meeting with Joey's team. Will hadn't come with me that day. It wasn't a Monday, and Monday was the only day our store was closed. Our new endeavor was not earning enough for additional employees; we were it.

The meeting was scheduled to be held in one of the other strange round buildings beside Algonquin. Joey, his main doctor, the social worker assigned to him, the chief nurse on duty, and I were all sitting around a table in a small, hot room.

Dr. H got up to open a window. "The design of these buildings sure doesn't allow the air to circulate. I hate to close the door, but I guess we should get started."

She proceeded to fill me in on Joey's progress. It didn't take long; they seemed to be traveling a slow road. Then they began talking about subjects that I suspected were the real reason I was there. I was pretty sure my job was to fill in the gaps. Joey wasn't a talker. They were probably having a hard time getting information out of him.

They touched on all the biggies — his relationship with each one of us, how he liked school, if he went out much with friends. If it was a question that they thought a mom could knowledgably answer, they asked it.

Somewhere in the middle of it, Joey went limp. It was now obvious that this limp stage meant Joey was leaving us. When he came out of his slumped-over ten seconds, the alter that arrived was angry. I think it was The Darkness. It must have been him because the room instantly filled with tension.

He slid down in his chair with his arms crossed, and his head lowered a bit, so that his stare was through his tensed eyebrows. He was obviously impatient and annoyed.

Dr. H glanced at him briefly, but turned back to me in an effort to keep the meeting going. "So Jamie, I understand you're renovating your home?"

"Yes, we've been getting ready to open an antique and gift shop in the front of our house."

The alter venomously sneered, "And God help anything that gets in the way of Your. Precious. Store."

It was like he had reached out and inflicted some sort of very efficient martial arts movement, one effective chop to my throat. I was stunned, and unable to answer.

I didn't want to let him get to me, though. As I recovered, I said, "You know, if there's something you need to say about the store, you can talk to me about it. I am not going to love you any less if you do, no matter what it is. Just get it out."

His face spread into a crafty smile. "Would you like that?" Then he just sat, leaning back with his arms crossed, glaring at me.

I tried my hardest to hold myself together, but I couldn't handle the feel of his rage. I attempted to blink back the tears, but they slowly slid down my face. I brushed them away, not wanting to show my emotions. I knew this alter would see it as weakness… but I couldn't stop those damned tears.

I had become one of my antique quilts. At a glance, I still appeared to be all in one piece, but here and there the stitching had let go, leaving my feelings to roam around into places they shouldn't. My edges had become well worn and frayed into dangling bits, and any little tug seemed to open a new, fragile hole.

The doctor had been taking notes, but now looked from me to the alter. She turned to the chief nurse. "Call someone to come over and get him... he needs to go back to Algonquin." He had overstepped the boundaries of acceptability, and she would not allow it.

A few minutes later, a young man came into the room, took the alter's arm, and stood him up. The alter began to stand, but then slid back down into the chair limply, while Joey returned. As my son's eyelids lifted, he saw I was crying.

Rubbing his arm, trying to ease the numbness that always came with my son's return, he looked at me with regret in his eyes and said, "Ah no, what did I say?" He looked from me to the doctor, and then returned his gaze to me. "I was gone, Mom. What did I say? Mom, I'm so sorry."

I couldn't find words at that moment. The young man was standing him up again by then. Joey's frustrated voice was more gentle than usual. "Whatever it was, I didn't mean it, Mom. Don't listen to it. It wasn't me!"

As he was taken from the room, Joey's pleading eyes didn't leave mine. He was obviously upset that he'd made me cry. All I could think about was that powerful line. I had no way of knowing if there was something to those words, "God help anything that gets in the way of your precious store."

Joey did hate change.

It was horrible... thinking that I may have done something to contribute to his breakdown. I didn't want to consider that. But I knew it had given everyone in the room something to think about.

I'm sure they did pursue the possibility that it was the sheer stress of that summer that had caused his condition, but they mustn't have uncovered enough to keep them on that trail because, after that day, the topic of the store was never brought up again. Nothing about our relationships or everyday life seemed to be setting off flares for his team. They were going to have to dig deeper — into his hidden memories.

Chapter 31

To reach Joey's hidden memories, his team needed help. So, at several weeks into his stay at Algonquin, Joey met with Dr. E. Her experience and training made her the city's specialist in Dissociative Identity Disorder.

Joey's first appointment with her had been scheduled for a Wednesday. I was headed to the hospital that day, but not because I had been invited to meet her. That wasn't the case. The meeting was for her and Joey to get to know each other. I wouldn't be involved. No, my reason for heading into the city was to visit. I had told Joey that we would go out for dinner, his choice, and then if he felt like it, we would do some Christmas shopping. It was mid-November, and I always like to get an early start.

I'd finished work at my day job sometime between four-thirty and five. As I got into my car, my mind was all over the place. During the drive to the city, in the gloomy November dusk, my thoughts battled each other. I felt a mixture of excitement and fear.

The excitement was brought by hope. Hope that this new doctor would find the cause, and unlock the answer that no one else seemed able to get at. The fear... well, the fear was easy to understand. I worried about how Joey would deal with whatever *was* uncovered. Was she about to lift a lid that Joey had struggled to keep tight for years? It was one thing to find what was beneath it all; it was a whole other thing to help him through it. Not knowing how horrible the secret might be made for a strange mixture of emotions. It had left me on edge a lot during the previous weeks.

Secret Selves

All I could do was hope. I wanted so badly to get my son back to a normal life. No, more than a normal life — a happy life. I'd always had this underlying nagging feeling that Joey was not a happy soul. Now I knew it was true. But what could I do to help? It was like seeing your child with an unbearable, excruciating toothache that made you wince just watching, and not being able to find a dentist who could fix it. I was completely frustrated with the lack of progress.

I think one of my biggest personality flaws back then was my obsession with fixing things. I was so preoccupied with results, always looking ahead, always trying to work towards the best possible ending. I would try to push and steer things in the direction I thought they needed to go. There was a good reason why Will had called me "The Fixer" at times. He was more the type who would just let life happen, and he could see my obsession with making things right. But I had no idea what "right" was for Joey. Maybe it was finding a menacing memory, and dealing with it. Maybe it was simply teaching him how to cope with stress.

Until his problem surfaced, I used to think my fixation on the outcome of things was an honorable quality — to strive for the best possible result in everything. I would think our little family problems to death. I couldn't see the obvious fact that there were times when I wouldn't be able to figure out what the *best* solution was, and worse yet, sometimes I would think I'd found it, but my conclusion might be miserably wrong.

As I drove towards the city, I thought about times that had gradually awakened me from my vanity. With Kip, I'd thought I'd be sheltering him from pain if we hid his change from our small town — wrong. I was causing extra pain by appearing to not accept him for who he was. I'd thought that making him seem a bit more girly when he was young would help him fit in — wrong. It just made him feel many times more uncomfortable in his own body. And, on top of that, it had made him resent me. I had only wanted him to be happy, but I had added to his pain.

So, what's a mom to do? You just want the best for your kids. The answer was slowly becoming more apparent to me. Don't try to steer everything; just do the right thing today. For that day, I would give my son a break from his problems, and the problems of the kids who were sharing his life. I would count on the doctors to do their jobs. Hope would be okay. It might even get me through this. Worry wouldn't help anything. Today, I would just have a nice evening with my son.

When I arrived at Algonquin Cottage, Joey greeted me with a friendly, enthusiastic smile. I appreciated his eagerness, but at the same time, it made me nervous. My son was usually a pretty reserved person. He didn't show his emotions very often. When I saw him smiling enthusiastically as I walked towards him, I hoped that living with other kids his age was bringing him out of his shell, but my gut wasn't convinced. I tried not to show my apprehension and as casually as I could, asked, "Joey?"

"No, it's Troah. How are you, Jamie?"

Damn. So much for having a nice evening with my son. My voice came out somewhat less perky than his. "I'm fine, Troah. How are you?"

Troah brightly replied, "I'm fine." Then his face became a bit more serious looking, not totally clouded over, just less carefree than it usually was. He reached into his pocket and said, "Joey asked me to give you this." He held out a piece of paper. Apparently Joey and Troah could communicate now… did that mean he was getting better, or getting worse?

I reached for what appeared to be a folded-up drawing. It didn't make sense. Joey didn't draw, ever. Confusion slowed my thoughts as I unfolded the paper. On the other side of the drawing, the side folded in, was a handwritten note.

"Dear Mom,

Sorry I'm not there. I needed Troah to come out today. It was a really rough day. I hope you don't mind visiting with him tonight. He really enjoys spending time with you.

I'll see you soon.
Love Joey"

I looked up from the note. Troah was looking at me, smiling shyly again. "Joey wrote that before he left. I drew the picture for you."

He was so harmless, and so good natured. I was disappointed, but I really did appreciate the gesture. I tried my best to sound genuine, all the while trying to hide that I was blinking back a couple little tears. "Thank you, Troah."

I hesitated a second and then, "I'm going to go talk to the nurse for a minute."

I was wondering what I should do. I'd never been greeted by an alter on visiting day before. Did we have to stick around when he was like this? Or could I take Troah out? I had to find the nurse.

"Excuse me, I was planning to take Joey out for dinner tonight, but...umm, he's Troah right now. Should I still take him?"

"Hi Jamie. You're quite welcome to take him out... as long as you're comfortable with the idea."

Although a little surprised at this answer, I was relieved. I still wanted to take him out. I didn't want to stay at the cottage. I didn't know much about the other kids who were staying there. Joey had told me that most of them were deeply depressed, and that three had attempted suicide. I didn't know what the boy who barked suffered from. Really, it didn't matter; they were all there because they needed help. I felt like an outsider when I was around them, and I liked giving Joey a break from the tension that filled the strange house.

Besides, Troah could disappear at any time. There was no standard length to Joey's absences. I could get my son back soon, or I could be with Troah all night. I hoped it wasn't the latter. I wanted to talk to Joey. I wanted to know he was okay.

It wasn't that I disliked Troah. Actually, after the initial discomfort with the fact that an alter had taken over, each time I saw him, he stirred my curiosity. He was like a newborn baby. He didn't understand anger or hate. He didn't pass judgment on anything. He absorbed knowledge like a thick, thirsty sponge. Since the night I met him at the Fear Factor party, he had developed so much. He was still shy in some situations, but you could see him always watching and listening, soaking up every experience.

He was like an underdeveloped intellectual. I remember chatting with him one day. "I had the weirdest dream last night, Troah. It was so crazy; there must be a full moon."

In a completely serious voice, I heard, "Jamie, I don't know that lunar activity affects dreaming."

Lunar activity? That was a phrase that Joey would never have used.

Troah fascinated me. If I had been forced to pick from all of them, I would definitely have chosen to be with Troah. I had spent some time with Jay. (Strange how that alter had said his name was Jay, the same name that I had tried to force on Kip.) Jay was a fierce-hearted teen with an arrogance or cockiness that annoyed me. He always treated me with a reasonable amount of respect, but he wouldn't hesitate to take a passionate stand if something rubbed him even a little the wrong way. It was like he was always ready to pounce. It made me uncomfortable. I hadn't spent much time with the rest of them. The Darkness scared me, that much I knew of him. The other two were still a mystery. But Troah was easy to get along with. If the nurse thought an outing was okay, I'd give it a try.

I walked back towards Troah, and said, "So, would you like to go and get something to eat?"

He lifted his shoulders and tilted his head down a bit, and in a quiet voice, said, "I guess so, if you think it'll be okay?"

I smiled gently. "I think it'll be just fine, Troah. Get your jacket, and we'll get going."

We got settled in the car and then, out of habit, I asked, "So where would you like to go?"

Troah looked lost. I'd forgotten he hadn't experienced a restaurant yet. He hadn't been out in public much at all. He was quiet for a minute, and then said, "Where would Joey want to go?"

"Well, Joey likes the sandwiches at Tim Horton's. They're made on dense sub buns. They're pretty good."

"I would like to try one, Jamie."

"Good... we have a plan."

As I drove, I answered questions.

"What are those lights for?" He was referring to the traffic lights.

"How do people learn to drive these cars?"

"What are all these big buildings for?"

As usual, Troah's brilliant young mind was always curious, always questioning.

As we entered Timmy's, I explained, "We have to order our food at the counter. You can either come with me or wait at a table."

He looked at the counter, then down at the tables, then at me, his eyes nervous, a bit frightened even.

I pointed to a table. "Why don't you sit down here and relax? It won't take me long."

When I returned with the food, Troah was sunk down in his seat looking very uneasy, as if he wanted to crawl under the table and hide.

"What's wrong?"

His head motioned towards another table. "Those people keep staring at me."

I followed the line of his sight to a table of teenagers. They were chatting and laughing. "It has nothing to do with you, Troah. People just tend to look at other people when they're out in public." I nodded to reassure him. "It's okay."

I didn't seem to be convincing him. Their periodic gaze had completely unnerved him.

I then realized that they might be looking at him a little more than usual because of the freaked-out look on his face. "Here, switch seats with me."

From my seat he had his back to them, and gradually he started to relax.

It was incredible to me. The other personalities seemed to have a full memory of everyday things, but to Troah, everything was new. It was very curious.

We finished our sandwiches. I'd gotten him Joey's favorite: double bacon, lettuce and mayo on toasted white. He enjoyed every mouthful, asking what the different flavors were, and what the delicious white sauce was.

I wondered what we should do next. I'd planned to take Joey to the huge, nearby toy store. They had an impressive electronics section, and I thought I could watch what Joey seemed interested in to get ideas for Christmas. It wouldn't work with Troah. He wouldn't know anything about the hot new stuff that seventeen-year-olds were into. But it was an hour or so before visiting hours were over, and I really couldn't think of anything else to do with him. We might as well go. If I was lucky, maybe Joey would come back when we got there.

I didn't get lucky. Troah and I walked around the massive toy store, his eyes wide, as he took it all in. We entered the electronics section. I hoped all the new games and equipment would encourage Joey back. Still no luck. Then the unexpected happened.

Troah leaned into me, and said quietly, "Jamie, I'm getting a little tired. Do you think we could go back now?"

I think he was a bit overwhelmed.

Why not? I had figured I could at least pick up a CD, or a movie for Kip while we were there, but my heart just wasn't in it. We left the store, and got back into the car.

On the way back to the cottage, I saw Troah go limp. He lifted his head as the car entered the hospital property, and immediately started rubbing his left arm. "Hi, Mom." Then he grimaced. "The numbness gets a little worse each time... how long was I gone this time?"

"I don't know. You were gone when I got to the cottage. Troah had your favorite bacon sandwich for dinner."

Joey shook his head. "Dammit, I hate it when they get all the good stuff."

I offered him a smile. "I got you something," and handed him a bag. While at Timmy's I'd picked up some of his favorite cookies for when he came back.

He smiled back at me. "Thanks, Mom."

I wanted to spend a few minutes with my son before leaving. "So... how was your visit with Dr. E?"

"It was okay."

"Did you like her?"

"Yeah, she seemed okay, but we didn't get very far."

It was just like Joey to only give me the basic information. Not getting anywhere, I changed the subject. "Troah gave me this note. What did you mean by 'It's been a really rough day'?"

He gave me his usual vague-ish type answer. "A lot went on today. One of the kids was really upset, and it set some of the others off."

Vague was probably better in this case. The more I knew about daily life at the cottage, the more I wished he didn't have to be there. There were constant stressors lurking in the unusual round house, and the effects were starting to show. Joey had started smoking regularly. A couple of years back, he'd thought smoking was a totally disgusting habit. But everyone at the cottage smoked — all the staff, all the patients. Everyone seemed to need this coping mechanism.

There were certainly things that Joey had dealt with that would push people to relieve stress any way they could. My poor son had followed a trail of blood one day. At the end of the sinister red drops, he'd found his very close friend, Allie, bleeding into a puddle on the floor. That would probably start me smoking too.

Joey lit a cigarette as we said goodbye that night. Before I headed back home, he gave me a big hug. That was new too. He'd started showing affection again. I was unbelievably grateful for that. I really needed those hugs. It was one little bright moment that I could look forward to when I was finding the presence of the alters, and the lack of progress, so hard.

On the drive home, I thought about the evening I'd spent with Troah. I wondered how long it would take them to find the secret that hid behind all this craziness.

In the meantime, Joey seemed to be able to completely wall himself off from the world whenever the need was there. Whenever his emotions were too strong, or his day too difficult, the appropriate alter for the situation seemed to take over.

So that Joey didn't have to feel. So that Joey was protected.

Chapter 32

"She's gorgeous, Mom. You should see her, she could be a model. Wait... she gave me her picture." Joey dug into his pocket for his wallet and pulled out a photo. "And she tells me *everything*. She says I'm a really good listener and that she can tell I care."

I looked down at a beautiful brunette who had a knack for seducing the camera. "Wow, she *is* gorgeous. So... is there a romance budding here?" I handed back the photo.

He shook his head. "That's not allowed. But we spend a lot of time together. We talk *a lot*."

"What's her name?"

"Angelina."

*   *   *

As the weeks passed at Algonquin Cottage, Joey seemed to have a mixture of feelings about the place. There were moments when he appeared to accept that he needed to live there for a while. And he liked the other kids. There was Angelina and Allie, and he'd become buddies with several of the guys. He told me that he knew he would miss everyone when it came time to say goodbye.

Most days, however, his temporary life drove him nuts. On a calm day, life at the cottage involved some schoolwork, a group session on a topic like coping with stress or dealing with anger, some one-on-one time with a counselor and some free time.

Not a day would go by without someone either being upset and crying, or angry and ranting. At its worst, a day at Algonquin meant total lockdown because one of the kids had been found covered in blood from their attempted suicide. There were strict safety rules, but every once in a while, a desperate kid figured a way around them. The amount of stress Joey was exposed to every day in those two months was enough to push a stable person over the edge.

Then there were the nights. Even sleeping was a challenge. Josh (the barker) was in the room next to Joey. In the middle of the night he would sneak into Joe's room, flick on the lights, and run out. Without fail, it would wake Joey up. While listening to Josh giggle next door, Joey would get out of bed, and turn the light off, only for Josh to sneak in, and do it again minutes later. Joey would finally get fed up, and confront him, saying, "Josh, you can't keep doing this, man. I'm really tired right now. I have to sleep. You have to stop... okay?!"

That would usually do it.

As Joey would just finally be getting back into a nice, deep sleep, a flashlight would shine in his face. Every night, a nurse and her glaring beam of light would visit to make sure each teen was breathing. This would infuriate Joe.

After several weeks of it, he couldn't take it any longer and, when blinded by the flashlight, began to rant, "I'm not suicidal! I've never been suicidal, so I'm *going* to be breathing... *every* night! So stop checking! If I were suicidal, I would wait until you checked on me, and *then* I'd do it, okay... so stop!!!"

The next day would start off with a staff member being annoyed because he couldn't drag himself out of bed on time. Those rough nights definitely did not help him to cope with the daily stress.

Finally, at the beginning of December, I heard the news I'd waited seven weeks to hear; Joey would be released in a week. I was so grateful. I wanted him back at home, away from the tension. It didn't seem at all like a healing environment to me.

Dr. E, the specialist whom he had been introduced to, had left for an extended Christmas holiday, so therapy with her had been put on hold. And his team had admitted that they still didn't know why he had broken into pieces. He might as well come home.

He wasn't leaving the hospital completely, however. For a while, he would visit for two or three days a week. It was called the partial program. He would have a new team assigned to him at one of the other round houses, to gauge his progress as he transitioned back into regular life. We would drive him into the city in the morning, and pick him up at the end of the afternoon. When he was ready, after six to eight weeks of partial, he would be completely cut loose from the hospital, but continue to see Dr. E for however long was necessary.

Returning to high school would be part of the transition back to "normal life." I booked an appointment to meet the vice-principal, and explain the situation. He wasn't totally in the dark; Joey's social worker had contacted him already, but I really wasn't sure exactly how much he knew.

The December afternoon of that meeting seemed like an especially dark day. To a sun lover, it always seems like there are months of overcast days that start in November and they're always a challenge for me to cope with.

That year seemed particularly gloomy. It didn't help my efforts to try to stay positive. I was having a hard time convincing myself not to worry about Joey's return to school. His alters were still showing up regularly, and I wondered what the kids in his class would say to him, and how much strain what they did say would cause. By then, it was obvious just how stress-related his condition was.

I walked toward the high school that day thinking that Joey should probably go back to half of his schedule. It would lessen the load that he would be struggling to control. There wasn't much chance of him getting his credits anyway. His teachers had sent some schoolwork to the cottage, but having missed two out of three months of the semester, there was little chance he would catch up. It would be especially hard, considering he'd be away at the partial program for several days a week for the rest of the term.

I was greeted by the vice-principal when I entered the high school. He led me into a tiny meeting room. Around a small table sat the principal, and a rep from the school board. We shook hands. Joey's social worker was on speaker phone.

I braced myself, trying to prepare for "That Look." The look that bluntly said, "You don't really expect me to be able to process this information, do you? It's just too much!" Telling people about Kip… and now explaining Joey's complicated problem, had led to an intimate relationship between me and That Look.

The vice-principal began the meeting. "So, what can we do for you today, Jamie?"

I took a deep breath. "I'm not sure how much you all know. I'm sure you know that Joey has spent some time at the psychiatric hospital. He's ready to come back to school a couple days a week. But there's a problem. He has several alternate personalities and they still present themselves. His condition is called Dissociative Identity Disorder."

Silence for a minute.

I could see that they hadn't been given much from the social worker. Their friendly expressions faded. They nervously avoided eye contact.

The vice-principal slowly started asking questions.

"How often can we expect to see an alternate personality?"

I needed another deep breath. I slowly exhaled, and said, "There's no answer to that question. We never know when one will come out."

"How long does it usually last?"

"It varies from half an hour to almost a day. Most of the time, it seems to be a couple of hours."

The principal just sat listening with a blank expression, looking as if I had just recited a limerick in a foreign language. Yep, there it was... That Look.

The social worker explained that Joey was progressing and described the partial program.

Then, I brought up the topic of classes. "He's going to be struggling to catch up. I think a half schedule is a good idea, at least for the rest of this term."

The vice-principal seemed to be trying to reassure me. "That sounds like a good idea, Jamie. Any suggestions on what two classes he should attend?"

The principal came to life at this point. "How about one of the shop classes?"

My mouth dropped open in disbelief. *Had she even opened his file?* Joey hadn't chosen one shop class in three whole years of courses. And she thought that plunking him in one that was already half finished would work? This woman was the principal?! *Jesus!*

I held back the urge to shake my head, and ask her if she had seen *any* of Joey's school record. "Joey really has no interest in shop. Maybe he should just continue with the two least demanding of the four courses he's already started?" It seemed like simple logic to me.

The vice-principal agreed, "Yes, that's a good idea. What two classes are his best?"

Finally a question that I had an easy answer for. "He's pretty good in Math and he likes Introduction to Entrepreneurship."

"Good. It's a plan then."

I called the cottage that night, and asked Joey what he thought. To him, it was as good a plan as any. I figured the whole "going back" thing must be making him nervous. As usual, from his voice, I couldn't really tell if he was uneasy about it. He did want me to join him on the first day of school, when his two teachers would be briefed, though. It was a definite sign he was nervous.

Joey's first day of school was December twelfth, and to add an extra element of strange to an already uncomfortable time in his life, nature decided to throw in an ice storm. That meant the buses wouldn't be running and the school would be more than half deserted. It was not exactly business as usual, but maybe it was a good thing. I knew rumors were circling about Joey's condition. The young guys he worked with after school at the grocery store had asked me questions when I shopped there. On this "snow day", Joey could ease his way into returning to class without the full force of a school filled with curious stares.

We started the day in the vice-principal's office. Around a small table in his close quarters, he assembled the two teachers involved, himself, me and Joey.

Suddenly, I realized that sitting at a table while his problem was explained might put Joey a little on edge. I looked over at him, and asked, "Joey, do you want to stay while I explain things, or do you want to wait in the hall?"

Without thinking, he answered, "I'll stay," but I had barely introduced myself, and said why I was there when he changed his mind, and interrupted with, "Well... maybe I'll wait outside."

As he left, his teachers casually discussed how weird snow days were at the school.

I took my cue, and as Joey closed the door leaving us alone, said, "Well, it's about to get a little weirder."

Blank faces looked back at me as I told the two stunned teachers about Joey's problem with DID. There it was again: That Look. I was getting used to it. People were never sure how to react. They seemed to want to cover their expression of surprise: my guess was to avoid offending me. Then they usually appeared unsure just what they should substitute in place of their puzzled look. The result was usually a lack of expression, sometimes accompanied by their mouth hanging open.

As the teachers pieced their thoughts back together, they asked a string of questions, and then the vice-principal invited Joey back into the room. The teachers politely tried to sound convincing as they told him they were looking forward to having him back in their class, then they wished him luck.

I have to admit that although I was really trying to live in the moment, to not stress about tomorrow, and appreciate that Joey was back home, pesky little worries were definitely slipping through my screen. Joey seemed more comfortable with the idea of regular classes than I did. I couldn't stop wondering how he would manage at school when Jay and Troah were still making regular appearances.

Joey seemed to manage fine through it all. Jay would come out when Joey felt uncomfortable or intimidated by something, and Troah would arrive for a particularly difficult lesson or assignment. Everyone knew about Joey's condition, and he was fairly open to questions from his peers.

I only remember one person who got on Joey's nerves a bit. He was a good friend of Joe's, and happened to be in the same Math class. The two of them would be working away in class, and this guy would lean over every once in a while and say, "Joey?"

When Joey answered, "Yeah, what?" the boy would simply say, "Just checking."

Joey found it funny at first, his crazy sense of humor enjoyed someone making light of the situation. But there are always limits.

After answering this question over and over, he finally became fed up, and got mad at the guy. His friend didn't stop doing it completely, but slowed it down to a reasonable amount. Other than that bit of annoyance, the transition went well.

I managed fine too, although it was hard to carry on as if things were normal. While at work, I wondered every day what was happening, and how he was making out at school. I decided to start a journal to track the appearances of the alters; maybe it would be helpful to the team at partial. I felt I had to do *something*. So at night I would try to get details out of my son: never an easy task. The little information I was able to get, I recorded.

According to my journal, Joey's first days of "normal" life went like this:

> *Mon, Dec. 12: Only one short event. Joey was outside having a cigarette, and he said that "The Darkness" wanted to burn Joey's arm with a cigarette again, but Mr. Giggles came out and stopped him. Mr. Giggles seems to protect Joey.*
>
> *Tue, Dec. 13: Joey was very tired. He said Jay came out at school but didn't last too long. Joey slept all evening.*
>
> *Wed, Dec. 14: Joey spent the day at partial, and then went to Kip's to spend the night — No events that Joey could remember.*

Thurs, Dec. 15: Joey spent the day at partial, and Earl went to pick him up. On the way home (around 3 p.m.), Joey dissociated into Troah. During the drive home, Earl began to ask Troah some questions about why his relationship with Joey had deteriorated. This seemed to make Troah uncomfortable because he asked Jay for help. The two alters shared the drive with Earl. Jay is very assertive, and Troah is very diplomatic. I think it took both personalities to deal with the situation. Jay made Troah tell Earl all the reasons for the distance between Earl and Joey. Troah was needed for diplomacy.

By the time I got home from work, Jay was with us (Troah was gone). Jay stayed for the whole evening.

Fri, Dec. 16: (Snow day — no school) Jay was still with us all day. Mr Giggles would blurt out comments here and there.

Sat, Dec. 17: No events. Joey did express that it was very difficult to live like this — missing whole days, or periods of his life, and not knowing what happened, or what he did.

Sun, Dec. 18: No events. Joey slept a lot, and commented how tired he was all the time. I asked him if he thought his depression was coming back, and he said, "Maybe."

Mon, Dec, 19: Joey dissociated at school in the afternoon. He woke up at home. We're not sure which alter it was. Later in the evening, I took him to a video store. I waited in the car while he was in picking out a movie, but then thought I would quickly pop into a store across the street. This is something that normally wouldn't bother Joey. When Joey came out, he saw that the car was there, but that I wasn't in it. I got to the car minutes later, and he was Jay. Jay said that Joey was scared that someone had taken me, and he had become very upset. Joey's never shown this type of concern before. It seemed very extreme. When we arrived back home, Joey came back.

Tue, Dec. 20: Troah came out during 1st period. By lunch time, Troah was *gone, and Jay was with us. Jay stayed for the rest of the day.*

This was our "normal" for the next few weeks.

Chapter 33

During those weeks, every once in a while, I would lie in bed in the dark, tears splashing onto the sheets. I'd wonder if Joey would *ever* be better again, and if I was strong enough to deal with this broken child. Would the day ever come when I could breathe easily again, and know he was okay?

In the daytime, I would stay strong, holding my family together any way I could. But at night, in the darkness, when no one could see, I would let everything out.

During those moments of doubt, as I rested on my wet pillow after the release, I would talk myself into an attempt to relax. The only thing that seemed to help was a technique I'd read about in *Simple Abundance*.

In the book my friends had bought for me, the book that allowed me to accept Jul as Kip, the author encourages people to keep a "Gratitude Journal." She has a beautiful blank book, and each night before she goes to bed, she writes down five things about that day that she is grateful for.

I have to admit that I didn't go out and buy a beautiful book to write in every day; maybe I should have. What I did do was use the notion on the hard days, the days that seemed hopeless, days I just wanted over, so I could rest from it all. On those days, as I lay in bed after a good cry, I would try to think of five things that I was grateful for. If those five things came easily, I would try five more. I didn't usually get past the third or fourth "five things" before I fell asleep. I would wake up the next day, puffy eyed, but ready to give life another go.

Those moments of gratitude seemed to take away some of the fear and pain. Some days my list started out simply — I was grateful for my health, the love of my husband, his health, Kip's strength and determination, and the fact that Joey wasn't living in Algonquin Cottage any more.

Sometimes I would get to the little things, like the sunshine that had peeked out that day, a lunch break spent laughing with my friends, a piece of maple sugar candy that just melted in my mouth, a good glass of red wine with dinner, a movie that made me feel.

They're all important: the big things, and the little things.

The author of *Simple Abundance* says that "Real life isn't always going to be perfect or go our way," (that's for sure) "but the recurring knowledge of what *is* working in our lives can help us not only survive but surmount our difficulties." It seemed to work for me. Remembering the good in my life gave me a little added strength, especially on those "less than perfect" days.

I used any little activity I could to get through that part of my life, and the weeks of partial gradually slipped by. Will and I took turns with the trips to and from the program, twice a day, a few days a week, each of us doing our share. Earl even gave us a break once every couple of weeks.

The one nice thing about all the driving was that Joey and I had a lot of one-on-one time to chat. It was nice, most of the time. Like any teenager, there were days that Joey drove me so crazy that I could have pulled the car over to the side of the road, and clobbered him right there! But in general, the time together was a good thing.

Out of the blue one day, on one of those trips home from partial, Joey looked at me, and said, "You know, Mom, you are the best parent I know… if it wasn't for you, I think I'd be in jail somewhere by now, or dead."

It caught me totally off guard. I was the tough parent. I was the one who forced him to sit at the kitchen table every night for years doing his homework. I was the one who nagged him to write thank you notes for birthday gifts because he didn't like calling people on the phone. I was the one who made him do his own laundry. Yet Joey sat there saying that he thought I was the best parent he knew. It made all those trips to the city worthwhile.

There were times, however, when the worry monster still haunted me. I wanted Joey to get better so badly. And I wondered, on some days, what people thought of me as a parent. I had two very different, somewhat "less than normal" kids.

Would people ridicule my ability to raise children? Would they somehow blame me for our challenges, and label me a bad parent? Maybe they would, but I tried to tell myself that people who didn't share our lives weren't important. This new label, Joey's label for me, that's what it was all about. How my children felt about me was the important thing. That label of "being the best parent he knew"... I could live with that. It was something I could hang on to, and save for the times I needed it.

I don't think Joey ever knew, until he read this book, how much that one phrase meant to me. It had the power to take me to a peaceful place for years.

On days when I needed to relax, I would sit in my favorite rocking chair, and remember. Reliving the moment of Joey's classic line in my mind helped me to let all the tightness leave my body. It was a simple moment; only a couple unprepared sentences. But they were such powerful words. When I thought of them, I would close my eyes, focus on the feeling of my body swinging back and forth in my rocker, and I'd start to relax.

My thoughts would move on to times in my life that had moved me. There is so much beauty and love around us, but we rarely take the time to slow down enough to appreciate it, to remember it.

I'd think about a day I spent with my dad when I was a kid. He had taken me for a drive in the country to look for places he could paint. We drove around, getting out of the car once in a while to appreciate the scenery, taking a snapshot or two of the view. I remember sitting down at a picnic table at the edge of the road, overlooking a lake. We sat watching the water ripple in the breeze, eating peanut butter sandwiches and drinking Pepsi. It's a wonderful memory, one that gives me peace. We need to use those simple memories… slow down and appreciate what we've had, and what we have now.

I'm sure there isn't a woman alive who doesn't wish for a simpler life. Well, I didn't have a simple life, that was for sure, but taking a few simple moments every once in a while to remember sure did help to make the rest manageable.

Chapter 34

Just smile, Jamie. At least try to smile, a little.

The kitchen was filled with my family. The smell of turkey gave the room that holiday warmth, but I still couldn't relax. I was locked in a damned birdcage. I was there with my mom, brothers, sister and their families, but at a distance, separated. Nerves had placed bars between us.

I hadn't talked about our situation with my brothers. I knew they'd heard Joey had been in the hospital, but I didn't know how much they understood about why.

"Hi, Jamie. How are you?"

I wondered if my sister-in-law could see my discomfort. "I'm fine, Emma. How are you?" I forced as much of a smile as I could.

Emma was one of those people who had a talent for small talk. "I'm well. I've been working on getting trim. I've started a walking program in the evenings. And you know, I can't believe how much more energy..."

My mind wandered off. *What must they be thinking of my crazy life? How much had Mom told them? Did they know about the alters, or did they just think Joey was depressed?*

"Are you in any type of exercise program right now?"

Her question brought me back. "No, with the opening of the store and... and everything, I haven't had time."

"I'm still doing my yoga, too. You should try it. You'd be amazed at how much it does for you..."

I don't care. I really don't care to make conversation right now. I just want all this to be over. God, I hope next Christmas is better. I wonder if Joey will be better by then?

I guess I should have warned my family about what could happen, ahead of time; I might have felt less tension. But I couldn't talk about it. My mom was getting up in years so I only gave her bits and pieces of information. I didn't want to worry her. Mel was the only person I shared some of the details with. Usually I tell her everything, but that winter I couldn't. She was dealing with her own problems, she didn't need mine.

I don't know how much good preparing them would have done, anyway. Kip had visited Joey at the hospital. He'd even met us for dinner one night at Pizza Hut on visiting day. He knew all about all the personalities; he'd even talked to Joey about them, but knowing hadn't prepared him for his first meeting with one.

It had been a few days before Christmas. Kip had come home for the holidays.

He sat in the kitchen at the table, chatting while I dipped peanut butter balls. The room was filled with the wonderful scent of warm chocolate. When the kitchen door opened and Joey walked in, Kip said, "Hey, Joe."

Joey walked right over to him and stretched out his hand. "You're Kip, right? Nice to meet you. I'm Jay."

Kip shook his hand, saying nothing. When Jay walked away, Kip's eyes landed on me. He still said nothing. His eyebrows sat high, and his mouth hung open slightly.

Kip was never lost for words.

"I take it that's the first time you've met one of them?"

The first time threw everyone for a loop. There really was no way to be prepared. But it was worse when you knew nothing of what had been going on. I held my breath for most of that Christmas.

We got through the day without any strange personalities visiting my family. During those days of Christmas, Joey seemed to show some improvement. The partial program was not running over the holiday week, and the absence of stress caused by going to the program, and struggling to keep up with school, seemed to be therapy in itself.

*   *   *

As the new year began, so did new hope. Joey's team at partial began to prepare for him to leave their care. His specialist had returned from her holiday abroad to visit family. She made a plan for Joey to see her weekly, once he was released from the partial program. I hoped she was our answer. Maybe I would even get an opportunity to ask some questions.

The personality changes appeared to be happening when Joey felt he was losing control of a particular situation. At those times, an alter would come out and look after things. When life was moving along without difficult moments, the other personalities didn't show up as much. The fact that he could remember these appearances some of the time felt like progress to me. Four of the alters had seemed to combine into one, who kept the name Jay. Only Jay and Troah were left — that had to be a good thing. He must be getting better. But, I wanted to hear those words from her.

The first time I heard Dr. E's Australian accent was during a phone call. Joey had met with her at Algonquin Cottage, but hadn't yet had his first official appointment at her office. As she told me when and where it would be, I felt a rush of excitement. This would be it; we were finally about to get somewhere. A specialist would be able to get to the cause of the pieced-together days we were living, and finally begin the real healing.

I was a tidy little bag of nerves the day of that first appointment. And, as if to drive home the point that this new part of his therapy shouldn't be taken lightly, nature again threw its unpredictable side into the day's events with a snow storm. It was enough to cancel the buses at school, and make me white knuckle the steering wheel the whole way to the city.

When we finally arrived at her office after our careful drive through the snow, we were a little on the late side of the hour. "Hi," I said, extending my hand. "I'm Jamie."

Dr. E greeted us with a friendly smile, "Hi there, come right in. You can sit down there on the sofa." She opened a file. "Terrible weather out there, huh?"

Feeling awkward, we sat down on the overstuffed sofa in the small room.

"It's awful. It was a slow drive, I'm sorry we're late."

She carried on in her broad, thick accent, "It really doesn't matter. Today's appointment is just to touch base with Joey again, and to explain the therapy I'm planning." She looked at me. "Actually, maybe I'll catch up with Joey first. Would you mind waiting in the next room, just for a few minutes?"

I moved out into her waiting room and tried to read the book I'd brought. I would stop every few lines as I realized I had no clue what I'd just read. Finally, I closed the book, and just sat looking around, waiting. Her easy listening music was just loud enough to prevent me from hearing what she said to Joey. I assumed it was probably there for exactly that reason.

Soon, the door to Dr. E's office opened. "Come on back in, Jamie. Joey, you can take a seat in the waiting area. We won't be long."

I entered her office, and sat down, sinking into the worn leather couch.

Dr. E was an odd looking woman, reminding me of a fifty-something free spirit who was showing signs of aging. I hoped she was more competent than the last hippie-type counselor whom Joey had met — the one who had thought Joey's problem was his very good imagination.

She seemed to have it together. And I liked the friendly, easygoing way she had about her.

She sat down in a chair across from me, and threw me a huge smile. Her eyes had a gentle feel. The first line out of her mouth was, "So tell me… do you think, if you had continued to have children, that they would be anywhere near as interesting as these two?"

I laughed. It was not what I'd expected her to start with. It put me immediately at ease. I blurted out, "I'm not sure. I'm just kinda glad some days that I decided to quit."

I laughed at myself, in spite of how bad it must have sounded. I mean, it isn't that I'm ever sorry I had either of my two children, but I did certainly, at times, feel like I had my hands ridiculously full.

She smiled at my reply, and picked up a file from the small table beside her. She began to describe her intense interest in Dissociative Identity Disorder (DID). "I'm always off somewhere, at a seminar in Canada, or the United States, trying to stay on top of the new therapy techniques as they're discovered or improved. It's a mysterious one, this disorder. As you know, it's common with survivors of a trauma. A lot of 9/11 victims suffer from it. People who have lived through a disaster, like a tsunami, are often plagued by it.

"But with teens, the ones who haven't suffered such an ordeal… why are they afflicted? Usually it has to do with something that's happened in their childhood: something that is far too painful to deal with."

I nodded my understanding. "How do you plan to help him?"

"Well, I'm going to start by getting to know him. I'll delve into his past a little through questions, looking for a thread that I can grab on to and follow. After that, there are options."

I had read a little about possible therapies. "Are you going to use hypnosis?"

"Hypnosis is one option. I prefer another therapy, however. It takes the patient to a state of mind that is halfway between hypnosis, and our everyday state. To get to that very relaxed consciousness, I use a specialized sensory machine. It alternates impulses from the right to the left side of the body. I can send small electronic impulses to Joey's hands, or we can use it with earphones, sending specific sounds. I prefer that technique… if you'll give me your consent?"

I immediately said, "You have my consent. How successful is it?"

She looked at me intently, and said, "Success will depend on a lot of variables. There *is* something that you need to consider, however."

I waited uneasily.

She looked right into my eyes. "Sometimes… when you go into the wounds, it's *very* hard. We may find something that neither of you wants to know about."

It brought my optimism to a screeching dead stop. The last thing I wanted was to increase Joey's pain.

I had to ask, "Is it really worth the risk then? He seems to be getting better. Four of his alters have come together as one, and he can remember some of their experiences."

She looked sorry about what she was about to say. "Well, there is just as much risk in *not* attempting to uncover the source of the problem. If we only work at bringing his personalities back together, and we don't get to the bottom of this, he could have a recurrence several times in his life, whenever his stress level becomes too much. If we can expose the roots of all this emotion, we can deal with it. If Joey can understand the cause of the problem and address it, the emotions creating his alters should diminish, hopefully even disappear."

It made sense to me, but it was still the most frightening conscious decision I have ever made.

"Yes, I see your point." God, this was so scary. The fallout could be horrible.

"Do you have any more questions, Jamie?"

I was sure that I'd had more on my mind, but my brain wouldn't cooperate. I couldn't concentrate. I wanted so badly for Joey never to have to deal with this problem again. I wanted to put him back together, and never look back. But thinking about what we might find while we were trying to do that... scared the absolute hell out of me.

Chapter 35

Each week when Joey came out of Dr E's office, I would ask him what they'd done.

His answer would be some version of, "We talked."

Unsatisfied, I would press. "Talked about what?"

"I told her about my week, stuff like that."

"Didn't you talk about... how you are improving?"

"Ya, she asked if the old Jay, Mr. Giggles, Inner Strength, and The Darkness were still one personality... and how things were with Troah."

"Is that it?"

"We just talked about life, Mom."

After quite a few weeks, I began to wonder when the sensory therapy would start. At the end of their session one week, I asked for a few minutes of Dr. E's time.

With as much patience as I could muster, I asked, "How long will it be before you try the therapy that you described when we met?"

Dr. E's body language gave away the fact that I wasn't the only one struggling with patience. She didn't hide the deep breath she took before answering. "To use that therapy, we need to first find that little thread in his memories to grab on to and follow. I'm searching for that thread." Then she added, "It might help if I could meet his dad, and ask him a few questions. I've been telling Joey I would like to talk to him for weeks."

I knew there wasn't much chance of getting Earl to visit her. He hated talking to therapists. "I'll give him a call and ask him."

Then Dr. E said, "What about Kip? I think it would be helpful if I could discuss their childhood relationship with him. Do you think that he'd be open to a phone interview?"

I knew Kip was comfortable talking to doctors. "I'll ask him, but I'm pretty sure he'll do whatever he can to help."

I was right. Kip said that he would have a chat on the phone with Dr. E, or he could go in to her office for a one-on-one if she wanted. He wanted his brother to get better, and if he could help, he would.

Earl, on the other hand, was not of the same mindset. I told him that Dr. E would like to meet him, and that maybe he could take Joey to his appointment sometime in the near future.

His reply was elusive. "Yeah, maybe when I'm not so busy with work."

It was the reply I'd expected.

I didn't give up, though. Every once in a while, Earl would phone me, and ask what kind of progress Joey was making. It annoyed me a bit. This was the man whose total financial support amounted to every second haircut and half of Joey's soccer registration, and his help with the driving to the city for appointments had ended months back. Yet he looked to me for information.

Why was I the go-between?

I told him that if he drove Joey to an appointment once in a while, he could use the last five or ten minutes of the time slot to get an update from Dr. E. Or, if he was too busy, he could give her a call. I tried to make it sound casual, not like I was trying to persuade or push. But I wanted Dr. E to have her opportunity with him.

Not surprisingly, neither the drive nor the call ever happened. Could he really not spare a few hours, or even minutes, out of his schedule to hear about his son's progress, or was there something he was afraid of?

Weeks turned into months, and still nothing: no drives from Earl, no answers, no hypnosis, no sensory therapy. My hopes were dwindling after several months of weekly appointments. The sessions had taken on a pattern, and it didn't seem to be getting them anywhere.

Then one afternoon, when I went to pick Joey up after his hour with Dr. E, I was greeted with the unexpected. Joey was crying — hard.

I felt my face go expressionless. I didn't know what to feel: hopeful (that they had found a memory), or hesitant (because it was an unthinkable memory). Joey didn't cry, ever. I looked from him to Dr. E, and with reservation asked, "What happened?"

She shrugged her shoulders, and flicked her eyes from him to me. Her voice was soft and quiet. "I'll let him tell you."

Being her last appointment of the day, the three of us got into the elevator together. There was a lengthy silence charged with a strange energy. I knew the words that had been left unsaid were going to be tough when Joey said them.

My eyes fell on him. He didn't even seem to be trying to hold back the tears. He looked completely derailed.

I shifted my sight towards Dr. E again. She looked back at me, but couldn't hold my gaze. She almost looked apologetic. Or was it embarrassed?

The silence in the elevator was excruciating.

When Joey and I got to the car, I immediately blurted, "What happened?"

With eyes still down, and tears dripping silently, he said, "Angelina's gone. She killed herself."

Angelina had been Joey's romantic interest at Algonquin Cottage. "She gave me her phone number and email address, and I never called."

I had automatically thought that Dr. E had located "the" memory. That wasn't the case. I understood Joey's tears now.

All the way home I heard his regret. "I feel terrible, Mom. I planned to call her. I planned to keep in touch, but it's too late."

What do you say in a situation like that? As tears welled up, I choked out, "Oh honey, I'm so sorry."

His words came out in a whisper. "I should have called her... checked on her... been there for her."

There were two people who Joey had wanted to keep in touch with when he left Algonquin Cottage: Angelina and Allie. They had both suffered from severe depression, and he'd worried about both girls. Allie wasn't a romantic interest. She was a friend, but a friend whom he had felt a strong connection with. He said she was like the female version of him.

My son had his own problems. I didn't want him to take on other people's stresses, but at the same time, guilt and regret can be so debilitating. I knew he cared deeply for his friends.

"Well honey, you can't turn back time. It's too late to call Angelina now, but you can learn from this. Call Allie. You've talked about contacting both of them. You can be there for her. Do what you can... and don't wait."

I knew how hard it would be for Joey to call her. Several months had gone by with no contact between them. Joey wasn't a phone person, even with people he was close to. I guess when the majority of your time is spent with a video controller or television remote in your hand, your social skills get a bit rusty.

He sat quietly thinking. Finally, in between deep labored breaths, he said, "What would I say?"

"Ask her how she's doing, if she was able to get school back on track, if she's talked to anyone else from Algonquin Cottage."

Then I came up with a possible solution to his phone phobia. "Why don't you ask her if she wants to get together? Your birthday's coming up. I could bring you into the city, and the two of you could go to a movie or something. I don't mind the extra drive, now that the weather's nice. It could be part of your gift from me."

Joey liked that idea, I could tell. If he didn't like something, he was quick to say so, but he just sat, thinking. I'm sure he wasn't in any shape to make even the smallest decision at that moment.

The best he could do was, "Yeah, maybe."

He called Allie a few days later. I was impressed. I knew what he had overcome; his uncomfortable feelings, but he did it. He made arrangements to meet her for dinner and a movie.

When I picked them up after the movie, they got into the car, chatting and laughing. It must have been nice for them to spend time together without the stress of Algonquin Cottage hovering in the air.

And Allie looked wonderful. She looked like she'd smoothed out her problems. She had a totally different air about her, a confidence. She'd decided to investigate a career working with troubled teens, and she encouraged Joey to do the same.

I was proud of Joey; he had learned that moments pass by quickly, and that you can suddenly lose an opportunity. That day he was making the effort to give what he could right away, because he had been taught that… tomorrow is not always a given.

Chapter 36

That June, soon after Joey's eighteenth birthday, after six months of weekly appointments, Dr E decided that once every two weeks would be often enough for Joey to visit her. It didn't really surprise me. I was long past having to try to balance the feelings of dread and anticipation that I had felt when the appointments had begun. Hope had kind of settled to the bottom of the mixed bag of emotions that the last few years had left me carrying around. It wasn't that I had completely given up on Dr. E finding the cause of Joey's extra selves, but with each passing month, it became clearer that it might never happen. It left me wondering, if she can't help him, what next? Was there anything left to try?

Troah and Jay still made appearances from time to time, but definitely not as often. Joey was doing reasonably well in school, and had started to share his free time with a group of boys in his grade. Some of them weren't exactly the type of influence that I would have chosen for him but I told myself that it was normal not to like *all* your son's friends. Compared to having a video game as his best friend, it was a healthy step in the right direction. At least he looked happier. That was a good thing.

As summer neared, Joey settled into the fact that he shared his body with two other boys. He said it was fine; they only came out when he needed them, and they were no trouble.

Then that changed.

One sunny summer evening I left work with a list of errands. My first stop was the bank to pick up money for groceries, then off to do my shopping. Once home, I counted the remaining money in my purse to see exactly how much damage I had done.

After being home for a while, I noticed the top flap of my purse sitting open. I hadn't left it that way.

I looked in the workshop for Will. "Hon, did you go into my purse for something?"

Will wrinkled his nose into a confused expression. "No, why would I go into your purse?"

I had a rotten feeling in my stomach. I went right over to the suspicious looking open bag, pulled out my money, and counted it again.

It was so strange. There were some days that I might have been unsure about the exact amount in my wallet, but that day, there was no question. I was sure a twenty dollar bill was missing. I saw red.

There were only the three of us in the house — Joey, Will and me. And to my knowledge, in over eleven years of marriage, Will had never lied to me. He certainly wouldn't lie about wanting an extra twenty dollars for something.

That left Joe. It was bad enough thinking that Joey had helped himself to money in my purse. He knew my thoughts on giving him unearned money. But on top of that, our store was still in its first year of business. We weren't suffering, but we were definitely on a tight budget. We were careful to watch where every dollar went, and Joey was very aware of that fact.

Now, my fuse is usually safely tucked way in. It doesn't light easily, or quickly, but that night it was glowing red-hot. I stomped up the stairs to Joey's room. I knocked and opened the door. My voice didn't hide my frustration. "Joe, I have something to ask you."

He was lying on his bed, facing away from me, playing a video game. He lifted his head, and looked at me. "It's Jay."

That figured.

I walked right in, so we were face to face. "Pause that game."

Jay pushed the pause button, and looked up at me with an obvious lack of enthusiasm.

Without hesitation, I looked him right in the eye. "Did you just take twenty dollars out of my purse?"

He raised his eyebrows in that arrogant way of his, as if to say, "Are you nuts?" and answered, "No." That was it — just a smug no.

My blood was boiling. My hand rested on my hip, and I just stood there for a while, looking at him.

He just lay there, looking back at me with an annoyingly cocky attitude. Then, in an impatient way, he said, "Are we done?"

I felt like choking him, or better yet, slapping that self-satisfied look right off his face. I took a quick, deep breath. "No, we are not done. Are you sure you didn't *borrow* twenty dollars? I counted my money a little while ago, and I just counted it again, and there's a twenty missing."

His reply was filled with that annoying arrogance. "Well... I guess you counted it wrong then."

I wanted to bring the cocky little bastard down a peg or two. I hated him at that moment. I needed to get out of there before I smacked him.

Will was waiting when I got back to the kitchen. He looked hesitant. "Well?"

I shook my head tensely. "It's Jay up there, and he denied it."

Will's eyes shifted to the floor. "Well, I don't want to make things worse... but I'm pretty sure five dollars went missing from my wallet last week." He raised his eyes to meet mine.

I couldn't believe it. If Joey, or Jay, or *whoever* it was, thought that we were going to turn a blind eye to this so that we didn't stress him, he had another thought coming. My fuse was well beyond the snuffing point.

I would wait for Jay to leave and Joey to come back, though. Some cool-down time was definitely necessary anyway. I needed to organize my thoughts.

I fought internally with myself as I waited. I wanted to be mad. Didn't I have the right to be? Joey hadn't committed the theft; Jay had. But whether Joey had been conscious of his actions or not, the fact remained that it had been *his* hand that had reached into my purse. Jay may have been the culprit, but Joey had to be held somewhat responsible. Didn't he? God, I needed that damned parental instruction manual again. *Shit!*

An hour or so later, when Joey came down the stairs, my anger had subsided a bit. But only a bit. Joey went to the fridge, and took out a Coke.

Although I was feeling calmer, my voice was still icy. "Joe?"

"Yeah?"

"Do you remember what happened earlier?"

He looked at me. "What do you mean?"

I managed to keep my voice in an unruffled tone. "I'm pretty positive Jay stole twenty dollars from me tonight."

Joey didn't say anything. He just stood there, looking at me.

He began checking his pockets. Suddenly, he pulled out a twenty. "Oh shit, this isn't mine."

I closed my eyes. I didn't want to see that twenty. I still wanted to believe, even against the odds, that I'd been wrong. I opened my eyes, and looked at him hard. "If this *ever* happens again, Joe, you're going to have to live with your dad for a while — at least a month or so. It doesn't matter if it's Jay, you, or some new personality: thieves aren't welcome here. I'm angrier right now than I've been in a very long time."

I'd never said that I wanted him to live at his dad's before, *ever*. He spent the odd night there when he was getting up early to go to work with his dad, but everyone knew he didn't want to live there. I didn't want him to live there either. I just couldn't think of another consequence that would have the same impact. "I'm dead serious, Joe, if it ever happens again, you're gone."

It was so frustrating; it wasn't as if I could punish Jay. He'd have a great time laughing at me if I tried. In a sense, we were raising three sons, but I really felt we could only discipline one of them. I couldn't handle this, especially after all we had been through together over the last year — all the appointments I had driven him to, all the compassion I had shown him, even after calling me the best parent ever — he could still steal from me? It felt as if he had taken all that for granted. I was angry... and hurt.

From the look I saw on Joey's face, I knew he understood the sting this had given me. His shoulders dropped. "That's it... I'll make Jay go away."

Confused, I stuttered, "What... what do you mean?"

"I think I can make Jay go away. I have more control now. I didn't see the harm in having him around until today. But that's it... now I'm going to try to get rid of him."

My voice softened. "You really think you can do that?"

He nodded slowly. "Yeah, I think so."

*   *   *

I didn't see Jay again that summer. For a short while, Troah and Jay merged into one personality called Trey. Trey didn't survive long. Joey said it was probably because Troah and Jay were just too different to be one. Troah believed in peace, and Jay was always ready to fight. It couldn't work, so they were gone. I'm not sure why Troah left when Jay left. I didn't ask. I was just relieved to know they were gone.

Finally, after about a year of not knowing what to expect from day to day, Joey was just Joey, and he seemed to be managing like that just fine.

Dr E didn't seem surprised by this new development. She said he was making very good progress, and he appeared more and more stable all the time.

She made it sound as though she was giving up.

His stress level still concerned me. By biggest fear was a relapse that would include a new alter. What if it were a violent one? After Jay and Troah left, there had been one, Leon, who had popped out one day. If he hadn't introduced himself, I would have thought it was Joey the whole time. That one night was the only time I ever saw that alter. It was a huge improvement. Still, Leon did remind me of an important fact: unless the root was uncovered and addressed, anything could happen, at any time.

I decided it was time to push for the sensory therapy. For hypnosis. For anything.

My mouth hung open when Dr. E agreed to try.

Finally!

On his next appointment, they tried hypnosis. Not quite successfully; Joe got to a very relaxed state, but not relaxed enough to go under.

Joey's next appointment, two weeks later, his mid-March appointment, was the last time he saw Dr E. Their last hour together consisted of talking about the future, about her upcoming extended trip abroad and about his great progress. She finally admitted that there wasn't much more she could do for him. She told us she was moving out of her office, and would find a new one when she returned from abroad. She didn't have a new phone number to give us, just her fax number at home. She would, however, call to schedule a visit just to check in with him, maybe once every six months or so. She wished him luck.

Then she cut him loose.

Chapter 37

I was lost. I felt deserted. Dr. E had tried hypnosis once, only once. And then nothing. I hadn't seen the sudden end of therapy coming. Giving up hadn't even crossed my mind.

It made me annoyed with her. At the same time, I was a little annoyed with myself. Why couldn't I see the end of Joey's regular trips into the city as a good thing? It had to be a positive sign, a step towards life being normal again, didn't it?

But no matter what logic I tried to use on myself, for a while all I could feel was let down. I thought about looking for another doctor. Unfortunately, I knew my son would fight like a gladiator about that. He was totally fed up with doctors and appointments. I knew suggesting that he start over from the beginning, especially when he was doing so well, would be like asking him to give up his weekends to repeat grade two.

It's just that I was having trouble living in the moment. I wondered if he would one day turn into six boys again, or eight, or even ten. He hadn't dealt with the root cause. Too much stress would always be a risk to him. I reminded myself that I had done everything within my power to help him with his problem.

I guess there are things that just aren't fixable. It's nobody's fault. It's just the way it is.

That year, I was forced to think of my relationship with my son in a new way. I needed to let him be, and love him that way. I was forced to realize that suffering makes us stronger. Difficult things in life force us to evolve. What my child was going through might be exactly what he needed to experience in order to grow. I needed to trust fate.

And really, how did I know if it would have been better if the doctors *had* located his buried trauma. Maybe, once uncovered, that elusive memory would have plagued him for the rest of his life. Sometimes when DID patients reclaim their painful memories, any trigger that reminds them of that trauma can bring on a dissociative episode. Would that be better than having to be careful with his level of stress? Maybe sometimes things *are* better left alone.

While I tried to get used to the concept of giving up the search, Will had other things on his mind. He was worried about Joey's future. Joey had started missing quite a lot of school. He complained about his teachers. He didn't see the point in it, since he was going to learn the trade of drywall from his dad anyway.

I understood Will's concern, so I sat down with Joe to try to reach him.

"I know you don't like school, honey, but once you're finished and you start working, that working career lasts for such a long time. You'll be glad later if you keep your options open. If you at least have your high school diploma, you'll have choices."

"I'll never use the stuff they teach us, Mom. I hate it. I don't think I can last much longer."

"It's only a couple more years, Joe. If you put your mind to it, it'll go faster than you think. You don't have to go to college right away if you don't want to. But you never know, you might even enjoy college. You'd be learning about something that interests you. It's completely different than high school. And you pull off such amazing marks when you like what you're learning about."

"I'm going to learn drywall, Mom. I like that."

"Well, you might not like it for the rest of your life. You can't get too many jobs without a diploma. I don't want to see you stuck pumping gas or something like that if you get tired of drywall."

"You worry too much, Mom."

God, the kid was taxing. "Maybe, but I've spent twenty-one years of my life working for the same company. The people are great, but other than that, it's just a paycheck, not work I enjoy. It's a job, that's all, and I want more for you. If you finish school, you can learn a skill that you'll be proud of, and be happy doing."

He just sat in a slumped position. "I can do that without school."

It seemed like a waste of energy. It looked like getting him through high school would be our new big challenge, but I had no idea how to motivate him to do that.

We turned to the same counselor we had asked so many questions of over the years. Will wanted to come with me, so I took a Monday afternoon off work, the day the store was closed, and we headed into the city to get tips on motivating teens without causing stress.

Side by side, Will and I sank into my counselor's worn leather couch. He had a good knowledge of all our relationships, so that didn't need to be covered. And he knew about Kip, so I didn't waste time there; I made my way right to Joey's hatred for school.

Sitting on the doctor's sofa that day, I took a new hard knock. It came in the form of logic, and you can't really argue with logic. My counselor, a man I totally trusted, reminded me that my son wasn't a child anymore.

"He's almost nineteen, Jamie. Joey's a grown man. You can't fight genetics and you can't change a personality type. He has parts of you in him, and he has parts of his dad. You can't will that to change."

It's that old debate: nature versus nurture. People try so hard to mold their children into what they want them to be. It just doesn't work. You can't change your kids. You can guide them, and you can help them to think about things before they take action, but you can't make them into something they're not.

What the doctor said made sense, but his next comment shook me to my bones.

"If he quits, maybe you should kick him out; let him experience how difficult it can be without a high school diploma."

"Ummm… maybe I should tell you about Joey's last couple of years."

My doctor hadn't been one of the therapists Joey had visited. And as strange as it sounds to me now, I hadn't seen him since Joey's alters had shown themselves. I guess I'd had too much on my plate to think about how *I* was dealing with the whole mess.

I filled him in on my son's condition and how stress-related it was.

"Well, maybe kicking him out isn't the answer just yet. It's a difficult situation. But it's definitely time to let him start making his own mistakes. You can't think for him for the rest of his life. Sometimes they have to learn the hard way. If he quits, make him get a job; charge him rent. Let him see how hard it is out there."

I guess I was naïve, thinking that I could find all the answers. Those days, I had an awful feeling that The Fixer couldn't fix anything anymore. I just thought that I'd failed at helping Joey discover the cause of his personality split, so I might feel like a good mom again if I could find a way to motivate him.

What I needed to remember was that Joey wasn't only my son, he was a person. He had his own anxieties, dreams and obstacles. He had his own opinions. They may have been right; they may also have been wrong, but they were his. I needed to see him for who he was, with all his virtues and talents, and all his flaws. They were all part of him. I could talk with him about the future. I could help him think about where his path might be taking him, but trying to force him to take a different direction would only make us both miserable.

As a parent, that was one of my biggest hurdles. When I had had my babies it was instinct to fight to be in control. We all do it; we have to. We do it to keep our kids safe, to take care of them. But at what point do we stop?

Some people never do. I remember being a young adult, and hating that my mom always wanted me to be someone I wasn't. I pretended to be a practicing Catholic for years after I moved away from home, thinking that it would please her. The only thing that it accomplished was to make me a liar.

During those days, I wondered why she couldn't accept that I prayed, and that I tried to be a good person every day, and love me for that. When I used to tell her that I was spiritual, just not religious, she'd say, "Well, Jamie, I just hope you're doing the right thing."

There were times when I told her that I was a bit jealous of Will; that I would love to work in our store full time like he does.

She'd look at me, cock her head and say, "You *do* work in your store."

That made me laugh. Sure I did, in what other people called their *spare time*. But when I said that I dreamt of growing my business instead of spending forty hours a week in a manufacturing plant, she'd launch into a dialogue about the security and benefits of my job, and what a great company it was to work for. It was a speech I heard many times. I had a job that she respected, and even though I was in my forties, she still tried to make me share her views on that subject, ignoring the fact that my job didn't make me feel fulfilled.

I didn't want to make Joey resent me by trying to force him to be someone he wasn't. But he had so much to offer. At one point, I wanted him to go to college so badly. I wanted him to do something that made him feel rewarded and satisfied at the end of the day. The kid had a natural way with animals, and was great with children. People with problems seemed to feel comfortable opening up to him. He was so good at math, and he was a natural performer. Maybe he could take advantage of one of those qualities.

But that was *my* agenda. As the mom of a nineteen-year-old, I didn't have the right to have an agenda for him. It was Joey's life.

I couldn't help but think about Angelina. I imagined how her parents must feel now that she was gone. Had they tried to push their daughter towards what they wanted for her, or had they asked her what she dreamed of, and helped her work towards getting it? Whatever they had done, it was too late to change it now, but it wasn't too late for me.

Joey was Joey. He had a unique way of dealing with stress, that was for sure, and he hated school. They were both parts of who he was. Somehow I had to accept that.

I'd spent the last few years of my life realizing that transgendered people had the right to be exactly who they were. But we're all entitled to that right. It's not fair to try to change someone. I didn't like it when people did it to me. I certainly didn't have the right to do it to others, even my kids. If I wanted a life that was truly without secrets between me and them, I would have to accept my children, not try to change them.

I needed to let Joey find his own way; I couldn't find it for him. I'd done all I could. I wouldn't stop trying to help him think through his options (it would kill me to do that), but I had to start letting him make decisions. Hopefully, if he made mistakes along the way, he'd learn from them.

I would do my very best to encourage him to finish high school, but beyond that it was really up to him. If he chose to keep going, I would help him. If not, I'd have to get used to it. I'd offer my knowledge, my time, my heart and my help. That was enough.

As a parent, my most important role was to love my son for who he was — exactly the way he was. What I needed to remember was that I had a big-hearted, funny, loving, giving, strong-willed young son. Couldn't that be enough?

Finally, I surrendered, and believed, it was enough.

Kip: Spring 2007
Chapter 38

"I'm going with full chest reconstruction, Mom."

It didn't register at first. "What? What do you mean?"

"They take your nipples right off, resize them, and move them out to the sides a bit. There's quite a bit more scarring but it really does look more like a man's chest in the end." Two years after starting testosterone therapy, Kip had gathered enough money and was finally ready to alter his chest.

I was glad we were talking on the phone, I was shaking my head slowly. Could nothing ever be easy? It sounded so invasive to me. "But honey, I thought you were going with keyhole surgery? Why do you want to do something that leaves you all scarred if you don't have to?"

I had prepared myself for the day when he would have his breasts removed, assuming he would have the less risky "keyhole" surgery. It involved an incision at each nipple, and the breast tissue removed through it. The incision is disguised along the edge of the nipple so the scarring is almost non-existent.

The thought of one of my kids having surgery for anything makes me edgy, but this... this seemed more complicated than it had to be. It seemed unnecessary. I knew how important this step was to Kip, and I was happy for him but... they were going to take his nipples *right off*?

"Mom, Dr. S has done a lot of both types of surgeries. He has a photo album with before and after shots of his clients. There must be hundreds of pictures. I spent a long time going through it. The guys with keyhole look like they have the body of a flat-chested woman. The nipples don't look right. It's not natural. I don't want that. I want a man's chest. I can live with the scarring."

I said the only thing I could think of, "Well don't rush into anything. Take some time to be sure."

"I will, don't worry. Hey, while I was there we talked about the other surgeries too."

He was referring to the choices for sexual reassignment surgery.

"Dr. S was impressed with all the research I've done. I told him there was too much risk involved. He said a lot of his trans patients need something done there, to feel whole. I told him that I have a 'Little Kippy' and it works just fine. I think I'll leave it that way, until they perfect those procedures."

I laughed. *Thank you, God!*

I had done a little research on the subject myself and the risks were horrible. Hormone therapy creates natural growth in that area, causing the clitoris to resemble a pre-adolescent penis, but for some trans-men, that wasn't enough. Several types of surgeries are available to make this area more like a typical penis, to allow the patient to void through this area, and to enlarge it to a more aesthetically pleasing size and shape. A prosthetic penis and testicles can even be added, but the long term success of implants has been poor.

The worst part was that there were considerable dangers with all the bottom surgeries. The patient could lose all sensation in that area. There was risk of serious infection, persistent tenderness and urine leakage. The body could even reject the new penis, causing it to fall right off! The list of complications was endless.

I was so grateful that Kip didn't feel incomplete the way he was. The way I saw it he was more a man than many of the men I knew, just the way he was.

*   *   *

To Kip, surgery meant that he would enjoy summer again without the many layers of restrictive, sweaty tensor bandages that bound his chest. To Cally, it meant they would finally get to swim together in our pool, something they had never done, since Kip didn't ever go shirtless. Even a wet shirt would have betrayed the secret underneath: the bandages that kept him strapped down; therefore to Kip, swimming was out of the question.

On a dark spring morning, at 6:30 a.m., Cally, Kip and I walked through the gentle rain towards the car. It was the big day: chest reconstruction. I was groggy during the twenty minute drive to the hospital. "Not a morning person" does not even begin to describe me at that time of day.

After arriving, we settled into the couch in the waiting room while Kip was checked in. There was a short wait and then, just before eight o'clock, the nurse came over to us, and asked Kip to follow her.

Once he was prepped for the procedure, we were invited in to wait with him. He seemed quite amused by something.

"That nurse is hilarious, Mom."

"What? Why?"

"When she got me in here, she asked me to get into this hospital gown. She was busy over there and I guess she wasn't paying attention when I changed." He was lying in bed as he told the story, covered with a flannelette blanket.

"After a few minutes, she came back over here, picked up my chart and started chatting with me. This is what she says, 'So…

you must have lost a lot of weight, huh?' I must have had the most confused look on my face.

"I just said, 'Excuse me?' She says, in a less confident way, 'Have you lost a lot of weight?'

"I just said, 'No.'"

It was early, and he hadn't been allowed to eat or drink anything, so his brain wasn't fully in gear yet. "I guess she wondered why a man would have everything tightened-up if it wasn't because he'd lost a lot of weight."

I could understand her confusion. When I looked at Kip's face now, there was no evidence he had ever been anything but a man. I guess the nurse mustn't have been able to hold back her curiosity.

"She looked scared to ask me, but she said, 'Well, do you mind me asking why you are having this done?'

"I told her I was a transgender. You should have seen her face. I thought, *Oh crap, I embarrassed her*. She looked away and said, 'Oh... Oh... Oh, well, I would never have guessed that!'"

In her embarrassment, she probably hadn't realized that Kip had been more amused, and somewhat complimented, rather than insulted. She had looked at him like any other guy. It was definitely a compliment.

"So next she says to me, 'I "need"' you to relax your arm. Okay, I "need" you to lift it up like this for me.' She was totally blushing when she raised my arm. Then she goes 'I "need" you to turn it palm up, so I can find a good vein.'

"I said, 'You're very needy, aren't you?' and laughed."

Teasing would have been the best way my son knew to tell her there was no harm done. I could just picture the devilish grin Kip would have been wearing by then.

The nurse smiled at that.

* * *

For the most part, the surgery went well. In fact, it was even finished quite a bit ahead of schedule. Without notice, his doctor had bumped his operation up three hours. The patient scheduled before him had chickened out: something that probably happens quite a bit in the life of a plastic surgeon. As a result, there would be no wait time. Kip usually only gets nervous immediately before difficult events. It was perfect. He'd had no time to get nervous.

A few hours later we were invited back in to sit with him in the recovery room. As the last bit of the anesthetic wore off, he began to feel the first throbs of pain. His nurse gave him a shot to help make him comfortable again.

He didn't look good. You could see the beads of perspiration forming on his face and neck.

"I know this sounds weird, Mom, but I feel worse since she gave me the pain stuff. Is that normal? And I'm hot, *really* hot."

I took off the extra blankets, thinking that that would do it.

Nope.

Several minutes went by, Kip shifting awkwardly in his recovery bed, constantly trying to get comfortable. He repeated, "No really... I really feel hot! I feel like I'm going to pass out!"

I grabbed a face cloth, and ran it under cold water. Dropping it on his forehead, I heard a long drawn out, "Aaahhhh."

The cloth warmed up so quickly. *Was this normal?*

I had tried not to let myself think about the fact that this was a pretty major surgical procedure, but I was definitely thinking about it now.

I ran the cloth under cold water again, and then again. Every time I dropped it on Kip's head, he sighed, "Aaahhhh" with relief.

I caught the nurse looking at Kip, then looking away quickly when she saw me notice, trying to hide her concern. I didn't look at Cally. I didn't want her to see my fear. If I was calm, she would be calm. Then the worry was given some power. The nurse told us that maybe we should wait in the waiting room.

We sat in the little room listening to a woman who was obviously suffering from allergy problems.

Hork.

I tried to read the book I'd brought, hoping it would take my mind off the fact that Kip was not bouncing back from surgery like I'd expected.

Hork.

I tried to focus on the page in front of me, but my mind kept drifting back to Kip. The nurse had said that everyone reacts differently, and that it would just take a little more time, but the tension in her face had left me rattled. I was nervous.

Hork.

Would you please shut up!

The sound that woman made with her throat wouldn't have been pleasant under any circumstances, but that day I thought Cally might just jump on to the couch and kill her.

Hork.

Hork.

God, it was hard to focus with those vile sounds. I thought I might just kill her myself. I *had* to get out of there.

"Cally... you hungry?" It was after 1:30 p.m.

We could escape the throat lady by going to get something for lunch. Before leaving, we checked on Kip — he was stable. Hallelujah! Trying to be positive, we thought we'd pick something up for him. He'd be feeling better soon.

After lunch we popped back in to check on Kip and learned that, after another dose of strong pain meds and a good vomit, Kip had discovered a new allergy. He was taken off the pain killers that had caused the reaction, and switched to Tylenol # 3 with codeine. Next came Gravol (also known as Dramamine) to settle his stomach. Then he was released.

As I drove home, watching my son carefully in the passenger seat, I thought, *God, what next?*

Not that it surprised me. He's been a magnet for unusual incidents his whole life. In high school, he'd been allergic to the library. Try explaining *that* to a teacher! He reacted severely to some kind of dust or mite that lives in old books. They didn't believe someone could be allergic to the library… until they made him spend an hour in it. His face swelled up until he resembled a young version of Frankenstein, and his hands and feet were huge. So I did what any loving mother would do — I sent him to school like that. They didn't make him go into that library again.

I just hoped that for now, the drama was over, and that we would make the twenty minute drive home from the hospital without the use of a brown bag.

* * *

We did make it home, and my son started to perk up. He had a sandwich, and kept it down.

I checked his drains — two little tubes, one from each side of his chest leading to a little bottle. This was for the normal healing fluids that are sent to, and have to drain from, any part of the body that suffers a trauma like this. The bottle didn't look too full — I could wait to empty it later.

Kip took his next dose of Tylenol, and settled in on the couch.

Things got back to feeling kind of normal, for an hour or two anyway. Then his Tylenol and his sandwich came up violently. We weren't having much luck with painkillers.

It didn't make sense, though. Why did the first dose of Tylenol # 3 agree with him, and not the second?

He looked so miserable again. And the beads of sweat were back.

Then it hit me — the Gravol had worn off. Gravol was added to his list of meds.

I stayed home from work the next day, just to keep an eye on things. It was a peaceful day. Kip in his Gravol-induced groggy state, me coming down from the rush of adrenaline the day before had brought on. We watched movies just like we had years ago, and enjoyed each other's company.

After another night of Gravol, Kip was starting to think that maybe just Extra Strength Tylenol would be enough. It might not dull the pain as much as Tylenol # 3, but at least he wouldn't need the Gravol and he'd feel alert and alive again. If he could tough it out for another day and a half, he would be seeing his doctor, and he could get a second opinion.

It made sense to me. I just hoped that the visit to the doctor's office wouldn't include another dose of drama!

Chapter 39

That Friday I drove my son to see Dr. S.

Since his surgery, Kip's chest had been bound with the familiar tightness of tensor bandages. "I can't wait to get a look under there, Mom."

We both hoped the drain tubes would come out that day. He was so afraid of bumping them, or knocking them out. He had to be so careful in every movement he made. It would be great to be rid of them.

I waited in the reception area, listening to piped in elevator music while Kip saw the surgeon. When he came out, his face was strange. It wasn't a look I recognized. Have you ever seen a movie where someone is lobotomized, and they walk in a trance-like state? That was Kip.

He walked toward the receptionist, and blankly turned his head toward me. "I need to book an appointment for next week."

Jesus, Kip, what's going on now? I had to stop myself from shaking my head as my eyes followed him through the room.

As we left the office, I figured out what that look was.

"It looks so weird, Mom. It doesn't look at all like I'd expected. I'm not so sure about this." His eyes stayed stunned and sort of glazed over until we got home.

I guess any life-altering change in your body is hard to accept, even if it's a good change.

The minute we got in the door, he turned to me. "I've *got* to show you. Come on!" He gently, but firmly, pushed me to the bathroom, and immediately took off his shirt. He undid the clips that held the tensor bandages in place.

As he unwound the wide strips of cloth, all I could think was, *Oh no… I know who's going to have to wrap those back around you. What if I do it wrong? Shit.*

He let the last bit fall to the floor, and stood there, looking concerned. His usual humor was not in the room.

He looked at me so seriously. "Tell me the truth… are they level?"

I wanted to giggle. I think maybe I did a little. He was kind of cute at that moment, sort of vulnerable looking.

His nipples looked level to me.

I stepped back, and took a careful look, so he would trust my answer. "Yes, they look a little weird, but they're level."

On top of each new nipple the doctor had stitched a fairly thick layer of gauze-like material. And below them were two bright red stitched lines, caked with dried blood.

Kip looked deep into my eyes. "Are you sure?"

I replied in my most authoritative mom voice, holding his eye contact. "Yes honey, I'm sure."

I was pretty sure I'd convinced him because, as I began to wrap him back up, the usual Kip reappeared. He looked down after I had gone around his chest a couple of times with the bandages. Everything was covered, but the sewn-on gauze made it look like Kip had humongous, hard nipples.

He looked at me, and in his dry way said, "Is it cold in here?", and looked back down at his chest.

I smiled and giggled as I finished the wrap job. As usual, I could count on that crazy sense of humor to help me through things.

When we went back downstairs to join the rest of the family, Kip looked at his brother. He must have needed one more bit of reassurance.

"Joey," he demanded seriously, "show me your nipples."

Joey, without hesitation, lifted his shirt, and stood waiting.

Kip's face relaxed. "Oh yeah... I guess they look the same." The nipple panic was finally gone.

Unfortunately, the drains were not; it had been a little too soon to take them out.

* * *

By the next appointment a week later, the healing fluids had stopped flowing, so the little bottle and its two drain tubes were removed. Kip said that after disconnecting the drains, the surgeon had left the room for a minute.

Kip had seen a little loose, dried-on blood around one nipple. He rubbed it with his fingernail to try to clean up the look of his chest. It hadn't been as loose as he had thought, and more came off than Kip had planned on. A thin line of fresh blood had trickled down his chest as the surgeon reentered the room.

Dr. S looked at the bright red line leaking out of Kip.

Kip said he could feel the look of guilt as he lifted his head and said, "I picked."

His doctor had scowled, "I see that. No more picking! Got it?"

Kip, embarrassed, replied, "I know. I won't. I think I almost picked off a nipple there!" and laughed nervously. He decided right then and there that he had better behave himself. It would only be another couple of weeks until the stitches were removed, and he did not want to mess anything up in the meantime.

* * *

Right on schedule, the stitches came out, and without incident (that was a first). Dr S had asked Kip if he wanted to keep the tensor bandages. Kip said that he didn't. As a matter of fact, he didn't ever want to see a tensor bandage again.

He had dropped them in the wastebasket with enthusiasm, and said, "There, take that!" After years of being tightly wound in tensors, he was way overdue for life without binding.

A week later, Kip and Cally were swimming in our pool. It was obvious how much Kip was enjoying his new freedom. I was proud of him for being comfortable enough to go without a shirt so soon. His nipples looked very natural, but he had a prominent red scar line that went almost clear across his chest, with only a short break in the middle. He said he probably wouldn't be able to go without a shirt around people he thought would be uncomfortable with the scars, at least until they faded a bit, but it was good to be able to take off his shirt at home.

As I sat watching them enjoy this new experience together, this first swim in a pool as a couple, I thought about how many simple pleasures and blessings we take for granted, or completely fail to notice in our lives. We miss so much, doing two things at once, rushing through simple moments: moments that will be tomorrow's memories.

I read a book once that talked about one of the most respected Vietnamese Buddhist monks in the west, Thich Nhat Hahn. He teaches about awareness and mindfulness. The idea is that you must be present in the moment. He uses drinking a cup of tea as an example.

If you're sitting down to a cup of tea, and your mind is all over the place, wishing you could change what you said to someone yesterday, or worrying about how you'll pay the hydro bill tomorrow, you won't enjoy the tea. You'll look down, and the tea will be gone. You will have drunk it, but you won't remember.

He teaches his followers to smell the tea, to feel the warmth in their hand, to really taste it. Be mindful and aware. Life is like that cup of tea. If we don't pay attention, we won't notice, or remember.

That's hard for me to do sometimes. I get so wrapped up in what I'm working towards that I forget to be mindful. I forget to be grateful. That day I was thankful that I was able to share that moment with Kip and Cally, and that my son and our relationship had come such a very long way.

Now when I think of the fear I'd had, the fear that this "change" might not be the right thing to do, it makes me laugh. If only I had known, four or five years ago, what I know now. I have a wonderful new son. And I'm not the only one to see the surprising effects of the change.

You always assume that the older generation will take this sort of thing harder than everyone else. Well, to my surprise, my mom commented to my sister, "Kip is such a sweetheart, and he is quite good looking too!" A comment I would never, ever have expected to hear come out of her mouth. She, too, can see the positive effects that his change has brought.

And both Will's mom and dad have accepted Kip's change with open arms. Will's mom has told me several times that "Kip is a real pleasure to have around."

There's a good reason for that; he's happy. He's being who he should have been all along. When you let people be who they really are, they sure seem to blossom.

You know, I have been asked by friends if I miss Jul, if I had to grieve the death of my daughter. I've always answered no. To be completely honest, I guess that's not the whole truth.

Like any parent, I miss the days when Kip was younger. I miss getting hugs and kisses as I tucked Jul into bed. I miss taking her to the beach on hot summer afternoons, swimming with her and helping her build sand castles. I miss going to auctions together, and seeing Jul's excited face when I let her do the bidding for me. Yes, I miss those days, but no differently than any parent who thinks back on their fond memories.

Do I want Jul back now?

Jamie Johnson

I can honestly say no, I don't. I haven't lost a daughter. I have gained a confident, strong, level-headed son of whom I am immensely proud.

Me: 2007
Chapter 40

During the spring of Kip's reconstructive surgery, I was in the middle of writing this book. At that time, it was perfectly legal to fire someone for being gay in thirty-one of the fifty-two states in the U.S. And it was legal to fire someone for being a transgender in *thirty-nine* of the states!

These laws didn't exist in Canada but, from things I'd read, I knew many employers were far from being supportive. People across North America were literally being forced to hide away the truth.

During Pride Month of that year, the head office of the global company I'd been employed with for twenty-one years asked for pride journals. They were to be published on the company's Lesbian/Gay/Bisexual/Transgender (LGBT) website. The website was called OPEN. The New York head office requested that employees write stories about how being one of these people, or knowing one of these people, had affected their lives and their careers.

Wow… what an open-minded approach.

I sent off an email. "I am the mother of a brave young man, a female-to-male transgender, and I would be happy to write about my experiences with my son if you would like me to."

The communications coordinator of the website seemed genuinely excited to hear from me. "We would love that!! I've been trying to get a good pride journal regarding a transgender person, but I haven't been able to get one published. I think the compassionate story of a mom is the perfect way to introduce the topic! Please send us your story!"

So, I wrote a journal. But the reaction to it was not at all what I'd expected.

My journal described the Monday morning when Jul called me at work with her plea for acceptance. It explained what a transgender person is and the incredible support I received when I finally shared the story of my brave new son with my colleagues at work. Finally, it described how I could then focus my energy towards my job, instead of towards hiding my secret.

Hiding my secret. Boy, how many secrets our home had held over the years. The energy it had taken to keep them private was so massive. There's so much more peace to life when they are taken out of the shadows and placed in plain sight. I was fiercely grateful that Kip had shared his with me. It had changed his life for the better in so many ways. And I had emptied the bag of secrets that I used to reach for whenever I felt unsure of myself. Ridding my life of those skeletons had given me the freedom to live as myself, instead of who people wanted me to be: something everyone should be able to do. I mean, really... shouldn't *everyone* have the right to be who they are?

The fact that so many people do not have the opportunity to be just that: who they are, is why I felt compelled to write my pride journal.

I heard from the coordinator of the website shortly after he received it. "Thank you, Jamie. It really is perfect. I'm sure it will be published. Could you please send me a picture of yourself? We usually publish a photo with each journal and I'd like to have a face to present to management along with your story."

My journal was approved by the sponsor of the website, and the first levels of management. Then the top managers of my company had the opportunity to read it. That was as far as it went.

Upper management replied, "We do not feel that the company is ready to talk about this sub-topic."

As I read these words, I couldn't believe my eyes. *Sub-topic?* What the hell did that mean?

The coordinator was genuinely apologetic. "I'm so sorry, Jamie. I was sure they would publish this story. But don't worry, I won't give up on the issue, and I'll keep you posted on how the "T" discussions progress."

It didn't make sense. We had a LGBT website, but we weren't allowed to talk about the "T" part?

In my opinion, OPEN was far from the appropriate name for that website.

* * *

A couple months later I heard from the coordinator of the website again. "I'd like to invite you to the Out & Equal Workplace Summit in Washington, DC."

My company had been one of hundreds of sponsor companies for the event. People from around the world came to teach, and learn about LGBT issues.

"Why do you want me to go? I mean… what would I do there?"

"The staff here at OPEN feel that if you go you might be able to help us find a way to break the barrier in communication on the "T" topic."

I agreed to go.

I left home wondering, however, if I would feel like an outsider at an event like this and, if I was wasting my time. I really felt strongly about being there, though. And I had this strange feeling that I was going for a reason.

Initially, when I arrived, I have to admit I did feel a little out of place. I felt as if it was obvious that I didn't fit in. I was in a sea of people who looked different from what I saw every day in our reserved small town, and I couldn't help but think that some of them might be wondering what I was doing there. But I was there to solve a problem, so I got organized, and went to my first seminar.

I had been worried for nothing. I didn't feel like an outsider at all. I felt welcome. I hadn't shared my reason for being there with anyone yet, but no one seemed to care. We were all just people.

That night I met the other attending colleagues from my company for the first time: a bunch of top executives and managers from assorted locations… and me. It was a little intimidating, to say the least. We took turns introducing ourselves. When my turn came the coordinator spoke up, telling everyone about my pride journal, and to my confused amusement, the whole table began applauding.

As they clapped away, my amusement turned into embarrassment.

What the heck is going on? They didn't applaud anyone else. I smiled nervously, and thanked them. Then I changed the subject.

I checked in with Will the next day on the phone. It was a funny conversation. He knew I'd been nervous about the night before, so right away he asked, "How did dinner go?"

I laughed. "Great. Actually, they were all really nice people… and they applauded me."

"Applauded you? For what?"

I giggled again. "I have absolutely no idea. It was the weirdest thing I've ever seen."

Over the next couple of days, I came to understand.

I realized that straight allies are seen as real friends, and straight parents who are allies are seen as special, and are very much respected. I was amazed at how something so basic as supporting your child was viewed as a thing to applaud. I was blown away.

I learned so much at the seminars I attended at that summit. My favorite was given by Amanda Simpson. She is a male-to-female transgender who has been the chief engineer for Raytheon Missile Systems for twenty years, before and after transitioning! She has also gone into politics, and has been successful even though she hasn't hidden the fact that she is a transgender.

That in itself is amazing, and for one very good reason: every transgender person lives with a catch twenty-two. If Amanda keeps quiet about her past, so she can be seen as 100% woman by all, people do not become educated. People do not learn that this is simply a medical condition that needs correcting.

But, if she does come forward to tell her story and educate, she risks rejection, judgment, and exclusion. She risks emotional pain that she doesn't deserve. Not by everyone of course, but enough people will judge and degrade her to make her question if it's worth it to share.

My son has chosen not to tell some of the people in his new life. He doesn't feel they need to know that he was born with the wrong body. Even though he's more comfortable and happy with who he is now, some people who learn the truth react strangely to him, now that he's changed. He is never sure if those people are stuck in the stigma associated with "transgender" or "transsexual," and are less than friendly to him because of that, or if he has done something to offend or anger them.

It's the uncertainty of how people will react that stops him from sharing. After he's shared his secret, thoughts run through his head… did that person just shoot me a sideways look because they think I'm less of a man now? Am I somehow unacceptable now… or did I imagine that look?

Then, of course, there is the risk of flat out prejudice by some, and not all prejudiced people hide it. Some people still make life uncomfortable for transgenders. And there is a real risk of physical danger, that's the scariest part.

I wonder what I would do if it were me? I think I would probably feel the same as my son.

If I were born with some irregularity in a private part of my body — I don't know, say a third nipple — and it made me uncomfortable, would it be necessary for me to tell everyone in my life about it? Clearly not. In many ways, that situation is no different than that of the young men like my son. For many of them, their bodies are a private matter, and the risk of judgment and discrimination outweighs their desire to tell.

Amanda has faced those risks head-on. She's been an incredibly brave woman. I was totally inspired by her. I've never met anyone like her.

And I was lucky enough to run into her again. It was the last morning of the summit, and I was exhausted. The summit had been an emotional roller coaster. The spirit and energy during the positive moments were very infectious. But during the transgender seminars, the rooms were filled with people who had changed, or wanted to, and the energy in those rooms was very different. Still positive in a way, but those rooms were filled with pain, and I could feel it. I hadn't expected to feel so much. Stupid. I should have been prepared for that.

When I arrived at the first seminar that last morning, I found a panel of four very prominent T's, and introducing them was Amanda Simpson. They each spoke about their lives — very admirable lives. They all had different experiences. One had lost her family, but kept her job. One had kept her family, but lost her one hundred and sixty thousand dollar a year job because she had transitioned. Each gave a very moving account of his or her challenges.

Then there was a question period. My hand went up amongst a sea of other hands. I figured they wouldn't have time to get to me. After all, many of the other raised hands belonged to transitioning people, and they deserved to be chosen before me.

But they did choose me.

I stood and timidly began to speak. "My name is Jamie. I have a female-to-male son. I work for a large multi-national corporation that asked for journals during Pride Week. They accepted one I wrote but top management wouldn't publish it." I blinked back tears as I spoke. "They said their website wasn't ready for this 'sub-topic.'"

I heard gasps from every corner of the room.

"Do you have any suggestions on how to break the communication barrier with my top management?" I choked on the last few words.

The panel member that answered didn't sugar coat. "Well Jamie, first of all, you have to put aside your emotions. They won't help your cause. Then you need to tell your story as honestly and insightfully as possible. Educate and teach. It's ignorance that makes people afraid or confused. Allies, like you, are a key component to education."

At the end of the seminar, when people began to leave, I bent down to put away my notebook. When I looked up, I was surrounded by people.

Several voices asked me questions at once. It was obvious they all wanted to help me.

But, I'm here to help you.

It appeared they'd recognized that, and were returning the favor with support.

As I tried to talk to seven people at once, I suddenly realized that Amanda Simpson was sitting beside me! I had to force my lower jaw to not drop onto my knees.

In her strong, patient way, Amanda looked at me and said, "Jamie, I know your company." (I was wearing a name tag and the company I worked for was listed on it.) "My sister works for them as well, so I know exactly what you are saying. Get your story out there... *please*."

I wanted to hug her. I wanted to let out all the emotion, and become a sloppy, blubbering mess right there in her arms, but I fought to hold it all back. I choked out, "Yes, but how?"

She looked at me earnestly. "Send it to Oprah."

I replied, "Okay" but I think my tone of voice said, "*Yeah okay, whatever.*"

My doubt had slipped out, and I'm sure she could hear it.

She looked right into my eyes, and said, "I know some of Oprah's employees, and they're planning a show on the parents of transgenders." She put her hand on my arm. "Send it to me," she said and she handed me her card.

It was such an amazing moment. I floated through the rest of the summit. I left that seminar feeling like I had been hugged by half that room.

The two high-profile female-to-male panelists approached me later in the day, thanked me for what I was trying to do and gave me their cards. Until I left, people passing by would come up to me and say, "Are you the mom?" and thank me.

The gratitude I was shown was amazing. It left me feeling shocked.

It was undeniably the most eye-opening experience I've ever had — to hear how often people are abandoned by their families. I left the summit wanting to open every mind I could find. They were right. I needed to get my story out.

You know, I understand how the parents of some of these people feel. Even though I'm an accepting person, I struggled with the thought of my new son at first. It's a process, getting through the feelings, and it's different for everyone. But I can't believe how many parents never make it to those last important stages — acceptance and support.

It makes me wonder why? Because their child isn't average? Because they aren't exactly what they had envisioned when they decided to become a parent?

If you think about life and all its struggles, you have to admit that we really are all very similar. We're all looking for a little peace in our lives. We have no right to pass judgment on anyone. So why do we do it? Because we are a little different from each other?

How can we look down on people for anything if we've never walked a day in their shoes, never had to fight their fight? We all, every one of us, have our ongoing battles in our lives, our crosses to bear. How can we judge the next guy's life if we've never had to live it? We don't know what he had to go through every day just to keep his courage, his sanity and his path in sight. And, although we think we do, we don't know everything our children silently deal with either.

During the years when Kip was changing, and Joey was several people, when I was struggling to keep my courage, I wondered how many people would judge me... and my kids. I would wonder who was deciding that we were a family to be looked down on. I knew there were people who would think something was wrong with us: people who had decided that I must be doing something terribly wrong as a parent to have two children with identity issues. I must be a bad mom.

At first, I wanted to hide from those people. If they couldn't really see us, then they couldn't pass judgment on us. Hiding in a private place seemed the easiest route — the safest, most painless path.

But I realized I couldn't do that. Courage is not about hiding. Courage is about being afraid, and trying anyway. So what if some people had misperceptions? It wouldn't change who I am. And you know what? I've learned that what doesn't kill you makes you the amazing person you are. I've gone from crawling around low, trying to stay out of sight, to spreading my wings and showing whoever cares to look that, in my own way, I'm a beautiful butterfly. And I want to share my transformation because, after all the things that I have learned from raising my kids, after all the growing I have done… I like me.

I have two kids that I love deeply. And I now enjoy hugs from *both* of them on a regular basis. Sure, everything about parenting isn't cut and dried. That's life. We don't live in a fairy tale. It is what it is. But I've learned to deal, and be happy with today. I've learned to appreciate my children for who they are on the inside.

I'm proud of both of them. They are each loaded with courage. Kip stood up for himself, to be exactly who he is: something most of us could learn from. Joey let me write his full story, even the parts that he is not *at all* proud of, because he thought that this story might help a few people to accept and love their kids for who they are.

I don't think my kids understand how brave they've been. They both sometimes joke about the whole thing.

Kip says that I always told him that he could be whatever he wanted to be when he grew up. He says that I just didn't realize quite how far he would take that statement!

Joey will make me shake my head at times. Just recently he was in the shower (alone), and I heard him talking. Will and I looked at each other, both of us a little uncomfortable. There will probably always be a little residual fear of a recurrence in the back of our minds.

I walked over to the washroom, and put my ear to the door. I scooted back over to Will and, trying not to panic, said, "It doesn't even sound like English!"

Will and I stared at each other for a second, and then both bolted back to the bathroom door. I put my ear up to it again. I looked at Will, wide eyed, and said, "Oh my God, it *is* English, but with a *really thick* Scottish accent!"

When Joey emerged from the steam of the bathroom, I sheepishly said, "Can I ask you a serious question, Joe?"

He nodded.

"Do you have any new alters?"

His shoulders dropped in a shrug. "Mom, I told you... Troah is around in the back of my mind sometimes. He helps me when I need him, but he's the only one, and it's not very often."

I couldn't contain my curiosity. "But I just heard you talking with a heavy Scottish accent."

He looked back at me with his amused little smirk. "Well, if you *must* know... there was a fly in the shower with me. I was telling him that he shouldn't be in there with me because if he wasn't careful, he might get killed. The shower is no place for a fly to be safe."

I laughed, shaking my head. "Was it a Scottish fly?"

My son smiled. "I watched "The Water Horse" yesterday."

The movie is set in Scotland. Joey has always been talented when it comes to accents. Every once in a while, out of the blue, he will mimic someone's style of speaking. It always makes me giggle. When I reply to one of those funny moments with, "You know, Joe, you're crazy sometimes," he will always answer with, "Well duh, EVERYONE knows that!"

We can all laugh about what we've been through now. Those days have made us stronger and closer. I feel lucky to have learned so much from my kids. And if people can't look inside, and see me and my children (or their own) for who we really are... then maybe it's time for them to do a little growing too.

Epilogue

In the summer of 2008, Cally, Kip, and I began to plan the day that I thought would begin the rest of their lives together. The ceremony was to take place in August of the next year, in the yard of a beautiful Victorian Bed and Breakfast.

By May of 2009, everything had come together nicely... except unfortunately, the weather. It had been a rotten spring. Rain every weekend. We booked a church near our charming B & B, just in case the drizzle continued throughout the summer, and ruined Cally's romantic plan.

A mere few weeks after I'd made the arrangements with the church, everything in my personal life began to mimic the crappy weather.

Then it happened... a lighting bolt struck.

The phone interrupted the Monday night television shows Will and I liked to watch. It was Kip.

"Hi Mom, can you talk for a few minutes?" His voice had an unusual, walking-on-broken-glass quality.

"Sure, honey. What's up?"

I heard a deep breath in. "Ummm... I might not be getting married."

It hit like something I treasured had been snatched away from me.

We were almost there. Kip's happiness was so close to being documented on photography paper. Some black and whites. Some color. All put together in a beautiful album that would reassure me when I worried that life was being hard on him.

We had booked everything: florist, DJ, photographer, hall, tuxedos. The three of us had sat with the caterer and sampled a variety of dinners, selecting our favorites for the big day. The invitations had gone out. Many of them had been returned. Our guests had booked overnight accommodations so they wouldn't have to drive after the reception. New outfits had been bought. It was just seven weeks before the wedding.

Now, after six years together, Kip tried to put what he had realized into words. "I love Cally, Mom. I'm just not *in love* with her. It's like a friendship."

I was floored. I can't say I'd been one-hundred percent positive that Cally had been "the one" for my son. That's a tough thing to nail down, but they'd lived together for five years and had shown no signs of trouble. They seemed to enjoy the same things. She talked a lot about kids, and I knew she was in more of a hurry to start the in vitro process than he was, but all in all, they seemed happy. And they had such a strong history. I hadn't seen this sudden insight coming.

I was in shock. "What?"

Kip sounded so uncomfortable when he replied. "I feel terrible, Mom, but I can't stop wondering... I mean, I just feel like... well, I'm settling, because of my... situation. It's not that there's anything wrong with Cally. She's smart. She's beautiful. But something... something important is missing."

I didn't know what to say.

Was this cold feet?

I didn't want him to get married if it wasn't right, but how could he be sure?

I'd always felt that Kip had bought Cally her engagement ring because he thought he should. That hadn't sat well with me. They had been together for five years at the time and he was feeling a little pressured. A man should buy an engagement ring because he wants to, not because he feels it's the right thing to do.

Why had Cally needed to push him? Had it been wrong all along?

Or was this just those damn last-minute jitters?

"Are you sure, honey? Maybe it's just cold feet."

"I don't know... I don't know what to do, Mom. There are things nobody knows about. There are things I've been ignoring, trying to put up with. I know it was wrong, but I'm facing it now, and I really can't say that I'm sure I want to spend the rest of my life with her."

"Oh honey, that's not good."

We're going to have to cancel everything. The hall, the minister, the DJ. How would we let all the guests know? Call them individually?

"It's been awful, Mom. This feeling has been eating away at me for weeks. And I know Cally could tell. It was like she was overcompensating or something... doing nice things for me, trying to make me snap out of it. But it won't go away. Mom, I don't think I can say my vows and mean them."

Shit.

I wasn't much help to him that night. The words didn't want to come.

Finally I managed, "Well honey, you have to follow your heart."

"It's just that ever since I've been Kip, it's always been 'Kip and Cally.' I think I need some time to be just me... so I can figure out how I really feel."

I wanted my son to be happy. I just prayed that, in the end, this choice wouldn't accomplish the opposite.

* * *

It's always hard to know, when you give something up, if you're making the right choice.

The night of the auction had been the first clear, sun-filled afternoon in what seemed like weeks of clouds and rain. I could have used a few hours of sun therapy that night. It was a gamble to forfeit a perfect deck-chair evening to sit in a noisy auction hall — we could end up walking away with nothing.

But I was glad we'd decided to go. The auction had given me something I was infinitely grateful for — it took my mind off the internal struggle I'd been going through when I thought about my son's choice, *and* all the wedding plans that needed to be cancelled because of it. Those few hours of fast-paced bidding, forcing me to concentrate on something else, were a real blessing that night.

As Will and I left the sale, we caught the last fifteen minutes of a beautiful multi-colored sunset, a reminder of the peaceful sun-deck time we'd sacrificed.

It hadn't been a waste of time, however. Into the back of our cargo-style car we'd loaded two small tables, various odds and ends from someone's collection of china, and an ocean scene oil painting called *Sudden Storm*. All our purchases fit — all but a lovely old corner china cabinet. That had been tied into our open trailer.

We drove home with our cabinet lying on its back on a thick, comfy furniture blanket to protect it from scratches. The sides of the blanket were snuggled up around the edges, so that no damage would be done as the trailer jumped along the bumps in the road. The glass door had been removed to prevent cracking — nothing worse than arriving home with a new piece of furniture... broken.

Once home in our driveway, we untied the rope to unload the country-elegant piece and, through the darkness, we noticed two bumps sitting in a spot where bumps shouldn't have been.

Curious, Will looked closer.

He picked up two pieces of the drawer handle. They were just sitting there, loosely, on top of the drawer, several inches away from where they were normally attached.

Antique drawer pulls are often made in several pieces; this handle was made of three: two decorative circles of brass that were threaded for the screws that held the whole thing down, and a third piece, the pull, that allowed you to open the drawer. The pull was nowhere in sight.

When we'd left the auction hall, the complete handle had been fastened down tight with screws. How had these two little circles worked themselves loose? And even more fascinating, how had they not blown away during the twenty-minute, one-hundred-kilometer-an-hour drive home? There was no wind protection on the sides or front of our trailer.

We were happy to see the two little circles, but really, without the pull, they were pretty useless. This sixty-year-old handle had a nice brownish patina to the brass. There would be no way to replace the pull without it looking similar to an old pair of weathered and loved sneakers with brand new, white shoelaces. We would never find a match. The whole thing would have to be replaced with a reproduction, and they never quite look the same.

It was so hard to find antiques that were complete, and in good shape. Losing a piece of it on the way home was heartbreaking. It was a rotten mystery. Not much we could do, though. The damage was done.

Will worked at getting the drawer open, and found one of the screws inside. The jumping of the trailer must have jiggled the screws loose, but the second one was missing. It didn't matter anyway; without the pull we would be forced to go with a reproduction.

We unloaded our injured prize, and found a temporary home for it in the garage. I tugged the blanket that had protected it, and the second screw hopped onto the wooden floor of the trailer. How had it gotten there — out of the drawer? It seemed impossible.

Was it possible that the pull...?

I flicked the blanket again and onto the wood rolled the third piece of the handle.

Incredible.

We had driven for twenty minutes at highway speed, at one point swerving wildly to miss a baby raccoon and his momma, and still, all the original loose pieces were there for us to reassemble. They'd been separated, but were still together. What were the chances?

Maybe my pieces of brass were a reminder that although sometimes we feel like our lives are falling apart, if something is right, really right, fate will look after it for us.

I had feared, as all mothers do sometimes, that my son may be making a bad decision. I wondered if calling off his engagement was a huge mistake. I knew it was the right thing for him to do, though. If he had doubts, he had to find his way through those feelings before taking such a big step. But I wondered if he would one day feel that he had lost, or damaged, a good thing. I didn't want my son to feel regret.

Maybe I was being told that no matter how much it seems like the odds are stacked against something, if it's meant to be, it will be. This little miracle made believing that we were right where we should be, right now, all the more easy to do. I felt as if my drawer pull was a message that everything will come together again, if it's truly the right fit.

* * *

A person can't help but assume that romance for a man like Kip might be awkward once it hits the point of intimacy.

And, as much as I didn't want to think about it, I have to admit that I worried that once this new part of his life — dating — hit that stage, the rest of his relationships might be short-lived. I figured I knew how most girls would react to his not-so-typical body.

And Kip didn't waste any time finding out. That may seem a little on the heartless side... seeing someone else after freshly ending an engagement, but Kips says, even for him, it happened without warning.

There was a girl where he worked — Paige — whom he had always had a strong attraction to. Apparently, the feeling was not one-sided.

They had been friends, working side-by-side for the same company for over a year. One night Paige asked Kip to stop for a drink on their way home from work. They spent a couple of hours together, talking about what each of their hopes for the summer were, laughing at Kip-style humor, and gossiping about work. When it was time to say good-bye, to Kip's complete astonishment, Paige kissed him. Not a friend-style, little-peck good night kiss. A real kiss.

When my son told me about this incredibly sharp corner in the craziness that seems to be his life, my mind instantly went to that place: that first awkward moment of intimacy they would share if the relationship continued. "Does she know about your past, honey?"

"That's the amazing part, Mom. I wanted to keep kissing her... but, I couldn't. I had to get it out. So I said, 'Um, I need to stop for a second. There's something I have to tell you.' I couldn't let my feelings develop further just to have my self-esteem stomped on when I told her everything."

The kid has guts: you have to give him that much.

I guess I can understand why he felt he had to be up-front right away. If they got close for weeks, or months, and then his truth brought the relationship to an abrupt death, it would be heartbreaking.

Why risk that disappointment?

So, he told her right there, a moment after their first passionate kiss. He told her about his childhood and his body injustices.

In my head, this was when the girl would decide to start logging miles for a marathon and run for the hills. Or politely say she was sorry she'd given him the wrong impression, but she wasn't interested in him "that way." Or quietly stand there wearing a shocked expression, with a too-difficult-to-disguise undertone of disgust. In my imagination, the possible scenarios were countless, and they were all horrendous. But Paige just listened.

He then looked her right in the eye and said, "So... do you think you will be able to handle that?"

Her reply had humbled me. She answered simply and honestly. She looked back with warmth and said, "I don't know. I guess we'll just have to wait and find out... eventually."

And I guess, when the time came, she handled it just fine, because, as I write this, they've been dating for eighteen months, and Kip seems happier than I've ever seen him.

He feels overwhelmed with surprise some days. He thinks of Paige as that perfect, unattainable, top-of-her-class cheerleader from high school, the one who only notices the brainy football or basketball players.

His curiosity got the better of him one day. Since he and Paige had been friends for quite a while, Kip knew the type of guy Paige was usually interested in — the lean, sporty, jock type. At 5 feet, 4 inches, Kip doesn't really look like the jock type. And, like his mom, he struggles to stay on the lean side. So, one day he just had to ask her..."What attracted you to me? I am so *not* your type."

Her reply?

"I'm attracted to who you are, not just the way you look. I like you because you're Kip."

That answer won her points with more than one person, let me tell you! Their relationship was an enigma, but in a good way... serendipitous doesn't describe it right. It was a happy thing, but definitely not an accident. I believe they are right where they should be.

I keep thinking of a day that confirmed that to me.

While standing in my big kitchen that day, making lunch, Kip stood beside me looking like a six-year-old who knew about a surprise party, and was dying to share his secret, even though he knew he shouldn't. "Mom... Paige popped my cherry."

I looked back blankly. I had no idea what that meant. Kip had been engaged. They'd lived together for five years. Surely he and Cally had been intimate? So, if that wasn't what he was referring to, what exactly was he talking about?

"She's the first girl who has seen me without *any* clothes on."

I'm sure I didn't say anything back for way too many seconds. My brain wouldn't process this little secret.

Kip had been with Cally for six years, and she had never seen all of him?

I had no idea. How loudly does that say something?

I guess that old saying "Everything happens for a reason" is true. Kip's engagement had ended because it wasn't where he should be. Cally had given him a lot, but her role in his life was finished. Paige was opening new doors for him. He was letting his guard down. Funny though, you could see by his lifted eyebrows and his wide eyes as he told me that even he was amazed at how he was reacting to this new love.

And I found it fascinating. It made me wonder... before Paige, what had kept him from being comfortable enough to really be seen?

I didn't ask for details, however. This was their life. These were their private, intimate moments. I didn't need to know everything. It was enough to know that my son felt close enough to this wonderful young woman to be completely himself with her.

I understand body issues. I am not the nude beach type. Hell... I'm not even the bikini type. Not even when I was sixteen, and my body was at its best. I just don't have the confidence. I can't even imagine how Kip, and young men like him, would feel. I'm not sure if male-to-females go through the same hesitation; my experience is strictly with Kip's female-to-male friends. Many of those friends won't even entertain the thought of dating.

Think about it.

Obstacle number one: find someone you really connect with (we can all relate to how daunting a task that seems at times).

Obstacle number two: tell the girl *you* used to be a girl.

Obstacle number three: hope that when you get to the point of touching, she isn't completely freaked out!

Many of these young men think their bodies are too different, that they will *never* find someone who will love them the way they are.

Kip "dropping his towel" for Paige gives hope to all the young men like him that fear intimacy.

To them, I have just one little bit of motherly advice... real love is out there, guys. Go find it!

Acknowledgments

It is with great respect that I would like to thank the many talented, creative and generous people who have contributed to this book. First though, I must thank my two boys. Without their open minds and giving natures this book would not exist. Next, of course, I owe so much, including my peace of mind, to my husband. He was my foundation, always there to help me navigate the land mines during the tough years. And his support was still going strong throughout the many tedious months as I learned to write.

I can never adequately thank my family and friends. They made me feel safe and loved during the years when I thought I might crumble at any moment. Many of the chapters in our story came from the need to thank them for the strength they gave me.

I would like to personally thank everyone who helped me with this project, but a complete list of all those who read countless drafts, scrutinized chapters and helped with cover design is impossible. There are too many; it would create an entire second book. My gratitude goes to all those friends, family members and members of my various writing groups who, during the development stage, offered help or encouragement every time I needed it.

There are a few people I must single out, however. I was introduced to Rhiannon Beaubien (through email) by a mutual friend. She went over every word of my manuscript with intense detail, and offered suggestions and inspiration – all for a complete stranger, and not one cent exchanged hands. Sigrid Macdonald, a professional editor, did my editing for a very small fraction of her normal fee because she wanted the world to hear our story. Elsa

Franklin, literary agent, helped me to believe in myself. By offering to help me with publishing, she gave me the confidence to believe that the literary world might just be interested in what someone like me had to say.

And finally, I cannot forget to express heartfelt thanks to my sister. She has always been there for me. This time she outdid herself. As it happened, she read my full manuscript for the first time when she was going through something difficult. She said it helped her to accept the situation and move forward. Her reaction to this was to begin sending monthly emails to Oprah about me. Although it made me laugh, her enthusiasm helped me to persevere and believe that one day our story might help others… and there isn't anything more rewarding than that.

PERMISSIONS ACKNOWLEDGEMENTS

Grateful acknowledgment is made to the following for permission to reprint previously published material.

Grand Central Publishing: Excerpts from

"Simple Abundance - A Daybook of Comfort & Joy"

by Sarah Ban Breathnach.

Copyright 1995.

Reprinted by permission of Grand Central Publishing.

www.ingramcontent.com/pod-product-compliance
Lightning Source LLC
Chambersburg PA
CBHW032100090426
42743CB00007B/185